To Adam
God is good
J Fulwood Jr
6-8-2005

Neicy
443-414-1110

Love Lifted Me

A Life's Journey

An Autobiography
By Harlow Fullwood, Jr.
With Herbert C. Sledge, Jr.

Harlow Fullwood, Jr.

Love Lifted Me

Love Lifted Me

A Life's Journey

By Harlow Fullwood, Jr.

with Herbert C. Sledge, Jr.

C. H. Fairfax Company, Publisher

Baltimore

Published by C. H. Fairfax Company, Inc.
Paul F. Evans, Publisher
Post Office Box 7047
Baltimore, Maryland 21216
www.yougetpublished.com
chfairfaxco@hotmail.com

Editorial Offices
Suite 205
2901 Druid Park Drive
Baltimore, Maryland 21215
410-728-6421

The Fullwood Foundation, Inc.
Post Office Box 47727
Baltimore, Maryland 21244
410-788-1313
www.fullwoodfoundation.org

Design and layout by Charles Lowder, Graphic Designer
211 E. Chase Street • Baltimore, MD 21202 • 410-685-5949

Manufactured in the United States of America
ISBN 0-935132-28-7
Library of Congress Control Number: 00-136051

Elnora Bassett Fullwood

x

To Elnora Bassett Fullwood, my inspiring and devoted wife; Paquita Fullwood-Stokes, our daughter; and Harlow Fullwood, III, our son, who have been pillars of encouragement to me through the years. Also, to Robert Harwil Stokes and Harlow Fullwood IV, our precious and gifted grandsons.

To the Fullwood, Bassett, Davidson, Ray, and Hamilton families: May you continue to be beacons of love, loyalty, and leadership. In the words of George Washington Carver:

How far you go in life depends on your being tender with the young, compassionate with the aged, sympathetic with the striving and tolerant of both the weak and the strong because someday in life you will have been one or all of these.

To the memory of Harlow Fullwood Sr., my father; Louise "Sis" Hamilton-Fullwood, my mother; and Annie Conley Fullwood-Floyd, my paternal grandmother, who was affectionately called "Granny."

To God be the Glory.

Annie Conley Fullwood-Floyd
"Granny"

Acknowledgements

I express my appreciation to many for their support and encouragement in helping me turn my dream of this book into an overwhelming reality. Although this book is an autobiography, it is also a collaborative effort of some essential people who provided substantial assistance.

I extend a special salute and much love to my wife of 37 years, **Elnora Bassett Fullwood**, for inspiring me to tell my story – so that it may inspire others to care and share. **Elnora** has been my source of strength throughout my law enforcement, business, and philanthropic careers. She has been with me every step along the way, and to her, I say thanks sincerely.

I am eternally grateful to my paternal grandmother, **Annie Conley Fullwood-Floyd**, who reared me and taught me essential lessons that have guided me throughout my life.

Luther Davidson, my first cousin, helped me research a series of photographs; **Robert D. Moore**, the son of my high school football coach, provided precious photographs and other material about his father, the late **Clarence Lee Moore**. I extend thanks to **Esther White** in the Office of the President – Virginia Union University; **Reverend Matthew L. Jones** for providing me spiritual strength and his prayers; **Julius W. Bassett**, my brother-in-law, for his outstanding dependability to assist me with many endeavors; **Paul F. Evans**, for his quality publishing skills; **Charles Lowder**, for his graphic arts and layout-design expertise; **Frederick Douglass, IV**, for his transcribing and writing services; **Dr. Marian Davis-Foster**, for editorial help on a draft of the book; **Dr. David Thomas Shannon, Sr.**, for the Prologue; and thanks to **Herbert C. Sledge, Jr., J.D.**, a dedicated friend and compassionate writer who superbly enriched this book. I salute all coaches, teachers, friends and mentors who helped me achieve success, and I extend gratitude to members of my extended family: Concord Baptist Church, Virginia Union University, Baltimore City Community College, Coppin State College, Baltimore Police Department, Alpha Phi Alpha Fraternity, Rotary Club of Woodlawn-Westview, Prince Hall Masons, KFC Corporation, and WMAR TV 2/ABC.

To all who have been acknowledged and to many others, I say thanks for lifting me with your love.

About the Author

Harlow Fullwood, Jr. is a scholar, former All-American athlete, former law enforcement leader, award-winning business entrepreneur, and a generous philanthropist. He is President of Fullwood Foods, Inc. and owner of several KFC franchises. A native of Asheville, North Carolina, **Fullwood** graduated with *highest honors* from Baltimore City Community College and earned his Bachelor of Arts degree from Virginia Union University (VUU), where he was a College All-American football player; he was inducted in *1990 into the Central Intercollegiate Athletic Association (CIAA) Hall of Fame*. He has been awarded three honorary Doctoral degrees.

Mr. Fullwood was drafted by the Baltimore Colts and the Buffalo Bills football teams in the same year. After a brief professional football career, he joined the Baltimore Police Department where he achieved *2nd Place Ranking* at the Baltimore Police Academy. He served for 23 years, specializing in police recruiting. He became *the most decorated law enforcement officer in the State of Maryland* in terms of community service, was honored by the *Baltimore Sun* as **"1979 Policeman of the Year"** and, upon leaving the department, he received the **"Distinguished Service Award"** — the highest-level honor that can be awarded to a living police officer.

Mr. Fullwood became a Kentucky Fried Chicken franchise owner in 1984 and became *the first African-American franchise holder to lead the State of Maryland in gross sales* and one of the first in the nation. Some of his more than 500 awards for excellence in business and community service include: 1999 *Baltimorean of the Year* by *Baltimore* Magazine; 1999 Rotary International – Woodlawn/Westview Chapter's Community Service Award; *1998 Outstanding Volunteer Fund-Raiser Award* by the Baltimore Chapter of the National Society of Fund-Raising Executives; *VUU National Alumni Association Alumnus of the Year; National Blue Chip Enterprise Award from Nation's Business magazine; the Alpha Phi Omega Fraternity Leadership Award;* the *Henry G. Parks Business Award;* named the *Paul*

Harris Fellow by the Rotary International Foundation; presented the *Jimmy Swartz Medallion Award* by the late Governor of Maryland J. Millard Tawes; and named 1992 Delta Lambda Chapter, Alpha Phi Alpha Fraternity - *Brother of the Year.*

Harlow Fullwood, Jr. is married to **Elnora Bassett Fullwood**, a native of New Kent, Virginia, and they are proud parents of two children, **Paquita Fullwood-Stokes** and **Harlow Fullwood, III,** and two grandsons, **Robert Harwil Stokes** and **Harlow Fullwood, IV.**

The **Fullwoods**, through their foundation, have contributed hundreds of thousands of dollars to numerous charity causes and have generated and awarded more than six million dollars in college scholarships to more than 500 Baltimore-area high school students. *The Annual Fullwood Benefit & Recognition Breakfast,* held every January, continues to be the largest, most spectacular fund-raising event of its kind in the United States.

Ralph Waldo Emerson said, *"We aim above the mark, to hit the mark."* **Harlow Fullwood, Jr.'s** aim has been to produce the highest quality results. *He has hit that mark many times.* His autobiography is not only a story about a dedicated and resourceful American who has *achieved* and *given back.* It is also a unique collection of principles and personal experiences about how individuals should *care* about others and generously *share* their rich lessons-learned and rich fruit-attained. In recognition of his achievements, on April 4, 2001, Baltimore's **Great Blacks in Wax Museum** unveiled and included the wax figure of **Harlow Fullwood, Jr.** into its *Famous African-American Business Leaders of Maryland* Exhibit.

Herbert C. Sledge, Jr., J.D.

About the Co-Author

I met **Herbert C. Sledge, Jr**. 14 years ago, when he was Foundation Executive Director for the Baltimore City Community College, my alma mater. He is one of the most brilliant persons that I have ever known. **Herbert** has written speeches and drafted legislation for numerous local and national politicians; he has written many *winning* grant proposals; and his news articles on diverse topics have been published locally and internationally.

Herbert is a graduate of Carver Vocational-Technical High School; Morgan State University; was a CLEO Scholar at Harvard Law School; and earned his Juris Doctor degree from the University of Maryland Law School. Herbert was a Division Chief for the State's Attorney's Office of Baltimore City, at age 24; a staff member for the United States Senate; and was a member of the Regional Counsel's Office of the U.S. Department of Housing and Urban Development.

The White House, City Hall, Maryland State Senate, Fullwood Foundation, Baltimore City Community College, Maryland Bible College and Seminary, and many other institutions have honored **Herbert** for his expertise in fund-raising and grantsmanship, marketing, and business management. His intellect is remarkable. **Herbert** is my friend. I love him like a brother. I am proud that he is my co-author.

Harlow Fullwood, Jr.

Dr. David Thomas Shannon, Sr.

Prologue

It is my pleasure to introduce this book. Its title, **Love Lifted Me**, is first and foremost a story of unconditional love of God that was operative in the life of a young man. Throughout his life, **Harlow Fullwood**, Jr. has used the gifts of love to lift others. As his former professor, his former pastor, a fellow Virginia Union University alumnus, and a witness of his benevolent energy, I will use this introduction to share my reflections on this remarkable man.

The title of this book is an appropriate description of the mind-set that motivates **Harlow** to give and keep giving. His autobiography is a story of one who was lifted by love, who got "out of the box" of prescribed limitations, and who has tirelessly sought to help others achieve success.

I was always impressed with **Harlow's** capacity to accept help from others and to use his opportunities to assist others. He was a student in my humanities class in the early sixties. I stated that each student had an "A" grade at the beginning of the course, and this grade would continue until a student provided me with work that required me to give a lower grade. **Harlow** maintained the "A" and also helped other students to maintain their "A's." Instinctively, he lifted others.

Harlow presented himself for membership at the Ebenezer Baptist Church in Richmond, Virginia, where I was pastor. I baptized him. In 1979, several years later, **Harlow** and I reunited when I became President of Virginia Union University. He was already active in the alumni association. It was during this time that I witnessed first-hand his generous support for the university in public relations, fundraising, and recruitment. Through the years, I have also witnessed his outstanding philanthropic support of other higher education institutions and numerous community organizations.

On Saturday, May 11, 1995, **Harlow** received an honorary Doctor of Humane Letters degree from Virginia Union University in Richmond, Virginia. In making the presentation, **Dr. Lucille M. Brown**, a member of the Board of Trustees, read the citation. She stated, "**Mr. Fullwood**, you have been an outstanding businessman, humanitarian, an excellent athlete, a highly decorated police officer, and a quintessential alumnus of Virginia Union University." Several other institutions, groups, and organizations have recognized **Harlow** as an exemplary law enforcement officer, a resourceful entrepreneur, and a selfless philanthropist. This is but a concise way to describe this man; he is much more.

As I reflect upon **Harlow Fullwood, Jr.'s** extraordinary career and his continuous charitable spirit, I recognize that he has taken seriously the new commandment that Jesus gave His disciples: **"I give you a new commandment, that you love one another. Just as I have loved you, you also should love one another. By this, everyone will know that you are my disciples, if you have love for one another."**

John 13:34-35 RSV

Dr. David Thomas Shannon, Sr.,
Eighth President of Virginia Union University, 1979-1985

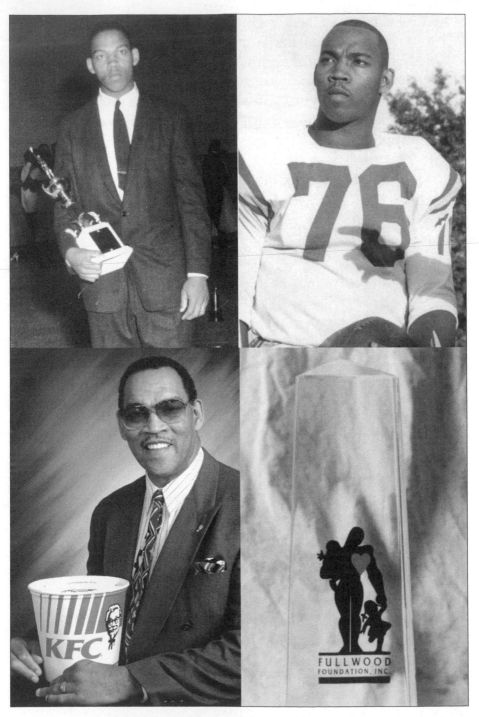

Harlow Fullwood, Jr. On the Move

Contents

Annie and Lucius Fullwood
My Grandparents and Family

The House I Was Born In

My Father and Mother

My Home Church

My Two-Room Elementary School

Mary Lee Percey, My
Step-Great- Grandmother, I and My
Grandmother Ollie Hamilton

Chapter One

Humble Beginnings

I was born in 1941, in Weaverville, North Carolina, in a two-room shack with outdoor plumbing. I was delivered by Mary Percey, my step-great-grandmother. I have three sisters, Joann, Gail, and Joyce, and a brother, Everett. All of them live in Baltimore. My mother, Louise "Sis" Hamilton-Fullwood, was a domestic worker, and my father, Harlow Fullwood, Sr., was a bus porter for Trailways. They did not make very much money. My father eventually went off to World War II.

When I was a child, we lost our home by fire. It was a five-room wooden house, and the lumber was very dry. I was about six years old. One day, I found some matches and started playing with them. I held a lit match up to some curtains. I burned down the house. We had no fire insurance. Actually, during those times, black folks were not allowed to have fire insurance. My family lost everything. We were suddenly homeless. Out of kindness, some black and white neighbors gave us clothing and a few other essential items.

We moved to Asheville, North Carolina. At that time, Weaverville was ten miles from Asheville. Today, it is eight miles away because Asheville's city limits have been extended. We

1

lived on Curve Street. There were three children — my brother, my sister, Joann, and I. We lived in a three-room house with a living room and a big bedroom. My mother and father slept in a bed on one side of the room, and the three children slept in a bed on the opposite side of the room. We had a small kitchen with a little stove that burned coal and wood. The house also had an indoor toilet. That was my first time to experience indoor plumbing. We had very poor living conditions. My father decided that he had to go north to seek better employment. In Asheville, there were the haves and the have-nots. My father went to Baltimore to seek work. After a short time, my father found employment and came back for the family.

I was doing very well in school. My father explained that we had to relocate to Baltimore where he had found work. His mother, Annie Conley Fullwood-Floyd, said to my father, "Look, I'll keep him." My grandmother had been keeping me on and off anyway. She told my father, "I'll keep him, and you go on and do what you have to do for your family." My mother and father took my brother and sister, and they went on to Baltimore. I went to live with my grandmother. At an early age, I understood the love that my mother had for me; however, the circumstances under which she left me made a life-long impression on me. I never displayed any partiality between my mother and grandmother.

My grandmother was part white and part Cherokee. She reared me with love, discipline, kindness, compassion, and commitment. She was born in Marion, North Carolina; however, she lived in Haw Creek, North Carolina, which was three miles from the Asheville city limits. That area had unpaved roads, outside toilets, and our mailbox was located about three hundred yards from the house. My grandmother had the best-looking, best-kept home in the community. The grass and landscaping were immaculate and precise.

Granny's parents were slaves. She took the last name Conley from that of the slave owners. Although her parents were slaves, Granny, as she was affectionately called, was not bitter about that. She had respect for persons of all races and creeds. She

2

conveyed that same humility to me as my legacy. She passed the torch to me to practice racial harmony. She would say, "Even in a segregated town, always remember that there are some good folk on their side of the fence. There are good and bad white folk; there are good and bad black folk. Harlow, I certainly hope that as you grow up, you will recognize the difference."

Granny valued education. She told her youngest son, "If you can't go to school, you can't stay here." Granny took great care in preparing me for school: she fixed my breakfast, dressed me in clean clothes, and she allocated time for me to study every night. Every school day, prior to my departure, she would say, "I am sending you to learn." That short, motivational statement inspired me significantly to do my best.

I attended a two-room school that had a potbelly stove. There were four grades being taught in one room. The two teachers, Manda Horn, who taught grades one through four, and Monie Jones, who taught grades five through eight, were committed to quality education, and they were highly respected in the community. My parents were not highly educated, but they motivated me to be a good student. We learned more with four grades in that one classroom than some students today may learn in high-tech, super-large schools. Parents sent their children to school to learn, and we did. It was strictly business.

When I was in the second grade at Mountain Street Elementary School in Asheville, I was far and above many of the other students. The school administrators decided to skip me to the third grade. I could not handle it. Mrs. Desiree Glover, the teacher, said, "Send him back where he came from." I went back to the second grade, and I did not mind it because suddenly the academic pressure was off me. That school had some tough teachers, but I learned a lot.

I remember when I was in the sixth grade, I visited Baltimore. It was like another world to me. Asheville was a "one-horse-town," and there was one way in and one way out of those mountains. Asheville was hard to get to. That is why it had a hard time developing economically. When I arrived in Baltimore, I thought the streetcar was a train. I had never even visualized many of the things that were there. The rowhouses with white marble steps fascinated me, and every block looked alike to me.

When I returned to North Carolina, I gained my first job in the sixth grade. I started caddying, carrying golf clubs. There were times when I caddied all day long, carrying two bags, in 95-degree weather. I was lucky if I made five dollars per day. When I would arrive at home, I would give a portion of my wages to my grandmother for her use. She would save the balance for emergencies.

Granny would not allow me to have an alarm clock to wake me up for school or work. She wanted me to learn responsibilities without mechanical means. We lived off the land, without needing to purchase certain essential items such as burning wood, sausages, hogs, chickens, eggs, and all. Granny canned vegetables, and she made quilts, soap, and clothing. She was very industrious. We had running water inside of our house, but we had no toilet facilities. We had a coal and wood stove. We had an outhouse that was about 25 yards away. I must tell you that it was some experience when you "had to go" in the middle of the night because you had to walk to that outhouse. However, when we later had an indoor toilet installed, we were one of the first families in the area to enjoy that convenience.

As I was growing up, I had a variety of chores that would last from sunup to sundown. Most of them involved yard-work that included raking leaves, putting leaves in the pigpen so that the pigs could have a good night's rest, feeding the chickens and hogs, mowing the lawn, chopping wood, and doing whatever else was necessary to help my grandmother. After I completed my daily tasks, Granny would give me a real good meal.

She believed that once you ate, working was all over. During my stay with her, she never forced religion on me. She was a loving and caring person. She was religious. One could tell this by the way that she lived.

After elementary school, I went to Hill Street Junior High School, where I completed the seventh and eighth grades. In those days, teachers administered immediate disciplinary measures. In the country, many young boys carried a knife of some type. Once, I took a hog blade to school. I was showing it off. I can remember that as if it were yesterday. Well, the teacher pulled me up and spanked my butt. Then, the teacher sent a note home. It was in a sealed envelope. I gave the envelope to my father. He opened it, read the note, and told me to go get a dogwood switch. I do not know what that note said, but after my father finished whipping me, I have never carried a knife since.

My father was strict. He would help me with my homework, and if I wrote letters too close together, he would crack my knuckles. Well, consequently, I acquired excellent penmanship.

During those days, times were different from today. We never saw teenage girls walking on the street pregnant, nor did we see a woman smoking in public. That was not the culture, then.

In my early grades, I really enjoyed participating in dramatic plays. It was easy to memorize my lines because I had a near-photographic memory. My first acting role was in junior high school as a country preacher. Until this day, many still refer to me as "Preacher." In fact, I am often asked whether I intend to pursue a career in the ministry. I guess it is because of my oratorical skills or perhaps my philosophical manner. I never did endeavor to become a preacher.

When I was sixteen years old, I worked at a fast-foods, drive-up restaurant. I earned fifty cents an hour. I started work at 9 a.m. and finished at 2 a.m. I was never late, nor did I miss any day from work unless I had permission. Of course, I was still in school, so most of my work time was on the weekends. I worked for a Greek married couple that spent a lot of time arguing with each other. He was a mobster from New York, and ever so often he would physically abuse his wife. He had a habit of taking the cash receipts from his business and disappearing for two or three days. Then he would return and do the same thing again.

One day, his wife decided that she could no longer cope with that habit. She asked me to take the weekend's cash receipts home. I considered doing that, but I was scared to death. After thinking it over, I agreed to do so. I cared for that money as if it were the only thing that I had left in the world. Foremost, I just appreciated the trust that she had exemplified in me even though I was so young. I took that money home and kept it in a pillowcase until the next day when I returned the money to her. After that first time, she would give me a bag of money every weekend. I would give it safekeeping at home and return it to her on each Monday.

That lady was always pleased with my honesty, integrity, loyalty, and my devotion to my job. My job involved some dirty tasks. I was continuously washing dishes, mowing the lawn, cleaning bathrooms, and performing numerous other exhausting tasks. Those bathrooms were so filthy that you would almost vomit when you entered them; however, I did not hesitate to clean them as best I could because that was my job. I knew that I was not going to be doing that forever; in fact, as I cleaned those toilets, I vowed that I would never have that job as my profession.

She knew that I wanted to go to college, and she indicated that she was going to do something to assist me. She encouraged me to focus on my studies and to pursue higher education because she saw a lot of potential in me. However, she died three months prior to my graduation from high school. She had a stroke and hemorrhaged to death. I was very saddened by her passing.

After I left Hill Street Junior High School, I attended Stephens-Lee High School. It was in high school that I discovered that I had the potential to become an outstanding student; I also discovered that I loved sports, especially baseball. At that time, I did not even think about college because I knew that it required money. We had a lot of love at home but no money.

I graduated from high school in 1959. My mother came to my high school graduation. I was very proud, and I know that she was proud of me after learning about all of my accomplishments. I graduated 10th in my class of 178. I was the first student in the history of Stephens-Lee High School to be elected captain of the football team and Mayor of the Student Council in the same year. I was a member of the newspaper staff, I was on the yearbook staff as a sports editor, and I starred in dramatic plays. At that time, I was such a good actor that I could memorize a one-act play overnight. I was voted by my classmates as the student most likely to succeed.

I attended Virginia Union University, an historically black, independent Baptist institution with a world-famous school of theology: The Samuel DeWitt School of Theology. I won a football scholarship to VUU. I earned my degree in sociology; however, I certainly did learn much about religion and philosophy.

Granny had sixteen children: eight boys and eight girls. All were grown and gone when I came on the scene. She outlived eight of her children. Granny divorced and remarried. About the divorce, she merely said, "I got tired of the man and the negative way he treated me."

When I was a youngster, my step-grandfather would make a pipe out of corncob and smoke the silk from the corn in that pipe. I know this will sound weird: When I was about ten years old, I sat on the porch with him with my legs crossed in the rocking chair and smoked that pipe with my step-grandfather. I would puff that pipe like a grown-up. Perhaps that is one of the reasons why, today, I do not smoke because I had that early experience of corn-cob-smoking with my step-grandfather. Also, there was one time that I took a little taste of white lightning, just to see what it was all about. Early in life, I quickly determined that I would not take that road.

While growing up, I stayed away from cigarettes and intoxicating beverages. My father and my uncles drank excessively. They drank enough corn liquor, also known as white lightning, to teach me never to do it. Their outrageous behavior toward each other when they were high on white lightning made a lasting impression on me — never to drink alcohol. Even in my college days, when I went to the parties and all, the guys I associated with knew that I did not drink. They would always give me a 7-up or Pepsi Cola. I was immune to peer-group pressure. Although I did not indulge in drinking, smoking, or doing any drugs, my associates still accepted me into their social circle.

When he retired, my step-grandfather had been employed at the Biltmore Estate, the nearby home of the Vanderbilts, for fifty years. He never drove a car. He walked everywhere. I remember once when my grandmother was in the hospital, he walked five miles to the hospital to visit and to comfort her. Then he walked the five miles back.

While I was in college, my grandmother called me to inform me that I could not come back home because my step-grand-father was very envious of the way that she treated me. He felt very jealous; however, he later changed his mind because he saw that he was breaking my grandmother's heart.

Early one beautiful Fall morning, while my grandmother was sitting on the porch, my step-grandfather was raking leaves. It was a few weeks after his retirement. He raked those leaves into a big pile, and he set them afire. While standing next to that pile of burning leaves, he had a heart attack and fell onto the pile. The flames engulfed him. My grandmother saw that, and she ran to his aid and desperately tried to rescue him. She tried to put that fire out with her hands. As a result of her efforts, she received first- and second-degree burns. My step-grandfather was later pronounced dead at the scene. Granny loved me, as she did all of her children, but I spent more time with her than any of her children. In her later years, she worked as a cook at a segregated elementary school about a mile from our home. Granny died at the age of 99 from diabetic complications.

I feel that my success is an example of what can happen when a person is nurtured by people with compassion. More than any-one, my grandmother inspired me. Granny did not have much education, but she taught me valuable lessons about morals and ethics. She helped me develop my character, provided love, and Granny empowered me to strive for excellence.

I was the first male on both sides of my family to go to college and to graduate. My mother had five children. My sister, JoAnn, was the first family member to graduate from college. She is cur-rently a science teacher at Northern High School in Baltimore. All of us had an opportunity to go to school. I felt really good about that. I do not recall any member in the family, on either side, giving me one dime to help me pursue my education.

My grandmother taught me how hard work pays off, and I am thankful for that. Often, the best things in life do not come without a sacrifice. Granny taught me the importance of helping others. I believe that success is a blessing. Possessing the ability to help others is also a blessing. I have never met a man or a woman who is successful and can truly say that he or she made it without some help from someone else. It does not have to be monetary help. It can be a compliment, words of encouragement, or a recommendation.

Weaverville, North Carolina, my birthplace, has a population today of approximately 2,107. The approximate number of families is 928. The distance from Weaverville to Washington, DC is 384 miles. The distance between Weaverville and Asheville is eight miles. The distance to the North Carolina state capital is 221 miles.

Asheville, North Carolina has a population of 66,700. It is located in Buncombe County. Today, Asheville has one high school, one middle school; one accelerated learning center, one preschool, five elementary schools, and one primary school. The student to teacher ratio is one teacher to every 17 students. There are 185 churches in Buncombe County. The Great Smokey Mountains National Park and the Blue Ridge Parkway offer unlimited recreational opportunities. In Asheville, George Vanderbilt created America's largest private home, the 255-room Biltmore House.

The Fullwoods
Harlow III, Paquita, Elnora, Harlow, Jr.

Paquita Fullwood-Stokes
Robert, Robert Harwil Stokes

"The Fullwood Tree"
From Grandson to Great Grandfather

Chapter Two

Abundant Blessings

My grandmother always said that if you wanted to meet someone nice from the beginning, meet that person in the church or at the library. Throughout my life, these two venues have been lucky ones for me. Elnora was my first date at Virginia Union University. I met her in Fall 1959. Both of us were freshmen. We dated off and on even though it was hard to tell whether she liked me. She lived off campus with her aunt; I lived on campus. She invited me to dinner, to go bowling, and to other social activities. She was very supportive from the beginning. If you find that a person supports you and sticks with you when you have few worldly possessions, that person's dedication becomes precious. Elnora is precious.

Elnora, the oldest of eight children, came from a Christian home. She is highly respected and looked up to as the leader by her brothers and sisters. When there is a crisis, they look to her as the problem-solver. She comes from a very close family. I have never encountered a family as close as theirs. I have witnessed Elnora passing on this kind of family strength and closeness to our two children, Paquita and Harlow III. Even with our two grandsons, Elnora has a strong presence.

Harlow and Elnora in Early Years of Marriage

I just knew that Elnora was the right kind of person for me from the beginning of our relationship. She has vision, she is very intelligent, and she has always worked hard. Very early in her personal development, she was taught to work hard. She earned two degrees, a bachelor's and a master's, from Coppin State College, and she became a public school teacher. Some people were born to do certain things. She was born to teach. She had the patience to work for many years with children who were physically and emotionally challenged. My wife has the patience of Job.

Elnora's parents, Edwin and Eldonia Bassett, recently celebrated their 62nd wedding anniversary. My father-in-law is a straight-up person. When I asked him for his daughter's hand in marriage, he said, very plainly, "I don't want you to marry her if you don't love her because she can stay here with me, and I'll take care of her." Now that's what one can really call the bottom-line.

Elnora has made the difference in my life. I am aggressive and goal-oriented. You have to have someone who can see things you cannot see or sees things differently than you. My wife can see storms before they happen. She has a unique gift for being able to forecast things and circumstances to avoid.

When my wife and I first came to Baltimore, we lived in a three-room apartment in the Cherry Hill community, which is located in South Baltimore. It was a nice place down by the river. It was in a new development. I was then working for the police department. I did not have a car. I rode the bus free. I had two police shirts. I would wear one, and my wife would wash one. I recall coming home from work one day and finding my wife in the bathroom with a bar of Octagon soap scrubbing my other shirt on the washboard. She always saw to it that I had clean shirts and socks. No matter where I worked, or how long or how hard, she always made sure there was a hot meal when I got home. That's the way her mother maintained a home.

Our daughter is just like her mother. She was born to teach, she is very creative, and she enjoys her work. She teaches computer math at Garrison Middle School in Baltimore. Paquita met Robert, her husband, at Virginia Union. Harlow III, a certified paramedic with Baltimore City, is a graduate of the Baltimore School for the Arts. He is currently studying computer engineering at the University of Maryland at Baltimore County (UMBC). Harlow, III is service-oriented and enjoys working with people, especially working with the physically and mentally abused. I am very thankful that my children have acquired the important qualities to teach and to care for others.

We tried to bring up our children in a nice environment. Sixteen years ago, we moved to a nice neighborhood in Catonsville. When I was in the police department, I resided quite a distance from the neighborhoods where I worked. This was for my family's privacy and for my privacy; however, I was always available to help in any community when there was a crisis.

We have friendly neighbors and live in a very pleasant neighborhood. It has a down-home atmosphere. The deer, rabbits, squirrels, and other wildlife remind me of the Great Smokey Mountains in North Carolina where I was born. We moved in on the deer. But, guess what? They did not move out when we moved in. They stayed. You can see them all around the neighborhood at any time of the day. I cannot landscape like I want because the deer eat tulips and everything.

In 1963, when I was a senior at Virginia Union University and an All-American football player, I was drafted by the Buffalo Bills and the Baltimore Colts. I chose the Colts. After a brief stint, I found out early that many are called — but few are chosen, meaning that I requested to be released from the team. At the time, it dawned on me that I had no job, and I had not completed all of the course requirements to earn my college degree. By 1977, it had taken me 14 years to obtain my Bachelor of Arts degree from VUU. On the journey to reaching that goal, I enrolled at the Community College of Baltimore now Baltimore City Community College (BCCC). I am very proud to say that I earned my associate degree from BCCC in urban sociology in 1974 — with highest honors. I was inducted into the BCCC Alumni Hall of Recognition.

I had become the most decorated police officer in Maryland in terms of community service. I had two college degrees, yet I woke up every morning broke. My job was rewarding, but it became a predicament when I could not educate my children from what I earned from my police salary.

My venture into business, the KFC franchise arena, was very risky. After 23 years of service in the Baltimore Police Department, I quit one and a half years away from full retirement. Now, that is taking a high risk. I could not afford to fail.

A decision had to be made. I had $30,000 in the city pension system accrued over 23 years. I was highly criticized for making the decision to use that money. I took some of that money and used it for the KFC venture. Guess what? Within three months, I had earned it back.

Even as I struggled as a new business entrepreneur, I was still doing community service. You can become very effective with your community service work when you have money to invest in it.

I do not think I could have been so successful without my wife. When we had our first interview with the Kentucky Fried Chicken official from Louisville, Kentucky, the first question was asked of my wife. It was, "If we give your husband a franchise, what will be your role?" Elnora answered, "The same as it has been for the last 20 years---supportive." My wife is quiet in her manner, but when she has to be strong, she can be very strong.

Many consider me as self-reliant, but there have been times when I have had to call on others for help. Once, an important KFC official from Louisville came to discuss our request to restructure our franchise obligations. That official saw that we saved our money, that we put great sums of money back into our business, and that we lived within our means. This really meant that we did not buy the most expensive home, or yacht, or cars, and we did not take the most lavish vacations. After reviewing our status, the official indicated that if we had been financially irresponsible, he would not have had the conversation with us that he did. Thus, we were able to receive help and to survive that rainy season. Our business was a blessing from God because we started from nothing.

Once, when it looked as though the business was slipping away, a young man said to me, "Well, it looks like you have to go back eating beans." My answer to him was, "That will be a problem for you but not for me because we have been there. Beans keep you healthy." If you fall, fall on your back because if you can look up, you can get up. J. Paul Getty once said, "If you owe the bank $100, that's your problem. If you owe the bank $100 million, that's the bank's problem."

If there is one thing that I regret, it is that I did not take more time during the growth years of my business to be with my family. I knew that opportunities like the business did not come every day. Not having had a background in business management made things difficult, but I had a very understanding wife. What I was striving to do was to give my family the opportunity to achieve a better quality of life. I had to work and work hard. No one was going to give it to me on a platter. I had to work to make it happen. I did, and it happened. Thank God!

Elnora and I have been in the Kentucky Fried Chicken (KFC) business for 17 years. During this time, we have experienced numerous difficulties and challenges. Life contains many speed bumps. There were times during the first five years of business when things were very difficult. We made it through the first five years, but it was the second five years that almost wiped us away.

In business life, I have never fired anyone. Some employees fired themselves. We set forth what the rules were in the beginning. There are certain things that I do not tolerate the first time. I often say to my employees: "Never be ashamed of dirty work as long as it is honest work. If a person is filthy and disrespectful at home, that person is going to be filthy and disrespectful at work. If you steal for the first time, you cannot work for us. If you are disrespectful to management and customers, you cannot work for us. If you cannot handle the product according to the guidelines, you cannot work for us. All of these things go toward having a successful business."

If a person is honest, comes to work on time, and is willing to learn, we can do something with him or her. It is hard for me to tolerate disrespect from my employees toward the customers or toward management because most people of my generation were not brought up that way. We were brought up to be respectful and to walk uprightly.

In my business-life with KFC, I was doubly blessed to meet and to hire Anthony "Tony" Cameron, a great guy who worked for 12 years as my operations manager. He is one of the best friends I have. Not only is he good at what he does, he is also truthful, honest and loyal. For those qualities, I was not able to pay him enough. I could not put enough dollars and cents on that kind of integrity.

Maybe I have become a workaholic since I went into business, but I used to be an avid golfer. In Asheville, we played golf just like the guys around Baltimore played basketball. I played too much golf. I played cards too; my main game was pinochle. Occasionally, I enjoy playing cards with a social group called the Swags. The membership includes business executives, lawyers, doctors, and community leaders. We play twice a month. Our card games involve sit-down dinners. It is nice to socialize with people who have achieved success in their own right. Our communication is candid, humorous, and honest. It is a beautiful relationship.

There is another group gathering that I go to every Thursday at noon. It is Rotary Club International of Woodlawn-Westview. I am a charter member of this service club. The membership includes men and women—black, white, and Asian. They are so uplifting. Rotary is an international service club that has raised hundreds of millions of dollars to immunize every child on the face of the earth against polio and childhood diseases. That's right, every child on the face of the earth.

Well, it is the new millennium, the year 2002. Of course, many considered the Year 2000 as the beginning of the 21st century while many others argue that the new century actually and numerically began on January 1, 2001. In any case, regardless of whatever time-measurement theory you accept, given what I have been through with my health in these last years...I am so very thankful that I have reached the new millennium.

Because of my progressive diabetes, I have worked at home these last several years. I have had considerable extra time to think about where I have been, what I have tried to do for others, what others have done for me, and how I can wisely and productively utilize my time. I have always preferred to stay busy and productive in all of my endeavors. As the famous poet Robert Frost once said, "The world is full of willing people; some willing to work, the rest willing to let them." Without a doubt, I have always been willing to work and to work hard. My family, friends, and colleagues can attest to this. Many say that I stay too busy.

One of the things I recognized several years ago was that my health was deteriorating. With that recognition, I understood even more clearly that a greater purpose exists for our existence. I believe that purpose is to offer whatever service we can to humanity. My grandmother always said, "Idle minds are the devil's workshop. The only way to kill time is to work it to death."

In reflecting on my health problems, I have concluded: sometimes we are so wrapped up in our own troubles and concerns that we lose focus on the big picture. As an insulin dependent diabetic, I am devoted to encouraging others to take care of themselves. Two years ago, I had a major operation on my eye and an operation on my left foot. I was hospitalized three times and had numerous laser treatments in both eyes. If it were not for the blessings of the Lord, using man through modern medicine, because of my diabetes, blindness would have been my fate.

The pressures of medical limitations have prevented me from working the job as usual, and they have taken a toll on me. Business-wise, we had to deal with variables we had no control over: drug infestation of neighborhoods where some of our franchises were located; vandalism; the exit of the middle class consumers from the city; closings of urban factories and businesses; the generally low economy in many areas of the city; and a shrinking work force. When we started the business, we did not have to deal with those concerns. Today, one can often see boarded-up locations that were previously thriving businesses. This is the reality. Trying to operate a successful business in any urban sector today can involve taking high risks.

When my health started to fail, I became even more dedicated to being able to see that my family maintained a comfortable standard of living. Many people say that I have plenty of money. That is not exactly true. I do not let money control me. I control it. I do not stockpile it. I have never seen a Brink's truck following anyone to the cemetery.

As far as my diabetes is concerned, I often have difficulty holding a pencil or a ballpoint pen. I call on my wife to help me button my shirts and tie my shoes and neckties. I must admit that after having been so independent, this is difficult. I go to three doctors on a regular basis—my foot doctor, my eye specialist, and my general practitioner. I look around and say, "Lord, it could be worse." Through it all, family and friends have been supportive.

If not given the proper attention, diabetes is a slow death. The disease brings on trouble with the legs, the kidneys, and the heart. It has been this way for me for the last five or six years. Some may shudder as I mention the word death, but it will come to us all. As Herb Sledge once told me, "Life is God's gift to you. The good that you do with your life is your gift back to God." During my illnesses, my family members have been very supportive and have been there for me. Although I am slower now in doing things, my general practitioner told me that I have as much energy as any diabetic he has had as a patient.

Religious faith is an important ingredient for success. When I speak to groups, I tell the story of the man who was on his deathbed, and his wish was to see his son for the last time. When his son entered the room, his father extended his hand and said, "Son, you are now holding the hand of the world's greatest failure." The son said, "Daddy, how can you consider yourself a failure when you made millions of dollars, hired thousands of people, and built a great railroad?" The father said, "Son, that is so true, but a man who leaves religion out of his lifeis a complete failure."

My greatest fear was working to give everyone else's child an opportunity and to lose the confidence of my children. Once my son and I were traveling to a football game. He was about 11 years old. He said, "Daddy, you and Mama are doing everything you can to help other people. What will happen to us if we ever need help?"

Once, my son, Harlow III, said to me, "Daddy, I want to be like you." There is nothing wrong with that, but I said to him, "I have made many sacrifices to give you opportunities so that you can be better and do better than I have done." If we are guiding our children properly, then one day your son or daughter will be better, or should be, than you.

One of my greatest sources of strength is from helping others. One of the most difficult things is when I get a call from a parent or a child for help, and I cannot help. If I had more resources than I have now, I might be dangerous out there with my generosity. The most difficult part is to say no to people. Philanthropy is difficult. It keeps me busy, and it takes up a good deal of time. This means that often when folks approach me about getting involved on committees and boards, I shy away. I prefer to deliver my own style of direct community and charity service through The Fullwood Foundation's activities.

The difference between the man in the penitentiary and me is that I had much help from many different people from all walks of life. Many of us look for an excuse as to why we cannot do something instead of why we can. My time is spent doing what I can do literally from dawn until dark.

Most of the time, I do not go to bed until one or two o'clock in the morning, and I get up at six. I take care of my personal needs and prepare my breakfast. Then, I am at my desk. Most of the time, I work until twelve or one o'clock in the afternoon. I stop to eat a little something. Then, I go back to the desk and work until midnight or one o'clock in the morning.

I plan our entire annual breakfast from my office at home. However, I have someone to help with the clerical work. All of my projects originate with me. What takes some people three months to complete may take me two weeks to complete. I believe in first class or no class. I do not give the students I am trying to help a philosophy that I do not practice myself.

Nowadays, I do not get involved in a lot of different organizations and committees. In order to be effective in my work with people, I cannot spread myself in too many different directions. I have confined myself to the development of the foundation and to the Kentucky Fried Chicken business. The business keeps everything else going. I realize this sounds very basic, but that is the way it is. However, I still support numerous charity organizations and try to be supportive of everything they are doing. This is certainly true, and the record shows it.

I have a long-range vision of where I want to be. I do not allow anything to divert that vision. I do not waste time. I work alone. I know where I am going and what route to take to get there. My commitment level is different. I am not saying that I am better than anyone is. My commitment level is merely different. I do not have patience with people who are spinning their wheels and not getting anywhere. I do not have patience with people who have the resources but who do not have the vision and humility to realize that they did not make it on their own.

I do not want people to think that I have not made mistakes in life. I have. I try not to make the same mistakes twice. To make one mistake is human. To make the same mistake again is the work of a fool. I am a very aggressive person. When you work alone, you have to be aggressive to get things done. Once a church deacon said, "You have a lot going for you. However, when working with people, you can catch more flies with honey than you can with vinegar." I strive to heed that advice.

The year that I had my operations, I raised more money for The Fullwood Foundation than in any other year. Some of my colleagues and family members ask me, "Why don't you slow down?" I say, "Why should I?" I prefer to stay busy. I need to stay focused, and that happens by staying busy.

One of the ways I stay busy is through my never-ending commitments to Virginia Union University, my alma mater in Richmond, Virginia. That is where I received my undergraduate degree.

I am also proud to say that I have been a generous donor to both VUU and BCCC. I have recruited more students for Virginia Union University than any alumnus in its history, and I have contributed thousands of dollars for scholarships and an endowment at VUU. I am very committed to supporting my alma maters and other institutions until the day I die. I have also reached back to help students attend BCCC by establishing that institution's first endowment and contributing thousands of dollars in scholarships for deserving students.

When I was growing up, I did not have many friends. I was an animal lover. I had a black cocker spaniel named Black Beauty who slept by my bed. He would wait for me after school and would scamper to me when he was called. One of the saddest moments in my life was when one morning I woke up and found Black Beauty dead, and I had to bury him. Since that day, even as an adult, I have never become attached to another animal like I was to Black Beauty. We have had two other dogs for companionship reasons because of the children, but there has not been that kind of attachment, that kind of association, to them like I had to Black Beauty.

Once my daughter observed me greeting a number of people at Memorial Stadium, and she said, "Daddy, you sure have a lot of friends." I said, "Your daddy has a lot of associates but very few friends." "Harlow, you are the same as you were when you lived in Cherry Hill," someone once told me. Still, even with that apt observation, I have accumulated very few close friends. Nevertheless, I can call on those few people, at any time, and I will get a favorable response. Everett, my brother, is one of my best friends.

I recruited Everett for the police department. He accomplished an exceptional record of service and retired after 25 years. Everett played professional football, and one year he was the last one cut by the Houston Oilers. He played tight end. He left Houston and went to Canada. After he left football, he stopped by the house when we were still living in Cherry Hill. "I am not going to give you any money," he said, "but I am going to pay all of your bills." That enabled us to save money at a faster pace and make a down payment on our first home. That was in 1965. We bought our first home in 1968. Everett's middle name is Carlton. He is now a top executive with the Baltimore Downtown Partnership. Being in law enforcement is a tradition in our family. My daughter's husband is a police officer. My niece is a police sergeant, and her husband is a police officer.

Edwin Bassett, III, my brother-in-law, is a dedicated friend. When I was in the hospital for 28 days at (what many of us called the "old Provident Hospital") Liberty Medical Center, on Liberty Heights Avenue, he drove to Baltimore from Richmond and spent two hours chatting at my bedside even though he was due right back home. Edwin could have called me on the telephone and talked to me, but he said, "It wouldn't have been the same as being in person." I have always remembered that loyalty.

I am proud to say I have the greatest set of in-laws that any man could have in life. Elnora's oldest brother Roscoe and I have been friends since I met her. When he got out of the military, his first stop was where we lived in Cherry Hill. We have remained very close.

"Because you are an individual who has played such a vital role of contributing to African-American history in Maryland, we would be honored to have a wax figure of you as part of our new display." That morning in July, 1999 when I opened the envelope I received from Baltimore's Great Blacks in Wax Museum and read the letter, I was stunned. I kept reading it over and over. I could not believe what I was being told. I was thrilled. I felt a tear of joy slowly streaming down my face.

Before I opened the envelope, I thought it was a "thank you" note for a recent pledge of support that I had made to the museum. After I read the letter, the true impact hit me. I laughed and cried at the same time. The letter was actually notifying me that my likeness, me, my wax figure would be created and placed on public display. I shouted, "Fantastic!" I called my wife, Elnora, and said, "Read this!...Can you believe it? They plan to make a wax figure of me that will be on display along with wax figures of some of the most outstanding individuals in history."

When I began to reflect on the significance of this honor, I recalled that this museum on East North Avenue, the first of its kind in the nation, contains life-like wax figures of such historic giants as Marian Anderson, Jackie Robinson, Henry "Box" Brown, Mary McLeod Bethune, Martin Luther King Jr., and United States Supreme Court Justice Thurgood Marshall. I was truly impressed that the late Dr. Elmer P. Martin and Dr. Joanne M. Martin, the museum's founders, and the museum's board, decided that I was worthy of this extraordinary honor. The letter announced the development of a permanent exhibit entitled, "Minding Our Business: The History of African-American Entrepreneurship in Maryland and Beyond." Perhaps it was that one letter that has helped me understand, more than anything else has, that I have indeed made some important contributions to the well-being of others. I remain humbled by this.

The Great Blacks in Wax Museum unveiled my wax figure on April 4, 2001 at Baltimore's Engineer's Club. I often think of myself as just a "po' ole country boy" from Weaverville, North Carolina. I wish my late grandmother, mom, and dad could have been there to witness this event. They would be proud, particularly Granny because she reared me until I was in my late teens. There is an old African expression: We Stand on the Shoulders of Our Ancestors. I believe this. My life goals have always involved following the examples that my grandmother and parents set and to pass those lessons and standards on to my children and grandchildren. The values that they preached have become my treasures.

When my wax figure was unveiled, I looked forward to my family joining me for that sensational occasion, but I must say again...I especially wish my grandmother could have been there. I was closer to Granny than to anyone else.

On that special day, I also wished all the teachers, coaches, and many others who helped me attain success could have been there including neighbors, church folks, and various civic leaders whose love, support, and encouragement lifted me and pointed me in the right direction to the highway of business success and community service. I wished they could have been there with me because their collective love lifted me.

In November, 2000, the philanthropic activity of The Fullwood Foundation was celebrated in the national spotlight. Elnora and I received the news that we were invited to be guests on the "Dr. Laura Show." Through arrangements made by WMAR TV 2 and the ABC Network, Dr. Laura Schlessinger provided us "red carpet" treatment, as we were flown first-class to Los Angeles, California to be on her popular television show. The format and purpose of her show was to discuss issues of morals, values, principles, and ethics. Dr. Laura interviewed us about our foundation's projects, our support for education, and she praised Elnora and me for our overall record of charitable giving. Dr. Laura also made a personal appeal to the millions of viewers to adopt The Fullwood Foundation's credo of "Caring and Sharing." A special part of that telecast involved a series of salutes coordinated by WMAR TV2, in which various local friends of The Fullwood Foundation provided on-air kudos. The well-wishers included college presidents, business leaders, pastors, and many others. I was deeply moved by everyone's thoughtfulness.

Today, I devote my time to my family, managing my Kentucky Fried Chicken (KFC) restaurants, and charitable giving. I have been recognized as a community leader and for bringing people together from all walks of life. My pride is to have been honored by such a variety of diverse groups and organizations. I believe that diversity is critically important.

I was recently invited to a church in East Baltimore, Greater Grace World Outreach (GGWO), and spoke before a congregation of more than 1,500 persons. What surprised me most was how culturally diverse that congregation was. I saw people of all ages and nationalities. I saw individuals dressed in expensive business attire --- sitting next to people in shorts and T-shirts. That huge crowd had the appearance of a patchwork-quilt of cultures. That experience enlightened me to the fact that the world is getting smaller. Cultures are getting closer to each other. The sermon delivered that night by the church's pastor, Carl H. Stevens, was dynamic. GGWO is a mission-oriented church with over 600 ministries around the world.

Every January, at The Fullwood Foundation's Annual Benefit and Recognition Breakfast, I am gratified by how diverse by race, culture, religion, and social achievement the crowd is. Among the more than 2,000 persons present are corporate CEO's, college presidents, Baptist preachers, Catholic priests, Methodist ministers, spiritual leaders from numerous other religions, wealthy folk, homeless victims, and people from all contemporary walks of life — all seated together — to participate in the traditional event that promotes "Caring and Sharing."

A child once said to me, "Mr. Fullwood, I want to be somebody, but I need some help." That is the cry of many young people throughout our great city, throughout the state, and throughout the country. This is their cry to people who are able to make a difference. It is our obligation to listen and to help.

My mother also placed an emphasis on family values and togetherness. Louise Hamilton-Fullwood was one child among eight, but she was the only one of her siblings who had any children. She died of cancer at an early age 61. It was her dream for all of her children to grow up to be productive. She lived to see that happen.

When I had the opportunity to go into business, the first one I looked out for was my mother. I was always taught loyalty begets loyalty. Daddy died before I went into business. He was 62 years and died of a heart attack. He might have been alive today had he listened to his doctors. Alcohol and cigarettes took their toll. He made every effort to provide for his family though. I am not as close as I would like to be with my sisters because of the age difference between us. We grew up separately. Very close bonding never really developed between my sisters and me.

What is success? Someone might ask, "Well Harlow, what does success mean to you?" What does success mean to me? Thomas

Edison summed it up beautifully when he said, "Show me a thoroughly satisfied person, and I will show you a complete failure." Socrates presented to his students three basic questions, "Who am I? Where am I going, and how am I going to get there?" When one can honestly answer such questions, one can have a good chance of being successful.

Many define having a good job, a good income, strong family, and a beautiful home as success. I think success can be achieved by setting goals for yourself and shooting for the sky. When I went into business, I looked around to see what it would take to be successful. I concluded, "Study, improve and never be satisfied." I looked to see why folks failed. For my business, I wanted a lawyer who knew the food industry. I wanted an accounting firm that would teach me the system. I gathered as much information as I could from a variety of individuals. I used what worked for them. One can learn by the successes of others and by the failure of others. Even today, I will listen to all kinds of advice. Then, I will make the final decision. If my plan sails down the Chesapeake Bay out of control, then, you know that I made the final decision.

Sometimes folks in my industry fail when they make money --- but do not prepare for a rainy day. One needs to understand that you cannot work a business by yourself. Surround yourself with good people, because loyalty begets loyalty. I work long and hard because I am afraid to fail. When you get to the top in your particular field, you have to work twice as hard to stay there.

I heard a person say, "In life you are going to fail. It is not the mistake that kills you. It is what you fail to do after you realize that you have made one." To make one mistake is human. Many of us worry about our setbacks and failures, but I am here to say that worrying is like a rocking chair. It will give you something to do, but it will not get you anywhere.

When I give a speech, I often say that it does not take much stamina or intelligence to win when all is on your side, but it does take courage when it seems everything is against your fondest dreams. True success is getting it when it seems impossible and doing it when there is not a ghost of a chance to succeed. Milton wrote poetry in blindness. Beethoven composed the Fifth Symphony when he was deaf. Abraham Lincoln became President of the United States, but before that — he had pursued different political offices and had never won an election. After every loss, he would go back and say to himself, "I will continue to study and prepare myself, and one day my chance will come."

My high school coach, Clarence Lee Moore, posing with high school state championship trophy, years later.

The Fullwood Family

Chapter Three

Fullwood Family Focus

I had an uncle, Pharman Fullwood, who had difficulty reading and writing. He left Asheville, North Carolina to go to Detroit, Michigan. He got married and did not have any children. My uncle did quite well for himself. He had a very nice home, a boat, a car, and many of the luxuries that one yearns for in life. Yes, my uncle was doing pretty well for himself. I guess, to me, to use the classic expression, that was my rich uncle. Well, he was not actually rich, but compared to my need-situation — he was rich.

During that period of my life, I was coping with a difficult situation at Virginia Union University. I was so destitute that I had to put pieces of cardboard in my shoes to keep my feet from hitting the ground. I had never previously considered that one day I would acquire a talent for being able to distinguish between various qualities and varieties of cardboard. But, believe me, when it is 20 degrees outside and snowing, one can suddenly become the world's expert on knowing how to keep one's feet warm. Of course, most people might say, "Cardboard is just cardboard." However, in my miserable condition at that time, I endeavored to find the thickest, most durable and comfortable cardboard that I could find. I would cut pieces from it and shape them into shoe soles to place inside my shoes. I know that I am dwelling on this issue, but this is the truth. In those days, cardboard was made really tough. It lasted pretty long. Wow! Imagine that. I guess I had become a cardboard expert. Sometimes, I would make my shoes so weatherproof that I could hardly squeeze them onto my feet, but my feet stayed relatively warm.

I knew my mother and father in Baltimore could not provide much financial help because there were three of us in college at the same time. My mother and father lived in the Lafayette Projects in East Baltimore. At that time, my father was a truck driver, and my mother did domestic work. I decided to make a telephone call to my uncle. I was certain that he could give me a little help so that I could at least buy a dignified pair of shoes. That particular telephone call was to become a most memorable experience for me.

As I slowly dialed the number, I was gripping the receiver and my hand was sweating. My confidence started building. I heard a familiar voice say, "Hello!" I got very nervous and could not speak right away. Actually, I took so long that my uncle had to say "Hello!" three times before I said anything. I carefully chose my words, and I said, "Hi uncle! This is Harlow, Jr. Uncle, I need your help. I *just* called to tell you that I *just* need you to send me *just* enough money to *just* buy a pair of shoes." After I said that, I thought to myself, "Why did I use the word *just* four times in one sentence?"

That was really the first time that I ever remembered asking someone to do anything for me personally. He said, "Okay! All right!" I gave him my address where to send the money, and we said, "goodbye" at the same time and hung-up the telephone. After I got off the telephone, I began to think of other things that I could and should have said before coming right out and asking for money. Oh well, it was one short conversation, but I was desperate. I had to make that call for help. After that day, I waited and waited.

Three days went by, and I waited. One week went by, and I continued to wait. After two weeks, I started hunting for new cardboard. Truthfully speaking, I was very hurt. I never did receive those shoes. Sometimes, an experience like that can test your faith. I learned that relatives could not always be dependable. That cardboard became symbolic to me that self-sufficiency was the most aristocratic goal for me for which to strive. I guess I could become very poetic about this, but I think during everyone's life some type of experience will occur, like my "cardboard-in-the-shoes adventure," that will really help steer the course of the rest of one's life.

I have always tried to remain optimistic, no matter what problems I would encounter. Sir Winston Churchill once said, "A pessimist sees the difficulty in every opportunity; an optimist sees the opportunity in every difficulty." Some people experience a problem and then strive to transform it into a positive result. This process requires deep faith and a very strong foundation. Granny built that strong foundation for me.

During my young adult years, Granny lived in Detroit with that same uncle. I went to visit her after I got out of school. I had gotten a job with the Baltimore Police Department. I guess my uncle was trying to clear his conscience. Prior to my visit to Detroit, he had his attorney call the police department to speak with me. That particular call really bothered me. His attorney talked to me about my uncle's intention to set up an endowment for my daughter.

My uncle also wanted me to do some things at Virginia Union. I was very surprised. I told the attorney that I would not discuss or answer any of the details then, and I wanted to wait to speak directly to my uncle.

When I went to Detroit, I had a chance to speak with him. He was busy getting his boat ready to go out on the lake. I approached him and said, "Uncle, I have something I want to ask. You had an attorney call me to tell me what you wanted to do for my daughter, for me, and other benevolent things. I appreciate your desire to help...but. Do you remember when I asked you to help me with a pair of shoes?" He said, "Yes, I remember." I then asked him why he had not helped me at that critical time when I needed help. My uncle stared at me for about thirty seconds, then he took a deep breath, and he said, "I just wanted to see whether you could make it on your own because basically that's how I made it."

I calmly explained to him that I really had needed those shoes. Then I said, "Whatever you plan to do for me, my daughter, and for anything else that you wish to do, I want you to know that I can provide for her and for me now. I do not need your help. If you still want to give some help, then give it to someone in the family who's striving and trying to do something with his or her life." At that point, my uncle turned red as a beet. I do not think he had ever heard anyone talk to him that way. Money and your position in life are important, but you must hold onto your values. I believe that charity should not be withheld in the face of critical need. When my uncle died, he ended up giving most of his money to the NAACP. At least, that is what was rumored.

When I was with my grandmother, I probably became closer to her than she was to her own children. She told me that she wanted to make a way for me to own her property. I thought about her offer. I reflected on it a lot. Then I told her that I was young and that I did not want to have to go through the complexities and headaches of dealing with her immediate children over that property. I told Granny that I preferred she did not consider leaving me that property.

Later, an interstate highway went right through that piece of real estate. Today, when I look back and think about that opportunity that I almost had, I say, "Man, I don't know whether I was too young, too good, or too stupid." I could have gotten rich from the value of that property. On the other hand, I can look in the mirror and say, "Hey, everything I have, I have paid the price for. That is the reward for working hard and working long."

After I got married, I had another chance to go to Detroit where my grandmother was living until her last days. I wanted her to have the opportunity to meet my wife. When I arrived and greeted her, she said, "I want you to leave and go do whatever else you've got to do, and come back in another hour or two. Then, I'll have something to tell you." I did just that.

When I returned, I was anxious to hear what she had to say. My grandmother never told me anything that ever turned out to be wrong. However, I was concerned that she did not feel I would graduate from college. This was not based on anything other than the fact that she felt that we did not have any money. She knew that it was expensive to do some essential things. She was insecure about our well-being. She did not readily understand about the opportunities that scholarships provided.

She said to me, after talking with my wife in private for an hour or more, "Son, this is it! This is it! This is going to be your backbone! I want you always to treat her with love, admiration, and respect because a good wife is a blessing from heaven." I can remember what my grandmother said about my wife, as if it were yesterday: "That's it. You cannot do any better. That's it." As always, my grandmother was correct. My wife Elnora has been right on time when I could not even see the time. There is nothing like a devoted and supportive wife.

My grandmother lived to be 99 years old. Just like it was with that KFC official who interviewed us, I guess my grandmother was able to see it also, Elnora's special characteristic of dedication. Elnora told that KFC guy, "If you give him the franchise, my role will be what it has always been: supportive." I will never forget those golden words of devotion.

My son Harlow, III attended the Baltimore School for the Arts. He really enjoyed it for a while. Nevertheless, again, he had people judging him because of what his mother and father did. Consequently, there were problems. He drove a nice car; he dressed well, and he presented himself well. However, folks always found a reason to try to lower his self-esteem. I believe if he had not had the strong support system of family, we would have lost our son's loyalty a long time ago. It is a sad thing to work hard to achieve and then to see your family's pride trampled over for no reason.

At the Baltimore School for the Arts, when he received his grade for Abstract Art, he received a grade of "F." I asked myself, "How can he receive 'F' in Abstract Art when he is drawing what he feels?" So, I went to the principal and calmly discussed the issue with him. I said, "Here he is in open competition throughout the city and state; he has either won or placed second for his exhibits, and his artwork had been judged by some of the most creative artists from the area. How can he get an 'F'in abstract drawing?" Believe me, I am not that type of parent who steadfastly defends his children no matter what the circumstances. I feel that my children should fight their own battles. However, this time, I had to step in and speak out. I mean, really, an 'F' in Abstract Art? No way!

Therefore, I took the matter to the superintendent where the decision was overruled. I should not have had to do that. That "F" grade really lowered my son's self esteem. Our young African-American men should be applauded when they express themselves in a positive way. Some accuse white America of being culturally insensitive toward young black men. It is hard enough to try to advance into adulthood as a young man. However, if you are black, the hill seems to be extra steep. Unfortunately, this is a fact of our society in this country. I am here to tell you that, to this day, my son has not gone back to that school since graduation. He has not answered any correspondence. It is like the school never existed.

Unlike me, who had many pleasant high school and college experiences, my son never did. That is one of the reasons why my wife and I have provided nice clothes for him and a nice car for him because we wanted him to know that we believed enough in him to say, "Here it is...Here it is." We wanted him to realize that he did not have to get into drugs or illegal behavior in order to acquire nice possessions and do well.

My son was enrolled at the Mount Washington School for Boys, the last military school in Maryland. It was run by the Catholic Church. My wife and I were very active at that school. I served on the board. One time when Harlow was very young, he marched in a parade. The Sun, Baltimore's daily paper, took a picture of him. It appeared in The Sunday Sun. He was in the second grade, and he received a lot of ridicule from kids and some adults, as well. Their conclusion was that the The Sun took his picture because of who his parents were. That sort of hurt him. I have always tried to encourage my son to strive to be at the top or near the top. I remember on one occasion there were some white parents who seemed not to enjoy having blacks attend the school. They did many subtle things to make it uncomfortable. I recall when the school conducted a fund-raising campaign that involved selling various consumer items. Prizes would be given to students who were the top sales achievers. I knew that my son was going to be number one. I was very confident in his will to succeed. When some white parents who were members of the fundraising committee realized that Harlow would become the number one seller, they pooled their resources to ensure that it would not happen. We were left holding the bag. At that time, the school was a place where black students would encounter many negative experiences full of racist overtones.

Some faculty members and students went out of their way to really make it difficult for my son. As a result, we transferred him to Arlington Baptist School, an institition that had a predominantly white enrollment. In my opinion, that school was even worse. When Harlow's experiences at Arlington Baptist School became difficult for him, I began to talk to him about the value of public education. However, I really needed to try to get him into a different kind of environment, one where people did not place much emphasis on what you had or did not have, or what your parents did or what your daddy did or whatever. No, I am not speaking of Utopia or some extremely tranquil and perfect world. There are good and righteous people in our society. I knew this already, but I urgently had to convince my son of this.

I wanted my son to develop to be his own person. Because of the schools that we had enrolled him in, it was difficult for him to understand that there are good people who do not constantly remind you of your race or heritage. By enrolling my son in those private schools, I guess I was basically trying to create success for him. Like many parents, I thought that a mere location, a venue, the mere name of an institution could mean that your child would be successful. I guess I was guilty of buying the name. To this day, I take a lot of blame for the predicaments in which my son found himself. One day, he said, "Daddy, I don't want to stand on the corner and get on a private bus while my friends are waiting for the bus going to the public school." He indicated that he wanted to go to a public middle school where his friends were. We decided to give him that opportunity with the hope that he would do well.

Here is an example of my son's experiences at Johnnycake Middle School, which is known today as Southwest Academy. I am revealing these facts not to criticize the school itself but to shine a light on what could be a pattern in our society, an unfortunate pattern that must stop. My son had played the clarinet since he could walk, and he was quite good at it. That school had a band. The band had what is called first and second chair. A white youth was given the first chair over him when all the students knew that Harlow had earned the first chair.

Children know. You cannot fool them. They know when they should be here or there. Harlow became very discontent, to the point where he gave up after he had been playing the clarinet for six or seven years. Since then, he has never touched the clarinet. That is because he felt that he had been the victim of prejudice.

Later on, my son came to me and said, "Daddy, I would like to be president of the student government. I know that you were when you were in high school. Will you help me?" I did. We bought some lollipops, and we formed a campaign committee for Harlow. When the school bus came, he had his committee pass the lollipops out. He had posters and all. He had a good mind for art.

His opponent was white, and the school was about 85 percent white at the time. Guess what? Harlow won. However, he received more ridicule from the faculty and staff, which was predominantly white, than he did from the students who elected him.

On one occasion at that school in the classroom when he entered, the teacher stopped what he was doing and said, "I just want all of you to know that this is a very fine example of how you buy an election." It hurt Harlow so badly that for the rest of his middle and high school tenure he never participated in any extracurricular activities. He went to Woodlawn High School, and he was having such a hard time. Sometimes, children can be very cruel to one another. That was not a good environment for him.

I am proud to say that today my son is a certified paramedic, working for a private company. He also works with young people who are experiencing difficulties in life because they are mentally or physically handicapped. His work is very rewarding. He is another family member in a line of Fullwoods who cared and who shared their lives for those who were in need of encouragement. Yes, my son has undergone many difficulties like many young people in his time. Harlow attends UMBC, the University of Maryland Baltimore County, where he is enrolled in the computer engineering program.

I always used to criticize him about his style of dress. I said to him once, "The way you dress, with your pants hanging down, and those big baggy pants, your shirt outside of your pants, and all of that, IBM won't hire you like that." And he looked at me and said, "Daddy, I want you to know, I know how to dress when I go to an interview. But, right now, I'm going to enjoy being the way I am." My son. My son.

My daughter is Paquita. In Spanish, her name means small. She is now an adult. She completed high school and college. She did very well, and I am very proud of her. She attended schools where my wife and I were very active. Actually, we have been active parents wherever our children attended school. At the elementary school, I was a member of the board of the Parent-Teachers Association. At that school, we noticed that for the first two or three years, Paquita was somewhat slow in her studies. My wife, being a teacher, recognized it. Paquita was missing many of the basic skills that she should have gotten early in school.

We went to Dr. Edna Mae Merson, the school's principal. She was very knowledgeable and had a Ph.D. degree. At that time, Woodmoor Elementary School had about a 98 percent white enrollment. Dr. Merson personally tutored Paquita in mathematics. Today, Paquita is a math teacher. What a turn-around.

When Paquita began her enrollment at Woodmoor Elementary School, she did not get off to a good start in that first year when she was in kindergarten. She was moving very rapidly, but my wife was able to detect that something was missing. Later, we found out from the principal that Paquita had a couple teachers in the first and second grades that the principal was trying to get out of the classroom and out of the school.

Well, we all know that it is easier to get teachers, but it is hard to get rid of them when you find that they are not doing the job, especially when unions are involved. Of course, I truly believe a bad teacher is worse than a person who goes out and commits mayhem. They cripple a young person for life. Many young people do not have a support system outside school. They are dependent upon the school to teach them the basics that can help them get off to a good start. Additionally, I have been able to see that if we do not teach young people how to read at an early age, we are asking for a disaster.

The contemporary ultimatum that I have in the back of my mind is: Either pay me now or pay me later. If we do not provide those opportunities early, then we are going to have to provide other provisions that are not something of which we want to really be a part, such as more prisons and other institutions that support those of us who did not receive an adequate, quality education.

I certainly feel that in urban American, 75 percent to 80 percent of all the problems that exist, in part, are due to the fact that some individuals lack education and training. Some do not possess any employable skills. Many of these persons have become lost in the system. Some dropped out of school, and, surprisingly, some completed school while illiterate. Many cannot even write a complete sentence and, perhaps, not even their own name. I am very concerned about this unfortunate syndrome.

My daughter's learning capabilities were discovered early, and then she excelled. Paquita graduated from high school. She had mail coming in from different private colleges and universities from throughout the country, such as Vassar and many others.

Once while I was talking with her, after seeing letters coming in from other colleges and universities, I asked her what her intentions were and what were her plans about college. She started crying and rushed upstairs. She would hardly speak to me for four or five days. When she finally got it together, she said, "Daddy, I was offended because I see how hard you work for the survival of historically Black schools, and you thought I was going to go somewhere else. I, too, want to go to Virginia Union University." I was deeply moved by that statement. I beamed with pride.

Her first year, or year and a half, at Virginia Union involved very unpleasant situations because she was around students who were doing drugs and drinking - students who were living a rough life and exhibited negative behavior. She even had a roommate who had some of those habits. Of course, it became very unpleasant to her.

I have always been very active all my life in trying to be supportive of education and, particularly, Historically Black Colleges and Universities (HBCU's). I am one who truly believes, from the bottom of my heart, that there is no place for a person who serves on the school board of public education, if that person sends his or her own children to a private institution. That tells me something. When I see principals and teachers sending their kids to private schools and all, that is also telling me something. I do not want to be part of that. It is hypocrisy and bad faith.

I feel that if a person believes in something well enough and endeavors to sell it to another person, then the person should follow through with that commitment. For instance, how can I sell the quality of Virginia Union University, but when given the opportunity, send my child somewhere else? I wanted my daughter to go to Virginia Union although at that time, I was not able to afford the tuition. I believed that if it were good enough for me, it was good enough for her, and she brought more positive tools to the table than I. She enrolled. I rejoiced. She did extremely well. I recall that when she graduated from Virginia Union, the professor said to me, "We really made something out of her." And, I said, "I can't give you all that credit because I sent you something to work with."

My daughter had also experienced problems growing up. There was jealousy because my wife dressed her well, kept her looking good, and she had good manners. She also had a good value system, good work habits, and effective study skills. As you can see,

I am very proud of her. Nevertheless, she too had unpleasant experiences growing up.

I served on the Board of Trustees at Virginia Union University for fourteen years. Ironically, the professors were abrupt with her mostly because of me. She was unable to get into a sorority, which broke her heart, because some things were done intentionally to hinder her from going on line. For a while, the experience was very unpleasant for Paquita.

However, because of all of those experiences, fortunately, she turned out a better person, a stronger person. Because of those experiences and because she had someone that she could share it with, she became strong. Elnora and I were always available to listen to whatever problems that Paquita had. Upon graduating from college, Paquita said that she wanted to work with me for a while because she knew that I needed some help. She did work with me for ten years.

Prior to completing college, she met a fellow named Robert Calvin Stokes; he was from Philadelphia, Pennsylvania. They fell in love while at Virginia Union where he was also a student. A couple of months after she came home from graduation, she said to me that she wanted to get married. She went on to say, "I want you to know up front that he's poor, but I love him." Without hesitation, I said to her, "Go get him because I have been there before. I understand where you are coming from. At least, the two of you will have a little more to start with than your mother and I did because we started out with almost absolutely nothing. We never asked anyone for anything. And, with regard to all that we've done and all that we've accomplished, I can assure you that we worked in a manner by which we never had to look over our shoulders to see whom we had mistreated."

Paquita was thrilled when she heard my comments. She already knew that I had very high standards; therefore, she was quite apprehensive about how I might react to her marriage plans. My candid and forthright reaction was unexpected. She thanked me, laughed with relief, and then she jumped with glee.

Robert worked for me for a while, and he was an excellent employee. It seems as though my family is all about serving humanity. Later, he decided that he wanted to have a career in law enforcement. Currently, Robert is working as a police officer with the Baltimore Police Department. From their marriage, they have presented Elnora and me with the most wonderful grandson that one could ever have. By all indications of his performance in the classroom now, I must say that Robert Harwil Stokes is one brilliant young man.

So often I wondered about my two children and how they would develop. As I reflect on the past, I wonder if I could have done anything better as a father. Maybe I could have, but I tried to rear them the way I was reared. I was strict, and I encouraged them to develop a positive philosophy. Sometimes, because of the change of time and the so-called modern styles of parenting, I did not know whether the old way was always the best way.

I remember the best advice my father ever gave me. Actually, I really did not have a close relationship with my father because I was with my grandmother most of my earlier life. However, I remember my father always saying, "A man who does not take care of his own is less than a dog." In the case of many of us who are striving to be successful, we try to provide our children with many of the things that we never had. I do not think there is anything wrong with that as long as we teach responsibility and accountability to go along with it. If I had all of the answers about parenting, I would not be in the chicken business. I would be at the right side of the president of the United States, giving advice so that we could all understand how important family is. My wife's family is an excellent example of unity. There are eight siblings. With respect to those brothers and sisters, I say, without a reservation, that theirs is the closest family I have ever met in my life. The family continues to be an inspiration to me.

I recall what my wife's father said when I asked if he would be gracious and bless us if we married. That succinct statement was very emphatic. He said, "If you love her, I don't have a problem, but if you don't love her, she already has a place to stay." Marrying Elnora has been one of the best decisions I have ever made in my life. I have not always been popular with the family, but I have loved my wife. Things have not always been like I wanted them to be, but I have always been independent, not depending on anyone. Once I married I had to look, for the first time, beyond myself and try to provide an environment in which my wife and I could develop. Marriage is a commitment. It is a partnership. The husband and wife have to discover the techniques and methods that work effectively for them.

Harlow Fullwood, IV
"Second Grandson"
(2 Years Old)

Elnora and I decided that we would pool our resources and budget. When we lived in a low-income area in the city, we decided that we wanted to buy a house. We were not accustomed to all the concrete and asphalt of urban life. We wanted a house with a yard around it. We determined that we could only find the type of house we wanted in the county. Today, we live in Baltimore County. Right now, I sleep in the county and do just about everything else in Baltimore City. However, after I finish work — I really enjoy going home. I enjoy going to my comfort zone, with its grassy lawn, beautiful flowers, fresh air, and open space.

That was our preference while we were living in the Cherry Hill area of Baltimore where I met some very wonderful, wonderful people who are still friends of mine as of today. In fact, on occasion, I invite them to come and play cards and have dinner. One of the first things those friends would say is "Man, you haven't changed at all." And, I say, "Yes I have. Just look around me."

In reality, my personality is still the same because I was always taught that you can rise to the top today, but tomorrow you never know. Therefore, you should treat people in a way that you can feel good about it later. I have always done this. I have many of the same friends I had when I owned very little of anything. I am still happy to call those individuals my friends.

We saved our money, purchased a home, and I went on to purchase a new Lincoln. My wife bought a new Oldsmobile. In Woodlawn, we had a small home, but it was furnished with everything that we needed in order to be comfortable. And for that, I was grateful.

I know this may sound sexist: a woman can make a home feel very relaxing, very special. She can create a comfort zone. When I got off from work, I always looked forward to coming home because my wife made a home feel like a home. It was not a house; it was a home. The unique personalities in the house make it the home. I know that sounds corny, but it is the truth. I will always feel that anyone who works hard ought to have a comfortable escape route, and, for me, that escape route is home. I was delighted to go home when I could not go anywhere else.

I am not saying that my life has been perfect. I have made mistakes and have skeletons in the closet, as anyone else might have. So often it is not the mistake that wipes us out; it is what we do after we realize we have made a mistake. One person said, "To make one mistake is human, but to make the same mistake twice is a fool."

I have never been a person so big and so mighty that I could not humble myself to say, "Please. Thank you. Forgive me. I was wrong." I tried to exemplify it in a way whereby a person could truly see that I was regretful or sorry for whatever it might have been. I guess I might be considered as an aggressive person. I like to get things done and get things done right away because tomorrow we will be seeing a different problem. If you have not solved the problems prior to that, it becomes frustrating. More frustration is one thing we do not need in our lives.

Much of my philosophy of life has been shaped by, and is essentially based upon, some of the rich lessons that I learned from my grandmother and others who took time to counsel me. She had a way of providing very brief lectures, very short verses, and symbolic phrases that have become a part of me. I think about her every day. Sometimes before I do something, I will ask myself, "Would Granny have done it this way?"

My grandmother would often say some of the following expressions: "It takes a lifetime to build a good name; however, if you are not careful, you can destroy it overnight." Relevant to marriage, she would say, "If you marry for money, ask yourself what would happen if you no longer have money. If you marry for sex, ask yourself what would happen if you could no longer satisfy the person sexually. If you marry for beauty, just ask yourself what would happen when the wrinkles show up."

Some additional memorable sayings, maxims, and pearls of wisdom that my grandmother left me are:
√ If you want to find yourself a good wife, look in the church or the library.
√ If you do evil and have no remorse or fear about it, then I feel that God has given up on you.
√ Never be afraid to stand up for what is right and just.
√ A good name is priceless.
√ You will never have anything in life if you expect to pay for everything in cash.
√ A good name is money in the bank.
√ You do not have to look for trouble; it will find you if you do not protect yourself against it.

√ When you live right, you do not have to spend a lot of time looking over your shoulders.

√ Never be too big or too proud to walk away from a troubled situation.

√ Good manners, a pleasant disposition, and good work ethics will open many doors that would ordinarily be closed.

√ Always be willing to give a helping hand to the helpless.

√ Never let money and success control you. You control it.

√ Regarding God, I prefer to die believing.

√ Honor your mother, your father, and God will richly bless you.

√ Always be prepared for a rainy day.

√ Sometimes God slows us down so that we can take a closer look at how fast we are going.

√ Sometimes it is better to travel alone than with someone who is in misery.

√ Sometimes when you travel alone, you can read the direction signs a lot better.

√ When a husband and wife work together, their potential for a successful marriage is unlimited.

When referring to me, Granny would say, "I want you to always remember that this is your home and will always be your. home, but never forget that this is my house. Never be ashamed to say to someone I am sorry and mean it. The greatest feeling in the world is to love and to be loved. Work a job in a way that when you decide to leave, the door is always open to you whenever you wish to return. Sometimes you can kill a person not by what you say but how you say it. An idle mind is the devil's workshop. The devil thrives on a person who is going nowhere, lost in misery. Learn to have faith in something else, other than yourself. Always remember that you have to give respect in order to get respect. Worry is like a rocking chair. It will give you something to do, but it will not get you anywhere. Always be willing to walk a mile with a friend. Never be ashamed of where you came from, and never forget the people who helped you along the way."

Clarence Lee Moore, my high school football coach, would often say, "Winning isn't everything, but it is way ahead of whatever is in second place." Thomas Harris, my college football coach, once said, "Show me a good loser, and I will show you a regular loser. I am going to take this football and teach each of you the real game of life."

My step-grandfather Owen Floyd once asked me what were my intentions upon graduating from college, what were my plans, and I said, "Well, I want to work a job, retire and then see the world." His reply was interesting. He said, "Son, I want you to take my advice and see the world before you retire because I am certain that you want to do more than just sightsee." Some of his sayings included: "Whatever you do, do it first-class, and if you cannot do it first-class, wait until you can. Sometimes the best that you do is not good enough. When you look in the mirror and you say to yourself, "I have done my best," then no one will know whether that is truly right but you. The difficult things in life are not always easy. Character is the one thing you have that no man can take from you. Obtaining education is difficult, but it pays great dividends. Let your light shine in a way that would lead others out of the darkness."

I am proud to share some of the memories that I treasure. Many of us can look back and recall the rich lessons that one or more of our relatives taught us. Perhaps at the time, we considered them to be nagging us. Perhaps we rejected that advice when it was provided, but when we mature we sometimes replay those statements in our mind. We go through a careful process of dusting off those pieces of gold and reshining them to a bright gloss. Next, we find ourselves handing-down those same words of wisdom, common sense, and perceptiveness to our own children and to others. Albert Einstein said, "Try not to become a man of success. Rather, become a man of value." My goal is to share my values with others.

Sometimes success can be elusive and may occur only after much effort, but one must never give up. Abraham Lincoln became United States president only after he had been defeated in 13 elections for various government jobs. He never gave up.

George Washington Carver once said, "Ninety-nine percent of failure comes from people who have the habit of making excuses." I am proud of my success, and I earned it.

At this point, I do not have any additional business goals other than to witness my children reach their goals. Their choices have not been to follow me into the KFC business. However, that business venture enabled my children to have opportunities to advance and to seek their own places in the world. They are doing that, and I am gratified.

Harlow Fullwood III and Harlow Fullwood, Jr.

Robert Harwil Stokes
First Grandchild
(10 years old)

Ms. Lucy Mae Harrison
"My Favorite
High School Teacher"

My High School
Football Coach
Clarence L. Moore

Replica of Stephens-Lee
High School
"Castle on the Hill"

In High School with State Football
Championship Trophy

Chapter Four

High School Years

O ne of the most inspirational persons that I have met is Frantz C. Wilson. I met him when I was a student in high school. I am honored to share his kind words about me. When Mr. Wilson learned that I was writing my autobiography, he sent me the following statement and asked that I consider including it in my book:

Every once in a while, one has the opportunity to meet a high school student who really has his head on right. I had just that opportunity in June of 1958, when I had just moved from my hometown to accept the executive director's position at the Market Street Branch Young Men's Christian Association (YMCA) in Asheville, North Carolina. I was in the process of putting together the counseling staff for the YMCA's summer day camp. I met with Mr. Joseph E. Belton, principal of the local Stephens-Lee High School, to get the names of students whom he would recommend that I interview. Without the slightest hesitation, he told me that, "The first person you want to interview is Harlow Fullwood, president of our student council and captain of the football team. This young fellow really has his head on right, and he is going to make a real name *for himself." Thus began one of my most rewarding experiences. I hired him, and soon Harlow was teaching Bible classes, coaching, teaching all the camp games, and setting the kinds of examples for the young campers that any father in the country would want for his son. Many of the young boys began calling him "brother." A few even began calling him "father."*

Over the last forty-two years, we have remained the best of friends. Harlow proudly points out to all that will listen that I gave him his first job. What he has not told to all who will listen is that he gave me my first real experience to witness a young man with his head on right.

When I was in the eighth grade, in my high school, football was a big thing. It was a big social outlet. We had good turnouts. I can remember an incident that occurred while attending my first football game. At that time, I did not know what organized football was all about. I saw the captain of the visiting team and the captain of our home team in the middle of the field. They flipped the coin. I asked the guy standing next to me, "What are they doing? Who are those guys in the middle of the field?" It seems like that incident occurred just yesterday. He said, "You dumb S...of a B...! Those are captains, and you'll never be one!" That hit me like a ton of bricks. I went on to become an All-State tackle and captain of the football team and played in the Shriners East-West All-Star game. That guy was negative, but he was also motivational.

When I went home, I went down on Eagle Street. That was where all the black folks would hang out. There were little shops, a barbershop, liquor store, and other businesses. And, there he was – that very same guy. He was standing on the corner. It was 20 years later, and he was standing on the corner. I pulled my car up to the curb, got out, and I took $50 out of my pocket. I walked over to him, shook his hand, and put the $50 in it. I got back in my car and drove off. To this day, I do not think he has ever realized what he had said to me. That was my way of saying, "thank you."

The ninth grade was where I met my first homeroom teacher. I could tell by her first reaction to me that she seemed to be thinking, "This guy is rough, but I believe that I can help him become somebody." That teacher was Miss Lucy Mae Harrison. She was very supportive. Sometimes you can determine a person's sincerity by the way the person speaks to you. Miss Harrison had a very reassuring way of verbalizing her compassion.

I remember when the Brooklyn Dodgers would come to Asheville, North Carolina each year to play an exhibition game against the Asheville Tourists, the Dodgers's farm team. We were always thrilled to see the Negro players. In my hometown, African Americans (or Negroes, as we were called during my high school years) could not sleep in the same facilities where white athletes slept and ate. Jim Crow was quite prevalent. It was always on my mind about how they (whites) could be so good but treated us so differently. The Dodgers had two of America's most famous baseball players on its team, Jackie Robinson, the first black major league player, and Roy Campanella, the first black catcher in major league baseball history. In spite of their national fame, these two men and other Negro players could not stay in certain hotels because of segregation. They either had to stay at the Savoy, the only black hotel in Asheville, or they stayed in private homes.

I always admired sports as I was growing up, particularly baseball. There was a player named Lou Gehrig. I read his story. I was so impressed by him, especially by knowing he was one of the best players that ever donned a uniform. He played first base for the New York Yankees. Physicians detected that he was dying of a fatal disease known today as Amyotrophic Lateral Sclerosis (ALS). It is an incurable, degenerative neurological disorder.

When the baseball world heard of Lou Gehrig's condition, about 60,000 fans gathered in Yankee Stadium to see and hear Lou Gehrig. He was to be on stage at home plate for perhaps the last time. Gehrig was called to the microphone at home plate, and this is what he said: "Even though I know that I'm going to die, I consider myself on this day, at this hour, the luckiest man on the face of this earth." I would like to paraphrase and apply the reference to my current status, to say, "Considering where I came from and how I got to where I am now, it is truly, truly a blessing."

In high school, I discovered that I loved sports. I wanted to go to college, but I knew I needed money. I also knew that my folks did not have any. When I was in the ninth grade, Coach Clarence Lee Moore, head football coach at Stephens-Lee High School, asked me if I was interested in trying out for the football team. Knowing that sports could be a vehicle toward gaining a college scholarship, I ultimately said yes. Coach Moore had been coaching for a long time. He coached football, basketball, and baseball. In my first year of high school, I guess I weighed about 170 -180 pounds. That was some size then.

My high school football days presented numerous challenges; for example, the school had no athletic field. We had to walk about two and one half miles to our practice field at a junior high school. There was no grass, and the field was all mud and clay. We started practice in August. School started in September. At that time, it was very hot up in the great Smokey Mountains, "The Land of the Sky." We practiced on clay, and the sunrays bounced back at us. We had such a good coach, but after the first practice, I said, "Man, this is too rough. This is too demanding."

We had to walk all that way and practice for a couple of hours, and then I had to walk about four miles home. I had to get up at 7:00 a.m. to ride the school bus for more than 45 minutes. We would pass several segregated schools to get to our school. That was rough to experience. I was in the ninth grade, spending nearly two hours every day riding a yellow bus. Still, I had to go home, perform my assigned chores, complete my homework, and study.

Riding by the segregated schools, knowing that if things were different you could already be in school studying, was almost too difficult to handle. Nevertheless, we had to cope. No one really thought about it, or at least we did not talk about it. That was just the way it was. Yes, we had problems, but for the most part, folks in Asheville respected one another. I know that if it had not been for white families, I do not know how my mother would have made it. My mother worked as a domestic for a white family that did many things to help her.

Getting back to the football part of it, after that first practice I said, "Whoa! This is too much for me!" Therefore, at the next practice, I began to make a judgement on whether I could tolerate the experience any further. I did not like doing calisthenics, running around the field and all that. So, what I did was to stand and wait, until the others finished.

Coach Moore was often referred to by students as "Prof Moore." He was enshrined into the Western North Carolina Hall of Fame. During 1944, Moore formed the Asheville Blues baseball team in the Negro Southern Baseball League. Under Moore's leadership, the Blues won the pennant in 1946-47. Moore's contributions to sports were acknowledged by the establishment of a permanent file on him in 1972 by the Baseball Hall of Fame Library in Cooperstown, New York. Moore had sent more than 100 athletes to college on scholarships. He said, "The joy I got out of coaching was seeing my boys make good and go on to college. That was the main reason that I coached. I wanted them to earn a good income. And now, when I go to other cities, the kids I sent to college can't do enough for me."

Coach Moore completed his undergraduate studies at Shaw University; he started out at Virginia Union University. Both are Baptist institutions. He later went to North Carolina Agricultural and Technical University (A&T) to receive his master's degree in chemistry and mathematics.

I went to VUU where Coach Moore's son, Robert, was a math major and a member of the football and basketball teams. I was very proud that one year we went to play North Carolina Central University (then North Carolina College) for its homecoming. I was also very proud to have gone to my home state as captain of the Virginia Union University Panthers, and Robert a member of the football team and captain of the basketball team. Both of us were from Stephens-Lee High School.

There was a friend in high school, Wilbur Mapp, who went to North Carolina A&T University. He graduated and is now a renowned artist and sculptor. He does work for folks all over the United States. He and I were good friends, and we were excellent ball players on our high school football team that won the 1957 North Carolina State Triple A Championship. There was one thing about those teams we played on; our coach had us dressed well. We traveled on nice buses, and our coach would always say, "We're going to look and play like winners." He really prepared us. In fact, he took the game of football and taught us the game of life.

I recall that Coach Moore always knew what our grades were before we did. He required us, once a month or once every two weeks, to meet him as a group on some church steps on Sunday. We would attend church as a group. Those of us who failed to show up did not dress for a game. I guess what he was trying to do was to get us to understand that as a team we do things as a team and when one was damned, all of us were damned. He placed a lot of emphasis on giving us the opportunity to look at different religions. He realized that we could be the best possible, but he also felt that we could not be successful unless we had some religion in our lives.

One of the best pep talks I have heard was made by Coach Moore. I was blessed to have had two wonderful coaches through my high school and college careers. I remember we were in the dressing room on Thanksgiving Day in 1957. We were getting ready to play Booker T. Washington High School out of Rocky Mount, North Carolina, which is located in the eastern part of the state, for the Triple A North Carolina State Championship. Asheville is in the western part of the state, so they had to come and visit us. During those times, we did not have what you call a weak schedule because often our schedule was established so that we could open up with the South Carolina State Champions and finish against maybe the Tennessee State Champions; and then, we played our schedule all in between.

The stadium was packed that afternoon. As I pointed out, high school football in my hometown was a tremendous social outlet, and everyone looked forward to it. We played our home games in the city stadium. It was impressive when you would come out of the tunnel on to the field and see all of the supporters.

Harlow Fullwood, Jr.

Coach Moore said that there was nothing that we could accomplish by playing weak opponents. He said that we could not grow off weakness, "We grow off strength." I would guess from those inspirational provisos, I played my best games. The tougher the competition, the better I played. We made many sacrifices. We did not have our own practice field, had to walk long distances, study, and practiced on a field that young folks today would not dream of practicing on.

Coach Moore would always say, "We're good because we have paid the price." In order to be successful in anything, you have to pay the price. As someone said, "Sometimes, you've got to give up blood, sweat, and tears." You have to sacrifice. Often folks see success, but they never see the sacrifices that were made before that success was attained. If there is any one thing that Coach Moore instilled in all of us, it was that we use the tool of the football to gain the opportunity to develop ourselves spiritually, culturally, socially, and academically. He knew that many of us had to depend on athletic scholarships in order to achieve the dreams and goals that we set forth for ourselves.

Prior to the Triple A North Carolina State Championship game, Coach said, as his pep talk, "I want you all to remember that you're not playing for me today. You're playing first for what you can get out of it; secondly, you're playing for your school and for the community that we live in; finally, I want you to go out there today and give it all you've got. I want you to look good. The greatest feeling I have is when you look good... because, then...I look good. So come on...and let's go out there and look good together." We won the game 25-6.

I think on that evening, and the evening the week before that leading up to the Regional Championship -- during those last two games in the year -- we could have defeated any high school team in the country. We were that good. It was the greatest pleasure in the world to win that game. There were three of us who advanced to play in the East/West Shriners Bowl in Greensboro, North Carolina. The West won for the first time. I was very proud to have made a winning contribution to that effort.

My grandmother and step-grandfather never watched me play in a football game, but they heard several of my games on the radio. Granny would say to me, "I didn't understand what was going on, but I know they called your name a lot." That made me feel very proud.

During my senior year, we were required to participate in a competitive essay contest. It was sponsored by the Civitan Club. White students and black students, high school seniors from throughout Buncombe County, North Carolina, competed in that essay contest. Writing an essay for participation in the contest was part of the requirement for Miss Harrison's course in English. I remember that we had a deadline by when to submit our essay, and I missed it. I had not even written it yet. Miss Harrison asked me, "Do you plan to graduate?" I said, "Yes Ma'am." She said, "You will not graduate." I believed her, so I went home and wrote the essay. It was a very difficult project for me.

While I was up late working on that essay, my grandmother came downstairs and put her arm around me. She said, "I know what you're doing is difficult. The real game of life is never easy. If you want to be good at what you do, you gotta pay the price." My grandmother was illiterate, but she had great wisdom.

Every time I brought the paper up to Miss Harrison, she would read it, mark it up with a red pen and say, "Go rewrite it." I did that about five days in a row. She told me to rewrite it again on a Friday. I was very angry, and I said to myself, "The hell with this!" I balled up that paper, threw it in the trashcan, and walked out the classroom. Do you know she had someone get that paper out the trashcan, had it typed, and turned it in? Moreover, guess what? I won second place in the entire county. Well, right then and there, I realized that Miss Harrison was trying to show me that if you want to be good, you are going to have setbacks. You cannot let the setbacks mess up your mind to the point where you give up. That was what I had done. Miss Harrison pushed me to excellence. The experience also taught me that I had to be willing to accept positive criticism.

I will always remember the name of that essay: "Citizenship Is a Process of Gradual Achievement." A 1957 article that appeared in the *Skylighter*, the school newspaper, described me as one of the most outstanding seniors in the history of the school. The Civitan Club at a Citizenship Luncheon held at the George Vanderbilt Hotel, a segregated hotel, honored the winners of the essay contest. For having placed second, I received a $50 United States Savings Bond and a Silver Medal. I felt very special on that day because I was the only African-American winner, thanks to Miss Harrison.

We had a policy at Stephens-Lee High School that no one could leave the school grounds without authorization or permission. As a member of the student council, I helped to enforce the rules and regulations that were set forth. We had to report any violators to the principal's office. The principal at that time, Dr. Frank A. Toliver, asked me to go to the store for him. Understanding school policy, I said that I could not do that. I recited the policy to him and explained that if I violated the rule, the students would not know whether I was going to the store for him or for myself. Granny always emphasized to me to follow the rules. A few days later, I was told that Dr. Toliver had a faculty meeting and recounted the details of that incident to the faculty. He stated how he was impressed with the remarkable way that I conducted myself. He told them that he did not like my refusal to obey his request, but he respected my mature attitude and good judgement.

My grandparents were up in age. My step-grandfather made $35 a week. I was making more money than that caddying and doing other odd jobs as a teenager. I had to walk a long way home, when I got off the bus. Frequently, it would be extremely cold when I got home from a game, football practice, or a social event. We heated the house with coal and wood. My grandmother would fill jars with hot water and would put them in my bed so that it would be warm when I got home.

During my teenage years in high school, I could go on a date, and it would cost ten cents per person to ride the transit bus, ten cents for a hot dog, five cents for a soda, and ten cents for pop corn. I could take one dollar and have the greatest time in my life. I always worked and had my own spending money. I never had a curfew growing up. Granny said, "You know the difference between right and wrong. If you abuse the rules, then expect drastic action." That was enough warning for me. I never abused the rules. Before I would go on a date, she would always state to me in a very direct manner, "Remember that thing between your legs has no eyes. It will go wherever you put it."

My grandmother often stated to me, "This will always be your home, but this house belongs to me." That was understood. There were high expectations and no deviations from them. When I was a teenager, Granny never told me when to come, when to go, or how to spend my money. She would fuss at me, but would say, "Yes, there is one thing for certain. We will never go to bed angry at one another."

At Virginia Union and at home I was taught to give my time and resources in service to mankind. I personally feel that character development is the greatest, if not the sole, aim of education. The best advice I was ever given might be summed up in exactly ten words: "Be honest with yourself and let your word mean something."

On graduation day, I served as one of the narrators for the commencement program. In a way, I hated to leave Stephens-Lee High School, fondly called "The Castle on the Hill." There were tears of joy and fear. Joy for having attended that wonderful high school and fear of facing the next step, college!!!

Academically, I graduated 10th out of a class of 178. I was the first student in the history of Stephens-Lee High School to be elected captain of the football team and Mayor of the Student Council in the same year. Also, I was voted the most versatile male in the senior class by my peers; I had leading roles in dramatic plays; and I was sports editor of the yearbook and school paper. Needless to say, I enjoyed every moment of my high school days.

The History of Stephens-Lee High School

In 1887, Isaac Dickinson, son of a slave mother and a Dutch father, was appointed to the Asheville City School Board. Vigorously campaigning for public schools for blacks, Dickinson helped organize the first school for blacks in an abandoned building on Beaumont Street. The school opened in 1888 with three teachers, and over 300 students were enrolled in the first five grades. Over 800 children were turned away. Paid $25 a month, which was less than half the salary of a white teacher, Beaumont Street's teachers concentrated on basic literacy. Dickinson helped establish Catholic Hill School 1891, the first public high school for blacks.

Catholic High School burned down in 1917, in one of the greatest tragedies ever to strike Asheville's schools. Seven students were killed; several others were seriously injured. In its ashes rose Stephens-lee in 1921, perhaps the best known of black schools. Named for Hester Lee and educator Edward Stephens, the new high school mirrored the philosophy of W.S. Lee who was certainly the dominant figure in black education after Isaac Dickinson. W.S. Lee was educated at Livingston College and at Columbia University in New York. An enthusiastic follower of Booker T. Washington, Lee emphasized a curriculum built around dignity, self-help, and Shakespeare. At Stephens-Lee, that meant courses in carpentry, radio repair, welding, home economics, cosmetology, English literature, music, and drama.

Stephens-Lee High School became a center for black culture and education throughout the mountains. When Yancey County's secondary school for the blacks burned down, students were loaded into a small, unheated bus and driven to Stephens-Lee. Blacks from Yancey County made a daily four and a half-hour drive into Asheville. With the only other black high school in the area being located in Hendersonville, a great many black mountaineers from surrounding counties found their way to Stephens-Lee.

The first graduating class was in 1924. Mrs. Ruth C. Carolina, who later became a long-time teacher at Stephens-Lee, and Mrs. Willie Knuckles Robinson, who later taught at the Mountain

Street Elementary School, were graduates of that class. Stephens-Lee quickly became known for its classical music program, drama production and, in the 1930's, its marching band. Only in the last decade of Stephens-Lee's existence did competitive athletics play a major part in the school's history. Coaches such as Oliver W. McCorkle and Clarence Moore always emphasized community programs and athletics as recreation, never as a system to promote the gifted few. Stephens-Lee enhanced the spirit as well as the intellect of black mountaineers. Plays, band concerts, and basketball games all drew large crowds.

The crisis over integration in the early 1960's and the subsequent decision to close Stephens-Lee challenged the very traditions of blacks in Western North Carolina. To them, Stephens-Lee was more than just a school. Representing the two strongest elements of black mountaineers — community and education — Stephens-Lee stood as a symbol of black achievement, independence, and culture. The hill where the school was built had been the center of black education for over a century.

It was here where the first "arbor school" for slaves had been built, where the first school for blacks was organized after the Civil War, where the only black high school known by many mountaineers had been for over sixty years. During the integration crisis of 1962-1972, the decision was made to close Stephens-Lee, thus resulting in the demolishing of the building where academic subjects were taught. Left standing was only the gymnasium and the fond memories of the teachings, pride, and dignity of all who passed through its doors.

Happy Birthday!
To My Favorite
Teacher,
Miss Lucy Mae
Harrison (94 years-old)

Stephens-Lee High School,
Ashville, North Carolina

*"A positive teacher who
helped me to visualize
and develop the spirit of
'Caring and Sharing' at
an early age."*

—Harlow Fullwood, Jr.

1959

1959

STEPHENS-LEE HIGH SCHOOL

ALMA MATER

O Stephens-Lee, dear Stephens-Lee
Our hearts are filled with love for thee;
A champion brave, thy youth to save - -
Thy children honor thee.
Home of truth we do believe,
Noble deeds thou wilt achieve;
In sun or rain we shall remain
Faithful to thee, dear Stephens-Lee.

O Stephens-Lee, dear Stephens-Lee
Our hearts are filled with pride in thee;
A warrior bold - - the right uphold - -
Alma Mater, dear.
When upon life's rugged sea
Oft our thoughts will turn to thee;
From day to day crimson and gray
Praise we Stephens-Lee.

Written by:
Ollie M. Reynolds
Music Teacher

Dr. Allix B. James

Robert Moore

Harlow Fullwood, Jr.

Napoleon Barbosa

Coach Thomas "Tricky Tom" Harris

Chapter Five

College Years at Virginia Union University

"Harlow Fullwood, Jr. advanced from economically disadvantaged circumstances to accomplish success in many endeavors. As a young man, he had few resources other than his faith, religion, and courage. As a student at Virginia Union University, he encountered many challenges that tested his will power and strength of character. He attributes much of his success today to the rich lessons he acquired both in and out of the classroom at VUU. Through hard work, determination, and valuable advice from faculty, staff, and coaches, Fullwood excelled as a scholar and athlete and graduated from VUU. This leading citizen in the state of Maryland, generous philanthropist, and role model for many is a proud VUU alumnus. He is an example of it's not-where-you-came from but where you are going. The story of his life is inspirational and should be required reading for all young people."

Allix B. James, President Emeritus,
Virginia Union University

The cab I took from where the bus dropped me off pulled into a circle in front of an old grey building. The cabbie said with a very raspy voice, "Here you are, buddy!"

I said, "What do you mean, here I am?...Where are we? Sir, I told you I wanted you to take me to Virginia Union University." He said with a voice that sounded like Louis "Satchmo" Armstrong, "This is it! This is VUU."

I was stunned. It felt like someone had slapped me, and my heart started beating fast.

I yelled, "No! This ain't it! It can't be it....Man, this is the raggiediest place I've ever seen!"

The cabdriver remained silent and reached his hand back for the fare. I paid him with a one-dollar bill and a hand full of change. I started crying. The driver did not even count the money; he just looked around and said, "Good luck at college, son. You have a lot to be thankful for."

I thought that was the stupidest statement I had ever heard. I slowly and reluctantly got out; the cab sped off. There I was, 18 years old and standing there crying. I looked up to the sky and said, "Precious Lord, what have I got myself into?" Sometimes in life, a scene can stay with you. I remember that incident as if it happened yesterday.

Perhaps you can remember a scene from a movie that you saw and can play that scene in your mind over and over. But this was no movie. This was real-life, and I was experiencing all kinds of emotions at the same time: fear, anger, self-doubt, regret, and just plain sadness. Actually, I did not really have a clear idea of what a college campus should look like, but I certainly did not expect to see only four grey-stone buildings.

I stood there for a while. I looked around and did not see anyone. It was so quiet that I could hear my own heart beating. Suddenly, an old, bald-headed man walked over to me. He asked, "What's wrong son?" I said, "Who are you sir?" He said, "I'm Coach Thomas Harris." I learned later that they called him "Tricky Tom." That short, stocky man with a cigar clenched in the left corner of his mouth shook my hand so hard that I can almost still feel his iron-grip today. The man probably never earned more than $14,000 a year, but his great wealth was his positive philosophy of life. He was very committed, and he generously shared his wealth of wisdom. But, at that moment, I was frightened. I said, "I'm Harlow Fullwood, Jr., and I have a football scholarship to attend this college. I didn't know it looked like this." With his deep voice, Coach Harris, said, "Son, I know why you are crying...Yes, this is Virginia Union University. I'm gonna tell you right now. I realize there's not much for the eyes to see at this place; however, if you give us a chance, we will make something out of you." Those words were powerful, and Coach Harris said them with such confidence and sincerity that I immediately stopped my crying. That first experience at VUU became one of the most inspirational events of my life. With his few words, Coach Harris prevented me from walking away from Virginia Union University and hitchhiking back to Asheville, North Carolina.

I remember registering for classes at VUU before all the other students arrived on campus. I went to the Registrar's Office, and someone gave me a pink form and told me to report three doors down the hall. When I got there, I was given a mop, a bucket, and my assignment. That assignment was to keep the hallway leading to the President's Office shining at all times. That was my job. When they handed me that mop and bucket, I thought I was going to die. I was insulted and devastated. I could not believe that I had passed up all of those other scholarships to other colleges and universities that would have paid for everything. And, here I was at a place where they gave me a mop and bucket. However, that was one of the best things that ever happened to me. That mop and bucket assignment introduced me to a new reality. It introduced me to the VUU standard, and that standard was basic: We do not give anyone everything. We will take care of your tuition, books, and fees, but you are going to have to earn your room and board.

I was very impressed by those first experiences at VUU. On my first day, I went to the campus library to read about the history of the university. I asked myself, "What is this place?

Why in the world do these folks have such high standards?" After reading a few paragraphs in a yearbook, I gained a new since of pride in being a VUU student. After my brief library research, I was able to totally understand what Coach Harris meant. I leaned that Virginia Union University was founded in 1865, the same year the U.S. Civil War ended, "to give the newly emancipated slaves an opportunity for freeing the mind in an ethical, humanistic environment." I realized that I was walking on the campus where "just-freed slaves" were educated. I was the first member of my own family ever to attend college. As a new VUU student and after reading about the university, I developed a strong sense of responsibility and determination to make my ancestors proud.

At VUU I had to work, complete my class assignments, go to football practice, and study every day. It was rough. I lived in a dormitory where the rooms were checked every day. There were two attendants, a husband and wife, who lived in the dorm. They would check to see if you were going to class, to see if your room were clean, and if your bed were made. Then they would post their findings on the bulletin board at the building's entrance for all to see. They would write on the bulletin board, for example: John Brown, bed unmade. Students, faculty, and even the president would look at that bulletin board. That daily process of public notification and potential embarrassment kept most students in line. Granny always taught me about cleanliness and cleaning up after myself, so I always had a nice room.

My name was never posted on that bulletin board. I was poor, but my room was as neat as anybody else's because l took great pride in being clean.

When we started football practice, I was very confident because I was All-State. I thought I was hot stuff. However, for the first time in my life, I competed with other guys from all over the United States who had also made All-State and All-American. They all strutted with confidence just like me. VUU had players on the team from California, Connecticut, Texas, and many other states. During that time, the top athletes that were black went to historically black schools. I always say that at our college the first ten or twelve players could have competed against anybody. They were among the best.

I had one coach who was responsible for everything; he was "Tricky Tom." They gave him that name because he was so creative and unpredictable that neither the players nor the assistant coach ever knew what he was going to do until game time when we got on the field. My experiences at practice were surprising because my high school was so poor that we did not even have a practice sled. At high school, we blocked each other. I was amazed at VUU to see how hard those guys from California, Pennsylvania and Connecticut were hitting that sled. You could hear the impact clear across campus. I remember the first time I lined up to shoot into that sled. I gave it my best shot, but someone said, "You don't hit it right, boy, and that sled is going to let you know something." I did not know what that meant until I ran into that sled, and the sled did not move. It was like running into a tree. I mean, it scarred my face all up, and all the guys started laughing. The more they laughed, the more it hurt. They said, "You big dummy. Where you from? You made All-State and all that, and you don't know how to hit a sled." I was absolutely disgraced and ashamed. No one had ever talked to me that way especially about lacking football skills. I was so mad that I could hear choir music.

Your peers can be very cruel. In Richmond, August gets so hot that you can smell the soil. On one of those hot days at practice, and after three straight days of that peer group torture, I said to myself, "That's it. I'm finished." I took my helmet off, threw it on the ground, and headed for the locker room. The players were laughing. Once I got to the locker room, I started pulling off all that sweaty football stuff. I was so hot and mad that I was steaming. I did not cuss, so I started reciting the Lord's Prayer. There I was, struggling to get relief from the heat, the hurt, and the humiliation. I started crying as I struggled to get my football gear off. Sometimes when you are angry, you just want to run away from circumstances.

I did not realize it, but Coach Harris followed me to the locker room. He hollered, "Fullwood, where you going?" I said, "I'm going home, sir." He said, "Son, what are you going back to?

The only thing a black man can do in your town is dig ditches and wash dishes. Is that what you want?" I said, "Coach Harris, I can't handle this. I cannot handle the ridicule and all that every day. I realize now that there are a whole lot of skills I didn't get, and it's because we didn't have any training equipment at my high school."

Coach Harris looked at me and said, "Fullwood, I knew that when you came here. I want you to learn something right now. You're big; you're one of the fastest guys out there; you're intelligent, but you are lacking key essentials that you need in order to be successful. You don't have a sense of commitment. That's the big difference between you being good and you being excellent. You have all the tools, but you haven't given me a chance to work with you. I'm gonna tell you, if you decide to stay at VUU, this is what I will do. I will work with you. All I have to give to you is my time. If you come back on the practice field, it's going to be very demanding. However, you are going to have to practice the regular two hours. Also, you have to arrive at practice an hour before the other guys and leave an hour after. That way, we can turn this thing around. Nobody is going to be working but you and me. That's all I can give you. Let me tell you something else. When I leave out of this room, you gotta make a decision. I can tell you that the decision you make this day will affect you for the rest of your life." I reflected upon those golden, motivational words for a few minutes, and then I decided to go back. Once again, Coach Harris stopped me from leaving VUU.

Coach Harris and I practiced every day. The guys then began to notice. They began to see that this guy Fullwood was serious. He's practicing four hours to our two hours. They were envious of my dedication and strength. I regained my confidence.

There were some good guys on VUU's team. We had a big guy on the team. He was about 6'5" and weighed about 305 pounds. He was a senior team captain. He pulled me over to the side and said, "Fullwood, I want to work with you too." There was a guy from Connecticut. I never will forget him; he was a guard. The coaches really taught fundamentals in Connecticut. He went to a school where he had access to plenty of coaching, equipment, and modern facilities.

Although I was a freshman, those guys really respected me. They looked up to me so much that when we got ready to go on the field, they would ask me to give the prayer. After the season started, I still had to come early and leave late. It got to the point where Coach Harris and I had to turn off the lights on the field. During my freshman year, I got a lot of playing time. I think it was around my fifth game when I hit that sled and busted the handle. The coach looked at me and said, "I think you're ready. So I'm going to start you." I was speechless. I as a freshman got to start in the game.

My first starting game was a classic one. On that beautiful Saturday afternoon, we played Howard University, at Howard's Stadium in Washington, DC. The sky was blue; the grass was greener than green and had that sweet, fresh-cut smell. The cheerleaders were trying to outshout and out-switch each other. Every seat in the stadium was filled. I was amazed. I was "pissing-vinegar-confident" because I was starting my first college game. I had so much adrenaline going that if they had stabbed me with a needle, I would not have felt it. My uniform was clean and shiny; I was handsome, and the cheerleaders knew it.

Well, my exhilaration came to a screeching stop. My brightest day became my darkest day. I was an offensive tackle. When I looked up, I saw the tallest, biggest football player I had ever seen in my life. That Howard University defensive tackle was 6 feet 9 inches tall and weighed 300 pounds; he was so good that professional scouts were there to watch this guy. His first hit not only made me see stars, but I saw stars of every color in the rainbow. He literally whipped me to death. Blood was running. I was hopelessly overmatched. He was a senior, and I was a freshman. My adrenaline was long-gone. I hurt so badly all over that I could feel the pain before he would even hit me, and this guy had no mercy. Howard was determined to win that game.

We had a policy at VUU that when you concluded that you

could not take any more punishment, you raised your hand and the coach would immediately take you out of the game. After the first quarter, I had enough. I raised my hand. My coach looked at me. I frantically raised and waved my hand, and my coach turned his back. I could not believe it. It was my worse nightmare; I had to play all four quarters.

Virginia Union won! VUU beat Howard by a score of 25 to zero. My team beat Howard, and that Howard defensive tackle beat me to death. VUU won. I was just there. I made absolutely no contribution to the victory.

After the game, I was badly bruised, embarrassed, and bewildered. All I could say to my coach was, "Why?" Coach Harris said, "I see that you need some more work on techniques. I saw you when you raised your hand. I just wanted you to experience what the Central Intercollegiate Athletic Association (CIAA) was all about." I could not believe what I was hearing. Coach added, "I saw some good things. You are big, fast, and intelligent. We will work hard, and one day you will be ready." There I stood, listening to these words. I knew that Coach was sincere, but I was in such pain that I could only ask him again, "Why?" I was so bruised that I looked like I had been in a boxing match with Joe Louis.

I now realize what Coach Harris was striving to do. He was showing me that experience cannot be taught. Experience must be gained. That Howard game, my first starting college football game, was an experience of a lifetime. This reminds me of a quote made by Tom Landry, the famous coach for the Dallas Cowboys, "Leadership is getting someone to do what they don't want to do, to achieve what they want to achieve." As strange as this might sound, I am glad that Coach Harris turned his back on me and made me stay in the game. Following the game, Coach Harris gave a congratulatory pep talk. He said, "Y'all go ahead and enjoy yourselves, but remember the bus is leaving out of here at midnight." I was too sore and angry to socialize.

On one occasion, I was already on the bus, and, as time went by, most of the other guys came back from socializing and got on. The coach asked the bus driver what time it was. The driver said, "It's midnight." Coach Harris said, "Let's go; it's time to move out." So, the bus pulled off. One of my teammates said, "Hold it! We're missing three of our players." The driver slowed down to try to let some players running for the bus -- get on. Coach said, "I didn't tell you to slow down." What he was showing them was that this was a team, and that you do not have different rules for some players. Everybody went by the same rules. From that point on, everyone on the team was on time for the bus. As a matter of fact, I don't know how they did it, but those three players beat the bus back to Virginia Union. They took Coach Harris seriously and were determined to demonstrate their respect for his leadership.

One of my finest football experiences was when VUU played a game against North Carolina College at Durham, North Carolina. It was that school's homecoming. I felt so proud. I was captain of the football team, and the son of my high school coach, Clarence Lee Moore, also played on the VUU football team. Robert Moore was also captain of VUU's basketball team. I know I stated this before, but it is worth repeating. This was very special for me and Robert because we had both attended high school together. Coach Moore was there to see the game as well as many students from Stephens-Lee High School. VUU lost to North Carolina College. For Robert and me, that prideful smile on the face of Coach Moore immediately took away the sting of defeat.

In my senior year at VUU, I was named to the All-Central Intercollegiate Athletic Association (CIAA) Team. There were 17 teams in the CIAA including Morgan State College, Howard University, North Carolina A&T, Virginia State, and Hampton Institute. Three players named to that ALL-CIAA team were graduates of Stephens-Lee. They were Wilbur Mapp, a center at North Carolina A&T College; his brother, Winston Mapp, an end at Winston-Salem Teacher's College and I. This was very noteworthy because it told all of the United States that Stephens-Lee was a high caliber high school for producing superior scholar-athletes.

Stephens-Lee High School closed after integration. Integration was good, but it did result in the closing of many historic black schools across the United States. In light of the local government's efforts to comply with federal guidelines, the integration process resulted in the merging of Stephens-Lee, my alma mater, with the white school known as Lee-Edwards. In order to comply with all civil rights and community-wide concerns, the new name of the school became Asheville High School and still operates today under that name.

Virginia Union University presented many academic and personal challenges for me. I had to study all the time. College was very difficult for me. I realized that I did not have a sound foundation. Many times, teachers made you feel that you were prepared because you were a good fellow. I suffered because of that factor. I always practiced good work ethics and study habits, but it was just so hard for me. God knows, at Virginia Union, I had some of the best instructors in higher education.

There are two very symbolic memories that I have about my years as a VUU football player that I will share. The first is with regard to a player named Napoleon Barbosa, my college roommate. Napoleon was the first black in the nation to be named to an All-American High School Team at the position of quarterback. After he graduated from high school, he went to work; he did not have an original intention to go to college.

My coach heard about Napoleon and went to Ohio to recruit him for Virginia Union's team. Napoleon was working in the coal mines of Ohio. My coach visited him, convinced him to enroll at VUU, and brought him back. I have seen and played with numerous football players, at high school, college, and professional levels, and I can emphatically say that Napoleon Babosa was the best all-around football player with whom I ever played. I am also proud to say that I introduced Napoleon to his wife Dorothy.

My second important remembrance involved one of the defining moments for me as I matured as a student, football player, and as a young man. My senior year at VUU was a very good year. VUU's team played Winston-Salem Teacher's College, and both of our teams were undefeated. Napoleon, my roommate, was quarterback; he was quite versatile because he also played as linebacker and punted.

Well, in that game, we were in the last quarter, and the score was 0-0. VUU scored a touchdown, but we missed the extra point, so the score was 6-0. At that time, VUU had one full-time coach and one part-time coach; on the other hand, Winston-Salem had many coaches for various positions. Accordingly, VUU's coaches were under considerable pressure as they endeavored to lead our team to victories. So, there we were, with a 6-0 lead, and there were only two minutes left. We could smell victory like it was an apple pie baking in the oven. I began to do a countdown of those 120 seconds in my mind.

At that strategic opportunity, my coach sent in a play for us to execute so that we could slam the door on Winston-Salem and win the game. When we huddled, we discussed the play, and the consensus was that it was not a very good play. To be more precise, we all thought that it was a stupid play to even use because we were ahead 6-0. Our team members seriously balked at complying with the coach's command. They encouraged me to ignore the coach and to call my own play. But I said, "Listen, yes, I am the captain, but we must follow through and execute this play as Coach Harris has instructed us to do...we must play it." He was known as "Tricky Tom" because the coaches of opposing teams never knew what new trick-play to expect from Coach Harris. However, we thought that particular play was the dumbest one that we could make under the circumstances.

Well, it was a passing play, and we executed it exactly as Coach Harris insisted. It was a deep pass, excellently thrown by Napoleon, and we were beginning to celebrate. Suddenly, someone tipped the ball, and a Winston-Salem player caught it and ran all the way. The score became 6-6. We were very upset. Like poetic justice, we blocked the extra point kick; therefore, the game ended with a 6-6 tie score. The apple pie had burned in the oven, and the smell of that burnt pie lingered. To us, that tie was a bitter defeat, and we were outraged and humiliated. After an undefeated season, it was very hard for us to cope with a tie.

The next day, there was a mood of overwhelming discontent on our team. All were silent as we reviewed the film. It was difficult for us to watch that film. The team members said that they did not want to play for Coach Harris anymore. They said, "Harlow, you tell him!" I was twenty years old, but I could feel my maturity developing as this experience was occurring. I said, "No, I will not tell Coach Harris that." They said, "If you do not tell him, then we will vote you out as team captain." I said, "Listen, Winston-Salem has many coaches. VUU has only two coaches. You have to understand that there will be times when Coach Harris might make a mistake." They replied, "All right, we will vote you out." I said, "Do as you please," and they did. I was devastated.

After that very intense experience, I went to Dr. Franklin J. Gayles, a faculty member, who was also Chairman of the Athletics Committee, and I explained the whole matter to him. He said, "Talk to Coach Harris..tell him." I did, and Coach Harris looked at me and cried uncontrollably. It was hard for me to watch that man cry. I cried with him as I told him that I had just been voted out as captain. With that additional news, Coach Harris was devastated. There we both were, two humiliated individuals. He was an unwanted coach, and I was no longer team captain. It was a very tough time for both of us.

Our next game was the last game of the season. Our opponent was Morgan State College for the CIAA Championship. VUU's president, Dr. Thomas H. Henderson, learned that I was no longer team captain. He was very disappointed, and he encouraged me to lead the team on the field anyway. I said, "No, I cannot do that." Dr. Henderson said that the team members wanted me to lead the team onto the field. Later, Coach Harris requested that I lead our team onto the field. Although it was a very ceremonial act, they desired our team to exhibit unity. I was reluctant, but I did so. Morgan State beat us by a score of 14-6 and won the CIAA Championship.

I am proud that we ran that play. I am proud that I did not bow to the insubordinate will of my teammates. If I had diverted from that play, and we had won, the victory would have been an empty one for me. Coach Harris was like a father to me. It was imperative that I, the team captain, followed his play command. He knew that, and he respected my judgement and decision. Of course, it cost me my team captain status; however, I did not compromise my position by going against the coach. That, to me, was more important than anything.

The loyalty between Coach Harris and me was unconditional. I was only twenty years old, but I had exhibited maturity and integrity. I am proud that I possessed such dedication and wisdom at such an early age. Sometimes in life, we must stand up and go against the numbers. I have never been afraid to stand up when I knew something was the right thing to do. My grandmother taught me that loyalty begets loyalty.

I encountered much difficulty with my studies. I was on a football scholarship that only covered tuition and books. I had to earn my room and board by working after practice. Then, I had to find time to do assignments and study. During that time, if you were placed on academic probation, you lost everything. You had to go home. You were given a candy bar and a bus ticket. The school did not waste any money. Consequently, I asked everybody on campus to help me. I went to see Dr. Thomas Henderson, the university president. He had an "open door" policy. After I had seen everyone else, I went to see him. He looked up over his glasses and said, "What are you doing in here?" I bowed my head when I told him about my problem. I was so ashamed to be on academic probation. He said, "Well, you know what the rules are." I said, "I can't go back home."

What led to this predicament was understandable to me. I was doing excellently until the peer pressure and campus social life got to me. Every time the guys passed by my room, I was busy studying. They would tell me, "Let's go out. Why don't you come with us and have a good time?" There were some nice girls around Richmond. After so many weeks, I broke down and went out with the fellows. It got so good to me out there that I started going out every night. When I got my grades, I said, "Oh Lord, what am I gonna do now?"

That is how I ended up in the president's office. He asked the secretary to bring him my first-year record and my high school record. He looked over them and said, "You're worth saving." He wrote something down on a sheet of paper and told me to take it to the business office. After reviewing everything, he said, "You've earned a second chance." That was my turning point, my awakening. That is why I tell young people today, what you do early in life can hurt you or help you. After having had a one-on-one session with the president of the university, I was not about to mess up again.

Many times, I could not go home when other students left for the holidays. I would stay on campus and take odd jobs. In fact, the only other students on campus with me were the students from Africa. Incidentally, those African students were very serious about education. You could see it when they graduated. They understood that this opportunity would never come again. They were here on visas. They got their education and went back to their countries. They did not go to football games, basketball games, and social events. They studied, learned, earned their degrees, and went home to share their knowledge.

On one particular morning during a holiday period, I was walking across campus. The president saw me walking across campus and said, "Fullwood, have you had your breakfast yet?" I said, "What breakfast?" He invited me into his house. He did not invite me in the back door. I went through the front door. I had on slick pants, the kind that have been ironed so much that they shined. My shoes were so worn out that I had to put cardboard in the soles and replaced that cardboard often. Well, you know the value of cardboard. In spite of my appearance, the president always treated me with dignity. He invited me through his front door, and I sat where other presidents had sat and had breakfast with him. After breakfast was over, he gave me some odd jobs around the house and paid me.

On the way out the door, his wife paid me too. She said, "That's not enough." She knew too that I needed a lot of help. At Virginia Union, you gained all kinds of experiences. I did not know that I was poor until I went to college. Where I came from, you ate the crops you grew. My grandmother canned vegetables and fruits, smoked meat, and even made soap. She could always find the fixings to cook a good meal and help us get by.

The first time that I experienced hunger, I thought I was going to die. On Sundays at VUU, you ate twice, breakfast and dinner. After that, you had to wait until breakfast for your next meal. This particular time, I missed my dinner. Students had to be at the dining hall at a certain time. That was the first time that I thought I was going to go to bed hungry. I said my prayers, drank some water, and got in bed. I heard a gentle knock at the door. I got up to answer it, and there was a special delivery package for me, a great big box! It was from Mrs. Erline McQueen, a lady that I used to help in her restaurant and never charged her anything. She remembered my act of kindness. She sent a note that said, "I thought you might need this at this time." I was so moved by that act of generosity that I called in some other fellows to share my good fortune. Man, that was some good eating. There was fried chicken, and lots of other good food in that box. My prayer was answered. Man, the chicken, that bird, must be my blessing!

Dr. David T. Shannon, who later became the ninth president of Virginia Union University, taught a Philosophy of Life course. On the first day, he asked me and the class to write one page on the question "Who am I?" After much uncertainty and after sitting there for at least ten minutes, I realized that I could not form one thought. I said to Dr. Shannon, "I don't have the slightest idea how to start writing on that question." He said, "After the course is completed, I'm going to ask you to write about the same question." On the final examination, he did. He was so impressed with my essay that he asked me whether I had I ever been interested in the ministry. Many folks thought that I would pursue the ministry.

Harlow Fullwood, Jr.   VUU 1960   "My Sophomore Year"

Elnora Bassett   VUU 1960   "My Sophomore Year"

I later discovered that one can share and make a difference in people's lives away from the pulpit. I do not think you have to be a preacher to make a positive difference.

At Virginia Union University, I was baptized by Dr. Shannon who was also pastor at Ebenezer Baptist Church. I remember very vividly that VUU was the place where I accepted the Lord Jesus as my Savior. At Virginia Union, I received many quality gifts -- gifts of love, understanding, and dedication. Folks took time to sit down and counsel me when I was going off to the left. I received a good education, academically and spiritually. One of my most precious gifts gained at VUU was the fact that I met a beautiful young lady in the library, where I often studied, who later became my wife. As I look back, I realize that God really blessed me with Elnora, a caring and supportive wife.

At Virginia Union, I majored in sociology and played football. I had very little time of my own because I had to study. I recall that I went on a football trip, and my term paper was due for a course in sociology. We had to read a book and write an essay about it. Unfortunately, through poor judgment, I had someone write the paper for me. In my hurry, I didn't take the time to read it. When I sat down for my mid-term examination, the first forty questions were relevant to that paper. I could not answer one question. I received a grade of "F." I also received a lecture from the instructor, Dr. Wendell P. Russell, who was also Dean of Students. Always try to be your own person. Never try to get something for nothing. That was the impression he left on me. While I was at Virginia Union, I had one particular professor, of many, who really helped me. He was Henry Hucles, one of VUU's outstanding basketball coaches. He led what they called the "Dream Team." He would beat teams that competed for national championships. Later, he retired and stayed on as an instructor. He was in charge of intramural sports and health education. He bought me my first jacket; before that, I was walking around campus broke and without a coat. We got to be real good friends. However, I abused that friendship. I did not go to his class or do the work. I earned an "F" at mid-term. He sat me down and told me, "Always remember in life, never abuse

abuse friendship. If I let you get away with it, then I'm not doing anything to strengthen your life. You have the potential to pass my class. Always remember, you can't get something for nothing." I said to him, "The second half of the semester, whatever I earn, will you give it to me and disregard the 'F'?" He said, "I think that's a fair deal." I never missed another day. That taught me something. Yes, I earned a "B."

I was in another course, zoology. That was one of the hardest. I attended class every day. The professor, Dr. Walter O. Bradley, gave us a test every week. He was also Director of the Division of Science and Mathematics. I had never made more than a grade of 65. Never. I said, "Lord, what can I do?" When I got my grade, I saw that I had earned a "C." I just knew that I had failed that course. I saw the professor walking across campus. I ran up to him, grabbed his hand, and said, "Thank you!" He said, "Fullwood, whatever you got, you earned. I saw how hard you tried. You were in my class every day, on time, and you tried hard. I would have had no compassion if I had flunked you." That statement lifted me.

Another memorable academic experience at VUU was when I took a math course. The professor, Dr. James E. Perry, a VUU alumnus, gave us a take-home exam that consisted of ten problems. They did not seem to be too difficult. There were 35 students in the class. I took the exam problems to my dorm room and worked hard on them. I never liked take-home exams, but I thought I did a very good job. I was astonished when I got my grade. I was the only one who got an "F." I learned that many of the students had some math majors help them with the exam. I studied alone. I just could not believe that I had failed that exam; I got six out of ten right. After class, I met with the professor. I discovered that they were not significant errors. The professor carefully explained to me what I should have done. A few weeks later, surprisingly, that professor gave the class that very same exam for the mid-term exam. I was the first one to finish. When I finished, I walked over to the professor, gave him my paper, and shook his hand. He said nothing, but he gave me a "wink of the eye." To me, that was equivalent to a high-five.

As I slowly walked out of the class, the other 34 students were still working. I was cool. It was then and there that I knew that I was not the worst student in the class. Yes, I got an "A." Yes, an "A." That experience taught me something very important. Virginia Union University professors were excellent, they had tremendous compassion, and they were of the highest caliber. This personal attention is what I most remember about VUU's faculty. They could turn the "F" student into an "A" student.

That is what I like about small black colleges. They work with you on a personal level. I have devoted all of my adult life to supporting education, particularly Historically Black Colleges and Universities because I remember when we could not enter many other schools. black colleges stand as symbols of black achievements. They are protectors of our heritage. The question is not, "Will Black colleges become extinct?" The question is, "Will we provide the vital support necessary to ensure their continued existence?" This we must do.

During my junior and senior years at VUU, I was captain of the football team. In our lives, there are often trials, tribulations, and even the negatives. I learned very early the true meaning of loyalty. I am referring to my college coach who coached 35-40 ball players with only one assistant and a part-time person. My college coach was committed to developing young men to go into the world and be productive. You could see it in the way he directed us. He placed a lot of emphasis on the things that many people have forgotten today. Now, there is so much emphasis on winning and very little emphasis on building character.

Not only has Virginia Union helped build my character, but it has also helped thousands of others to succeed. As a VUU alumnus, I am proud to note that 22 Virginia Union University alumni have served as college or university presidents (more than any higher education institution in the United States can claim), including CEO's at Chicago Theological Seminary, Fisk University, North Carolina A&T University, and Virginia Union University.

I am also proud to note that I served five years as President of the Miles W. Connor Chapter of the Virginia Union University

Alumni Association, Baltimore, Maryland Chapter. The Miles W. Connor Chapter was founded by the late Dr. Miles Washington Connor, and later named in his memory. Dr. Connor was a graduate of VUU and the first president of what is now Coppin State College. I have been recognized for personally recruiting more students to attend and ultimately graduate from VUU than any other alumnus. During my tenure as president of the alumni chapter, I helped raise over $300,000 to provide scholarships to enable Baltimore City youths to pursue scholastic excellence at VUU. With me at the helm, the chapter became VUU's most active, financially supportive and productive alumni group in the nation. For my commitment, I received the first Presidential Citation from President S. Dallas Simmons in recognition of my financial support, strong volunteer recruitment leadership as Chairman of the Board of Trustees' Student Affairs Committee, and my assistance in enhancing alumni relations. I was selected by VUU to chair the National Alumni Leadership Committee that will assist in raising $25 million for the New Beginnings Campaign at Virginia Union University. I demonstrated my commitment to this project by making a substantial pledge.

This small Baptist institution has inspired academic excellence and leadership development for 135 years. Today, VUU's Internet web-site home-page (www.vuu.edu) presents a unique statement: "VUU consistently produces graduates who succeed in a variety of fields and hold positions of leadership through-out the country and world, including U.S. Congressional representatives, physicians and scientists, attorneys and judges, ministers, state legislators, professional athletes, educators, business executives, 22 college presidents, and the first elected African-American governor in the United States. Our goal at VUU is to help students visualize, and then realize, a bright future. In short, we want to help students discover what's possible."

Yes, Coach Thomas "Tricky Tom" Harris was right. If we give VUU a chance, VUU will make something of us. Coach Harris was a native of Arkansas, attended Tuskegee Institute, where he was cited as a football All-American at the age of 16 and was graduated from Wilberforce (Ohio) University. His coaching career began there from 1938 to 1942. After serving in World War II, he coached tennis, track, boxing, and football at Tennessee State. After coming to VUU in 1950, he won four CIAA basketball championships from 1951-55 on the way to a 273-230 record and was 98-83-5 in football. He also coached the Union golfers to six CIAA titles. Harris retired as football coach in 1972, as basketball coach in 1973, and as athletic director in 1979.

Coach Harris died in 1982, at age 74. The extended family of Virginia Union University, more than 2,000 strong, from across the campus and around the country poured into Barco-Stevens Hall on the afternoon of Tuesday, March 3, 1982 to honor him. Dr. David T. Shannon, one of five presidents who served during the more than thirty years when Harris was the heart and soul of the Union athletic program, eulogized him. Coach Harris died in the Norfolk Scope, the city arena, while leading his girl's basketball team to the CIAA championship and a NCAA division II championship tournament bid. It was his second championship in three years of coaching the girls after his retirement as athletic director.

I am a proud alumnus of Virginia Union University, and I have had the pleasure of personally knowing seven of its eleven presidents.

Virginia Union University was founded in 1865. At the end of the Civil War, a number of groups established institutions for educating newly emancipated slaves. Mary Ann Lumpkin, a former slave, the widow of Robert Lumpkin, a white man who was a well-known Richmond slave dealer, leased Lumpkin's Jail, a building she inherited from her husband. Robert Lumpkin had used the jail as a holding facility for slaves waiting to be auctioned. By agreeing to lease the building, Mary Ann Lumpkin was instrumental in laying the foundation for a great university. In the 136 years since its founding, Virginia Union University has been teaching, working, improving, and growing into a highly respected private liberal arts institution. Located on Richmond's historic north side, Virginia Union University has an enrollment of 1600 students. The university has the nationally acclaimed Samuel DeWitt Proctor School of Theology. Lawrence Douglas Wilder, a VUU graduate, made national history by becoming governor of Virginia, thus the first elected African-American governor in the United States.

Bernard W. Franklin, Ph.D.
10th President
(current)

VIRGINIA UNION UNIVERSITY
"ALMA MATER"

O, for the happy hours we spend
On that cherished and sacred hill
Our "Dream of Joy" to us attend,
With truth and virtue to instill.

Thoughts of bygone days at thy shrine
Fill my raptured soul with ecstacy.
Alma Mater, my praises are thine!
You are God's gift to humanity.

CHORUS

Union, We'll e'er revere the cause for
 which you stand;
Union, Majestic light, send rays throughout
 the land;
Thy hallowed grounds and dear old walls,
May they forever be,
Dear Union, we still love thee.
Thy hallowed grounds and dear old walls,
May they forever be,
Dear Union, we still love thee.

VUU Campus Landmark

Lenny Moore makes Presentation

Wilbur "Weeb" Ewbank Scouting

Chapter Six

Drafted By Two Professional Teams

I was drafted by two professional football teams, the Baltimore Colts and the Buffalo Bills. I am very proud of that. Throughout high school and college, I devoted many years to enhancing my playing skills, won numerous awards, and was featured in many sports news articles. I had earned the reputation of being a "scholar/athlete" and a leader. I had the right stuff. However, people often ask me, "What happened; why didn't you become a pro star?" My answer is an easy one.

When I was drafted, many things were going on in my life. In fact, I was not mentally or physically prepared for a professional football career. I know that may seem strange. Many of us know this famous quote from Shakespeare's "Hamlet": *"This above all: to thine ownself be true. And it must follow, as the night the day, Thou canst not then be false to any man."* We studied "Hamlet" in high school, and I often wondered what exactly that quote meant. However, when I reached the professional football level, I suddenly learned. We must be true to ourselves before we can be true to others. Self-discovery is crucial. *A man must know his levels of excellence as well as his limitations.*

Where am I leading with this? When I think about my brief pro football career, I always use the expression: "Many are called, but few are chosen." When I reflect on those pro days, I feel that perhaps I was chosen to do greater work. Life-after-football has been good for me. For that, I am blessed.

Bob Terrell, a sports writer for the Asheville Citizen *Times*, wrote this in an article about me entitled *Crossing The Alps*:

"Harlow Fullwood, 6-feet-3, 255 pounds, fourth draft choice of the Baltimore Colts, is a young man with a physique of an Atlas and the mien of a minister, soft-spoken yet quietly containing the confidence of a Hannibal.

You get the idea that if this guy wanted to cross the Alps, he'd crank up a couple of elephants and go right over, or that when the time comes late this summer, he'll find his right position in the Colts' offensive line. Fullwood came out of Stephens-Lee High School here in 1959, captain of the team in '58 and anchor of the state championship line of 1957. He went to Virginia Union, where his high school coach, Clarence Lee Moore, had played years ago, and became one of Union's great linemen, filling out to supersize and attracting professional scouts by groups. He captained the college team two years. "I had a lot of fun at Virginia Union," Fullwood said. "I weighed 255 and played beside a tackle who weighed 270; his name was Roger 'Big Red' Anderson who was from Oxford, North, Carolina. Roger played for the New York Giants for several years. Our line? Oh, we averaged around 240, I guess. Had some pretty good-sized boys."

Fullwood was signed for the Colts by Buddy Young, one of the all-time great Colt running backs. Young picked him for his "Dream Team" last fall and at the same time, Fullwood was named to the Pittsburgh Courier All-American team.

Harlow Fullwood, Jr.
Freshman Tackle   235 pounds   VUU Football Panther

I left Virginia Union at the completion of my senior year without a degree. I was the first athlete in the history of Virginia Union to be drafted by two professional teams at the same time.

In Terrell's article, he quoted me as saying, *"I expected to get drafted, but not quite that high." The fourth round is high in the pro draft; it includes men the club really wants. Buffalo of the American Football League also drafted Fullwood, but he signed the Baltimore contract, "because guys just naturally like to play for the best."*

One of my most cherished parts of that article involves Terrell allowing me to explain my philosophy on the fact that *education is first*; he quoted me as saying:

"One day, I won't be playing football any more, and then what will I have to fall back on? My education, of course. It's something I'll always have. A lot of boys don't realize that you have to start your education in the lower grades. Too many of them want to wait until they get to college to start studying. But, they'll find they can't do that. I was an honor student at Stephens-Lee and, man, I still had to dig at Virginia Union." Harlow didn't pick the path of least resistance in college. He's studying social science and specializing in Sociology. He passed up an invitation to play in the East-West Shrine Game in San Francisco, in order to participate in the Crusade Bowl, a game that matches two teams of draft choices. The game was played at Memorial Stadium in Baltimore.

"I was scared at first," he laughed. "I couldn't sleep at night, for thinking about those guys from the big schools, Ohio State, Michigan State, and so on. However, after the first contact on the field, I felt just as good as they did. Those teams had very fancy uniforms and a coach for every position; nevertheless, once I made my first tackle I saw how many feet I knocked that player's back – and saw how he sat there on the ground trying to realize what had hit him and where he was – suddenly realized that, "Hey...we put our pants on the same way...one leg at a time. It doesn't matter how big they are or where they come from, you hit 'em hard enough, they'll fall."

From that bit of philosophy grew a boundless confidence deep within Harlow Fullwood. The fact that he is big and fast, third fastest man on the Virginia Union team, added to his confidence. He always tries to outthink his opponent, and that is in his favor. You can't always block or tackle a man, unless you get to him. There is one thing Harlow Fullwood, Jr. regrets about his college football career.

"I've got a younger brother," he grinned, who plays end at Morgan State. He's a freshman and his name is Everett. We played each other in the last game last fall with the Central Intercollegiate Athletic Association championship at stake. I kept waiting for the 'pulling'' assignment, so I could get him just once, but I never got it. And you know, they beat us 14-8 and took the title."

Everett was All-CIAA in his senior year. He was the last one to be cut by the Houston Oilers of the American Football League. After he was released, he played for the Canadian Football League for three years.

The outstanding fact of being drafted by two pro teams just blew me away. I had no idea as to how I would deal with this honor. So I went to my coach and asked him what to do. I always trusted the candid advice that my various athletic coaches gave me.

I received a telephone call from the Buffalo Bills. They were in the American Football League (AFL). They were all going to merge soon and become the National Football League (NFL). In terms of football history, the American professional football organization was formed in 1959 to rival the older NFL. AFL teams in 1963 included the Boston Patriots (later the New England Patriots), Buffalo Bills, Denver Broncos, Houston Oilers, New York Titans (later Jets), Oakland Raiders, Dallas Texans, the San Diego Chargers, and the Kansas City Chiefs. The Miami Dolphins were added to the league in 1966.

When I got that call from the Bills, my coach lent me $20 and said, "Well, I'd like you to have that experience. However, I want you to promise me, give me your word that you will not sign a contract." I listened closely to this advice. Actually, my coach was very concerned that I should not put all of my eggs in one basket; he was mindful that the AFL was new, and he worried about whether it would remain in operation very long as a competitor to the NFL.

To my grandmother and my step-grandfather, one's word was everything. They could not read or write, but, when you shook my step-grandfather's hand, the commitment was final. His word was his bond. My step-grandfather's handshake was just like currency. When he shook your hand, you could "take it to the bank." So I gave my word. I promised my coach that I would not sign a contract.

That trip to Buffalo was my first airplane flight. I boarded one of those huge, old, funny-looking planes. That flight scared me to death. Anyway, I traveled to Buffalo. When I arrived at the airport, they had a limousine waiting for me. I was thoroughly impressed. Just picture this. A guy from the back hills of North Carolina, riding in a limousine. I looked pitiful, and I knew it, but I was dressed in the best that I had at the time. My suit had been ironed so much that it was slick. It used to be wool but looked like it was sharkskin. My poor necktie was slick too. As for my shoes, I need only to use one word to describe their condition, and you will certainly get the point: "cardboard." Buffalo was really cold in December, but my shoes had been weatherproofed.

They took me to the stadium that seated about 60,000 football fans. My hometown's population was not that big. From there, we went to the brand-new Hilton Hotel. I had learned a little Latin and Spanish, but the restaurant was French. Therefore, I didn't know what was going on with that menu. I was lost.

The waiter came over to the table next to us. I was quickly trying to figure out what to do and what to say. That situation was very embarrassing. However, I noticed that the lady at the next table had chicken, so I pointed to her plate. I said, "I want that." You know, it has always seemed like chicken, that trusty bird, has always bailed me out. I guess, to me, the chicken could be our national bird.

I was there with the coach and the general manager of the Buffalo Bills. For the first time in my life, I felt really intimidated. Here was a man with so much wealth, and he offered me a contract of about $18,000 per year plus a bonus. The general manager started slowly putting $100 bills down on the table as the bonus. I think I counted $2,500. He said, "This is yours. All you have to do is sign the contract." Without hesitation, I said, "No I don't think I can do that."

That guy did not realize that money didn't mean that much to me. I really did not know what it was to have a lot of money. As I indicated earlier, I had not even realized that I was poor until I enrolled at Virginia Union. I guess that guy expected me to grab that money off the table, but I did not touch it. Then he paused, took a deep drag on this long cigar, blew a couple of smoke rings, and put more money down on the table.

He said, "You can use it, can't you?" I said, "Yeah, you can look at me and tell that I could use it." Well, we did not agree to anything then. So, he gave me $100. I had never seen, let alone touched, a $100 bill. He said, "Go out and see Buffalo. Let's meet here in the morning to try and work this out." Man! I took that $100.

I was not about to spend all of that money. Furthermore, I was in a city I had never been in before. My better judgement told me to be careful, don't celebrate, and get a good night's sleep. So, for excitement, I bought me a couple of magazines, *Life* magazine and *Sports Illustrated*. That was the extent of my spending spree. I think that was actually the first time that I had ever purchased two magazines at the same time. I went back to that plush hotel room they had for me, and called Elnora. I said, "Honey, I don't have a contract, but I do have $100."

The next morning I met with the general manager. He asked me whether I had made a decision. I promptly said, "No, I cannot sign the contract." He was very surprised. Then, he offered me more money. Again I said, "I cannot sign that." He said, "I must ask you, why not?" I said, "I don't really expect you to understand this, but there's a football coach back in Richmond who is just like a father to me. I gave him my word, and that's all that I have." He said, "Well, we can change that." I said, "No, we can't. You can't offer me enough money to force me to go back on my word." He said, "I'll tell you what, you take the money and the contract back to Richmond, sign the contract, keep the money, and mail the contract back to me." I looked at him, and I slowly repeated those exact words right back to him. I am not sure why I did that. I guess I just wanted him to hear his own so-called logic. Then, I said, "I can't do that either. That would be just like signing it now. No contract means no contract." My integrity was emphatic and absolute. I had given my college football coach my word.

My grandmother taught me that a promise is a promise. This reminds me of a situation that occurred that I will never forget. I had a chance to witness the degree of integrity that my grandmother possessed. I was about eight years old. We needed some eggs, and my grandmother took me with her to buy two dozen. We went to Mrs. Jane's house which was about a quarter of a mile from our house. Mrs. Jane was a white lady. She raised chickens, and many people bought eggs from her.

The walk was mostly uphill, but the weather was nice, and we walked at a slow pace. It took us about twenty minutes to get there. Although "Granny" had planned to buy two dozen of eggs at ten cents a dozen, she suddenly realized that she was short ten cents, so we could only buy one dozen. Granny asked Mrs. Jane if she could take the additional dozen and pay her for it on Friday. Mrs. Jane said, "Yes." It was Wednesday. Friday was my grandmother's payday. Granny thanked Mrs. Jane, and we took the eggs and walked back home. The walk back was easier because it was downhill for the most part.

When Friday came, it was raining very hard. We lived in the back hills of the Smokey Mountains in North Carolina, and when it rained, the red clay would get so muddy that when you stepped down, it would cover your shoes. Your feet would just sink into that red mud so much that you could not even see your feet. Each time you made a step, you had to pull your each foot out of the mud. I saw Granny put on her hat, then her scarf, then her coat. I said, Granny, where are going in all of that rain?" She said, "I'm going to pay Mrs. Jane the ten cents that I owe her." I could not believe that she was preparing to make that uphill walk in that rain and muddy red clay. I said, "Granny, you should wait until tomorrow. Mrs. Jane can afford to wait." Granny leaned down, looked me in the eyes, and said, "Listen son, I made a promise. When Mrs. Jane gave me those eggs, I made a promise, and today is Friday. When I got those eggs and when I gave my word, it wasn't raining and it wasn't muddy." Granny then left, to walk in that hard rain to go make good on her promise.

I remember that as if it were yesterday. That was my first lesson on what integrity means. Integrity can be defined as steadfast adherence to a strict moral or ethical code, honesty, soundness, and the quality or condition of being whole and complete. These words describe and define the noble person that Granny was. She taught me more about integrity than any scholar at VUU, Howard, Harvard, Morehouse, Morgan, Hopkins, or Yale could ever teach me.

Well, back to my professional football experience. The next day, Don Kellett, Colts' General Manager, called me and wanted me to come to Baltimore. I was drafted by the Baltimore Colts. Later that year, Mr. Ewbank was fired by the Colts and went to the New York Jets; Don Shula replaced him as head coach of the Colts. I was drafted by Ewbank and reported to Shula's training camp. When Mr. Ewbank became coach for the Jets, he asked me to come to New York and join the team. Some Colts did follow him, but I decided not to. I thought I would see what Shula was all about.

For those who do not know, here are some interesting facts about Wilbur "Weeb" Ewbank. This coach led Joe Namath and the Jets to defeat the Baltimore Colts 16-7 in Super Bowl III giving the AFL its first title. Mr. Ewbank died in 1998, at age 91. I remember reading that, ironically, two days before he died, Weeb Ewbank watched the New York Jets-Indianapolis Colts game from the owner's box at the RCA Dome in Indianapolis. Ewbank coached both teams to national fame and league championships. He was inducted into the Hall of Fame and was the only coach to win titles in both the AFL and NFL.

It was my dream to be a Baltimore Colt. I remember that every Baltimorean walked a little taller in 1958 when the Colts won the game. As you know, the game, The 1958 NFL World Championship, is still known as "The Greatest Game Ever Played." The Colts defeated the New York Giants in sudden death overtime. I remember that the game ended when Colts fullback Alan Ameche scored on a one-yard touchdown run. Ameche, whose nickname was "The Iron Horse," played as a fullback with the Baltimore Colts for six seasons (1955-1960); he founded Gino's Inc., one of the nation's first fast foods chain of restaurants. Among Ameche's numerous civic commitments was his role as Corporations Chairman for the United Negro College Fund. Alan was elected to the National Football Foundation and College Hall of Fame in 1975. Alan passed away on August 8, 1988.

The 1958 "battle royal" introduced the Colts to the world as one of the most rock solid teams in America. I believe it was that game that inspired the Baltimore slogan, "Unitas We Stand!" I cannot recall who coined that phrase; I don't know if it were the late renowned sports commentator Charlie Eckman, Baltimore Afro-American Newspaper sports writer Sam Lacy, Baltimore *Sun* sports writer, the late John Steadman, or Colts announcer Chuck Thompson who invented that phrase. I do remember hearing the roar of the fans in Baltimore's Memorial Stadium enthusiastically chant that slogan whenever John "Golden Arm" Unitas would throw a winning touchdown.

Was I proud to have been drafted by the Colts? Yes, absolutely! I felt that I was becoming a part of history. For me to have been drafted by the Colts seemed to me to be equivalent to being inducted into a special society of champions. To the true football fan, just mentioning the names of former Colts who are NFL Hall of Famers creates images of some of the most powerful and charismatic athletes in the history of professional football. The Colts included such legends as John Unitas, who many declare as the greatest quarterback of all times; Raymond Berry, the exceptional pass catcher who set an NFL title game mark with twelve catches for 178 yards in that 1958 overtime game; Gino Marchetti, who was named top defensive end of NFL's first 50 years; Art Donovan, the defensive tackle who was the first Colt to enter the Pro Football Hall of Fame; and Lenny Moore, the durable flanker/running back who scored a record 113 touchdowns and eighteen in straight games from 1963-1965. The mentioning of these names creates a mental "video replay" image of that exciting, powerful 1958 gridiron championship game.

Don Kellett sent Colts owner Carroll Rosenbloom's private jet to pick me up. I was really treated like a super star. The only ones on that plane were the pilot and I. My hope was that he would just stay alert, straighten-up, and fly right. I was so terrified that I don't think I made a sound during that entire flight, except when we landed and I just kept saying, Amen, "Amen, Amen!" When we arrived at the airport, the pilot got on the telephone and said, "Your boy's here, but he is as sick as a dog." The plane had been dancing around in the air like a butterfly. I'm sure it was the wind turbulence, but it seemed like that pilot either was a stunt pilot or was crop dusting. I was sicker than I had ever been in my life.

When I got there to the office, Lenny Moore, Claude "Buddy" Young, and Jim Parker were there. I knew about Buddy Young's accomplishments; he was described as one of the smallest and one of the biggest men in pro football history. Young, at 5'4-1/2", was an All-American at the University of Illinois, spent time in the Navy, and returned to lead Illinois to a 1947 Rose Bowl victory. Young later signed with the New York Yankees of the All-America Football Conference in 1947.

Buddy Young was one of the first blacks to play pro football after the "unofficial" ban from 1934 to 1945. He experienced great humiliation and prejudice. Young joined the Colts in 1953. He hung up his cleats in 1956; the Colts retired his number 22. In 1966, Buddy joined the NFL staff as the administrative assistant to commissioner. At the time of his death in 1983, he was Director of Player Relations for the League.

It was an awesome experience for me to be in the presence of these football idols. I had met Jim Parker earlier that year at the annual Athletic Banquet held at Virginia Union. Coach Tom "Tricky" Harris had invited Parker, the ace lineman of the Colts, to the university to demonstrate to VUU's football players techniques of pass protection. I still have and treasure a news article that included a group photo from that banquet of Coach Harris, Jim Parker, Herman Howard, Virginia Union's assistant football and basketball coach, my teammate Tom Harris, and Dr. Thomas H. Henderson, VUU President.

Jim Parker played for Baltimore from 1957 until 1967. At 6'3" and 273 pounds, Parker was the first full-time offensive lineman to be elected to the NFL Hall of Fame. He was charged with the duty of protecting Johnny Unitas, and he was quite successful at his job. I remember once when Weeb Ewbank was giving Jim Parker a pep talk to prepare him for a game at Memorial Stadium and he said to Jim, "When you go our there, don't be intimidated by the size of that crowd. There are 60,000 people up in those stands." Parker replied, "Man, you must have forgotten where I came from. At Ohio State, I practiced in front of 60,000 people."

Jim Parker and I played the same position. One time he told me, "Harlow, don't worry, I'm going to look out for you. By the time I finish, I'm going to make sure that you will be able to take over everybody's position on the team except mine." Jim Parker was the quickest that I had ever seen at two yards, and the slowest I had ever seen at ten yards. Actually, Marchetti was the fastest I had ever seen cross the line of scrimmage.

There was also another fellow at the Colt's office on that day. I admired that gentleman's record of success very much, and his presence at my contract meeting made it a very meaningful experience for me. Earl Banks, the nationally acclaimed and legendary coach of Morgan State College, was there with me when I signed my contract with the Baltimore Colts. It was indeed an honor for me to see him there. I have always had the utmost respect for him. Coach Banks was one of the greatest college football coaches in the United States; he posted an incredible 839 win-loss percentage. His dedication to scholastic and athletic excellence and his winning record made him the envy of college coaches nationwide.

From Morgan State College, Coach Banks sent Willie Lanier to the Kansas City Chiefs, Leroy Kelly to the Cleveland Browns, Mark Washington to the Dallas Cowboys, John Fuqua to the Pittsburgh Steelers, and Raymond Chester to the Los Angeles Raiders. While at Virginia Union University, I played against some of Coach Banks's most powerful teams. VUU's record against Morgan when I played was two wins, one loss, and one tie. The loss was 14-6 for the CIAA Championship played at Hughes Stadium in down-pouring rain.

When it was time for me to sign the Colts contract, I had my mind made up. Yes, that's right. I signed that contract as fast as I could because I knew that I would not be doing anything with Buffalo. I couldn't see any future with the Bills. I felt that I would be unable to work for an organization that only saw me as an economic component or that was unable to respect me as an individual. Here I was, signed with the Colts. A dream had come true. I was a member of the same team that had won The Game. I was a fourth-round pick.

I had my bonus money, and I was very satisfied. In today's football market, a fourth round draft choice can almost certainly become an instant millionaire. The first thing I did was to give my family some money. My mother and father lived in the projects in Baltimore. I remember when I went there, they did not have any food. Christmas was approaching. I took that bonus money and gave them the best Christmas they ever had. I was very generous. To make a long story short, when I got ready to go to camp, I was broke. However, I was happier than I had ever been in my life. I spent very little of that bonus money on myself. I brought a pair of pants and a suit for church. I didn't fly off the handle with wild spending.

I was proud and benevolent because I used most of that money to help as many other folks in the family as I could. That measure of kindness gave me a unique and warm feeling. Just seeing the look on their faces provided me with considerable fulfillment. Even today when I provide charitable contributions to others, I feel that exact same way. It is hard to explain. Albert Einstein said, "A person starts to live when he can live outside himself." I really believe this. I am in constant pursuit of new ways to give of myself. *Money is not everything, but it sure is way ahead of whatever is in second place.*

My short-term career as a Baltimore Colt can be best described by accounts made in various news articles that I will share with you. I will never forget that 1963 *Baltimore Sun article: "Fullwood*

— 4th Round Pick!" That article described how, I, that 250-pound tackle from Virginia Union University was acquired by the Colts on a fourth-round choice surrendered by the Chicago Bears. That article quoted me. I knew I was good, and I was anxious to tell the world about it. I was not arrogant; I was merely confident. The article said, *"Fullwood told Buddy Young, the front office man who signed him, that he was the fastest lineman on the roster. He could run 100 yards in 10.4 seconds, which was excellent time for a man of his size, 6'3". He told Buddy Young, "I'm a quick learner."*

Another news article stated, Colts' Signer: *"The Baltimore Colts recently announced the signing of Tackle Harlow Fullwood of Virginia Union University to a football contract for the 1963 season...he was a fourth draft choice of the Colts and was also drafted by the Buffalo Bills of the American Football League. The Baltimore club will employ him as an offensive guard. Fullwood is a native of Asheville, N.C., where he graduated from Stephens-Lee High School."*

A Baltimore Sun article about the Colts' 1963 training camp stated, *All opening practices are eye-openers, and today's was no exception as the 18 rookies and 15 holdovers were timed for the 40-yard dash. Harlow Fullwood, a 250-pound plus tackle candidate from Virginia Union, sped the distance in 4.9 seconds.*

This caused Shula, who was conducting his first practice as a head coach to remark, "He's fast enough to be a defensive back." Cameron C. Snyder, the sportswriter, said, "Faster than you were when you played in the Colts' secondary and is some 50 pounds heavier." Don't say that so loud, grinned Shula, who is justly proud of his playing career.

A few days later, another newspaper article appeared: *Fullwood Quits Grid: "Shula thinks he has a representative rookie crop, and some of these fresh faces give the impression they will be around for a while no matter how the battle thickens. One who will not, however, is Harlow Fullwood, big tackle from Virginia Union, who went to the coach and gave up voluntarily. He needs only six hours of study to get a degree in sociology and will return to his alma mater to obtain it. The Colts have put him on their reserve list."*

I was going though a lot of difficulties during that time. For example, two weeks after I left the Colts, I was notified that the Federal Bureau of Investigation (FBI) was looking for me. That's right, the FBI. When I moved to Baltimore to play football, I had forgotten to notify the Selective Service of my new address as federal law required. My former college coach, Clarence L. Moore, was a Commissioner on the Selective Service Board for Buncombe County, North Carolina, that included Asheville; he called to tell me that the FBI was looking for me. I had not left a forwarding address. That was quite a complex ordeal. They thought I was a draft dodger. I was informed that I must report to the Army camp known as Fort Holabird, and that I should be prepared not to be going back home.

When I reported to Fort Holabird, I was in the best physical condition I had ever been in. I was fit. My body was as hard as a rock. They selected me to be the leader of my group of draftees. I easily passed the physical exam. All of the others were dismissed but I. Then, I was told that the captain wanted to see me. I was proud to serve my country, and I was ready to go.

The captain informed me that the Army would not accept me. I was surprised. I asked, "Why not?" The captain gave me three reasons in his explanation. First, I did not meet the height/weight requirement, in that my height was not in proportion to my weight. I had never heard of such a standard for military service. Second, I was recently married. Third, I had applied for and was accepted at the Baltimore City Police Academy as a new recruit. With that explanation, I decided to attend the academy and pursue a career as a law enforcement officer.

Football has been an important part of my life. I know that this will sound trite, but football has been good to me. It provided me with a college education through a football scholarship. At my high school, I was captain of the football team; I played for four years and received a letter for each year. I had received many scholarship offers from colleges and universities from around the nation before I selected Virginia Union. I was a college All-American.

However, once I reached the professional level, the money was good, but I did not really enjoy the experience. Of course, playing on a team with world-class players made me feel almost invincible. Nevertheless, deep down, it was not for me. I suddenly realized that after my college days, I had no real desire to play football as a profession. I was a fourth round pick by the Colts, with a contract worth $18,000, and a $4,000 signing bonus, but I was not truly content. Today, a fourth round draft pick is an instant millionaire.

No matter what professional opportunities that I have had, I have always measured my potential for success by whether I enjoyed what I was doing. I was not mentally ready to be a Colt. As strange as this may sound to some aspiring athletes, I did not enjoy it. As we endeavor to determine a career path, it may be wise to take inventory of our conscience and ask ourselves, "Is this what I really want to do?" I walked away, and I have no regrets. My goal was to focus on my wife and my family. Quite often, professional athletes and others strive for success too soon and discover too late that they should have taken another path.

As an athlete, I never smoked, drank, or was caught using profane language. I took my role as an athlete seriously. I tried to make every effort to lead by example because I never wanted a child to look at me and say, "I don't want to be like him." I always wanted a child to be able to say, "That's my role model. That's my role model." I was a leader on all of the teams where I had an opportunity to play. I never liked to hang with the crowd. I remember my grandmother saying, "If you get in a jam and you're by yourself, it's a lot easier to wiggle out of it -- but, when you get in a jam with a group of other folks, you never know what direction it will lead to."

Thanks to my grandmother's teachings, my faith was strong, and my priorities were in proper order. As that old expression goes, "The road to success is always under construction." To sum up my recounting of my pro football experience, I believe that this quote by John D. Rockefeller, Sr. best describes my philosophy, *"If you want to succeed, you should strike out on new paths -- rather than travel the worn paths of accepted success."*

Elements of the game of football are symbolic of life's challenges. Here are a few motivational metaphors and analogies that I once outlined in a high school senior class commencement speech in Ocean City, Maryland. These words had their origin from an author unknown. I delivered this statement to a crowd that included many young persons aspiring to success: *"In the game of football, there are many rules. We can take those same rules and apply them to the real game of life. Personally, I would like to see each one of us rededicate our lives, based upon the rules for the Game of Life. It goes something like this:*

➤ *You are given the ball, and each of you is named the quarterback for your team.*

➤ *There is only one schedule to play; it lasts all of your life and consists of only one game.*

➤ *It is a long game, with no timeouts and no substitutions.*

➤ *You will play the whole game -- all of your life.*

➤ *Each of you will have a great backfield.*

➤ *Each of you will be calling the signals. However, the other three persons in the backfield -- with you -- all have great reputations.*

➤ *They are named faith, hope, and charity.*

➤ *You will work behind a really powerful line.*

➤ *End-to-end, it consists of honesty, loyalty, and dedication to duty, self-respect, study, cleanliness, and good behavior.*

➤ *The goal posts are the Pearly Gates of Heaven.*

➤ *God is the referee and sole official. He makes all the rules, and there is no appeal from them.*

➤ *There are ten rules. We know them as the Ten Commandments.*

➤ *You play them strictly in accordance with your own religion.*

➤ *There is also an important game-rule. It is: Do unto others, as you would have them do unto you.*

➤ *Now, here is the ball. It is your immortal soul. Hold on to it, get in there, and let's see what you can do in the real Game of Life.*

Harlow Fullwood, Jr.
Police Officer/Recruiter
Baltimore Police Department
1970

Chapter Seven

Life In The Baltimore Police Department

After my pro football experience, my main goal was to acquire a full-time, good-paying job. I started some intense job-hunting. I would get up at 5 a.m., bathe, get dressed, and leave home by 6 a.m. just as if I were going to work. Seeking employment became my full-time endeavor. I had a little bit of money, and it would soon run out. After pro football, my police career did not start right away. There were some tough times in between.

When I left the Colts, it seemed like I had the weight of the world on my shoulders. I was under a lot of pressure. Elnora was still in Richmond, and I was living with my mother and father in Baltimore in the projects. I was busy, taking all kind of unusual jobs. I was struggling, trying to earn and to save money. I needed a job to support Elnora and me. I no longer had time to be running around trying to join a professional football team. I needed to support my wife and plan for the baby on the way. I worked some jobs many people would not even think about working. I was trying to see the bigger picture and plan for the future.

Before I was accepted at the Police Academy, I was job-hunting diligently. I got a job way out on Pulaski Highway. I did not have

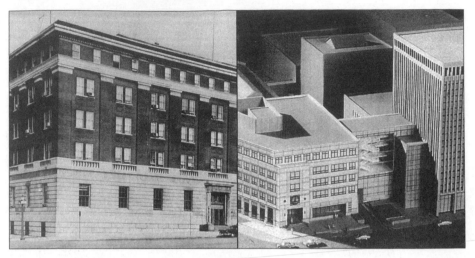

Old Headquarters   New Headquarters

Commissioner Bishop Robinson (left) and Deputy Commissioner
Edward Tilghman present me with the department's highest level award

any transportation. I was hitchhiking. One morning, I was standing there hitchhiking. A black man driving by stopped. He said, "Son I've been coming past you quite a few days, and I decided to stop today because you look troubled." He asked me where I was working, and I told him. He said, "I have to go by there every day. I'll take you and bring you back." He never charged me a dime. The last time I saw that man, he said, "I'm going to tell you something. One day all this is going to turn around. You've shown me something that I think a lot of other people have seen. Your work ethic is outstanding." I never saw that guy again. I wish I knew how to find him. I didn't know his name. I did not know anything about him.

One morning, I went down to City Hall to look at the employment opportunity bulletin board. I figured if I wanted to find a good job, City Hall might be the best place to start. Why not start at the top? I read everything on that board. I paid particular attention to the various jobs for which the city was testing. I saw a job advertisement for Baltimore City Police Officer. The minimum education required at that time was eighth grade. At first, I thought that was easy and that I could sail through the application process. I must tell you. I later found out that many of those eighth-grader applicants were some really sharp people.

I forgot to bring a pencil and paper with me, so I had to memorize everything that I read. While I was busy rereading that job advertisement, I saw a white fellow out of the corner of my eye. He was standing about three feet from me and was staring at me. That made me nervous. I later found out that he was a Maryland State Senator. He was disabled. I think he had polio. He came over to me and said, "Boy, what do you want to do?" I said, "What did you just call me? Now, where I'm from, that 'boy' stuff just doesn't work." I lit into him verbally. In no uncertain terms, I emphatically told him where I was coming from and then told him where he could go. He quickly said, "I'm sorry. I'm very sorry. I did not mean it the way you took it. I was not disrespecting your manhood or maturity, nor was I throwing you a racial slur. It is just a generation thing. I must be about

30 years older than you. It's just that I tend to call young black or white youngsters boy. What I was trying to find out was how I could help you. What are you looking at?" I said, "The police department job notice." He said, "I'll tell you what you do. They're giving a test. Be sure to take it." We shook hands and wished each other well. The senator's words were very motivational. He asked my name, and I said, "Harlow Fullwood, Jr." He merely said, "Thanks, and good luck," and we went our separate ways. Before that day, I had never considered seeking a law enforcement career.

I took the examination. There were about 2,000 people in the Baltimore Civic Center, now the Baltimore Arena, to take the test. The test was given in phases. There was a penmanship test, reading interpretation, and then you got into the "meat" of it. After each section was completed, it would be graded, and they who failed would be eliminated. The crowd was becoming smaller and smaller. Soon, there were about 500 people left. Anyway, I passed the test and advanced to take the physical. When I took the physical, I had a problem with one of my eyes. My vision did not measure up to the exact specifications. However, the testing agent said he would overlook that. I really think the senator had a lot to do with it.

I was selected to attend the police academy. For the first time, I felt that I had a steady job. At that time, I did not really think that was the profession that I wanted to pursue as a career. However, it was an employment opportunity.

There were about 35 trainees in my police academy class. There were five other blacks. I'm the only one living now. The academy was quite a rigorous experience. There had never been a black to graduate "at the head of the class." Based on my exemplary performance in all areas of training, I was destined to be the first. Some white administrators were very prejudiced. They committed a series of deceptive and unfair things. They did not want to see a black person ever graduate "Number One."

I remember that there was a white lieutenant who wrote the Digest of Laws for Baltimore City. He was not a college guy, but he was as smart as they come. One afternoon, he called me to his office and said, "Fullwood, I want to let you know I'm not part of this, but I don't have any real control over it either. I know that it is tough for you now, but you've got the stuff that we need around here. Always remember that there are some good people on both sides of the fence." It was reassuring to hear him say that. I graduated second in my class of 35. It was a real honor, but it wasn't what I actually deserved and had earned. From where I come from, you get what you earn. If you didn't put anything into it, you didn't get anything out of it. If you were the best, you were proclaimed as "Number One."

My experience at the police academy brought me in direct contact with racism and politics. Yes, I had encountered racial prejudice and discrimination before in the South but never in a competitive environment. I had become accustomed to the "level playing field." My academy experience was a rude awakening. At least, that lieutenant's statement helped me adjust to the inevitable.

Elnora and I lived in a real nice three-room apartment. It was in Cherry Hill near the water at a section called Harborview. As a new officer, I only made $4,500 per/year and was taking home about $110 every two weeks. Elnora had a teaching job. Therefore, we were able to manage.

I did not drive to the police department. I would take the bus to work, hitchhike, or whatever. Hitchhiking was nearly impossible because if people saw you in a police uniform they would not stop to pick you up. Sometimes they would slow down, build up your hopes, and then speed off. I can remember sometimes running about half-a-block to get a hitchhike, only to see a car that had stopped speed off when I just about got to the car door. That cat and mouse experience really ticked me off. It was cruel. People can be cruel.

I did not know how to drive. Therefore, I had to take the bus everywhere. Uniformed officers could ride transit buses free, so at least I saved some money. In my hometown, very few black people had cars; therefore, I never learned how to drive until I got to Baltimore. I bought a car, but I could not even drive it; Elnora had to drive it. I said, "Lord, this doesn't make sense. I'm a grown man, and can't drive." I taught myself. In fourteen days, I had my driver's license. At last, no more hitchhiking!

When I became a police officer, I learned so much and was exposed to so much new information that it was unbelievable. One of the things that I picked up right away was the need for me to become more culturally aware and sensitive. I soon gained a friend in the department named Officer Charles Markiewicz. We became good friends. He was of Polish descent. At that time, I didn't know that one could tell the nationality of a person by his or her name. It was just hard for me to understand that folks could look at a name and determine a person's national descent...that this person is Polish, that person is Jewish or Italian. In North Carolina, a person's last name was basically either Jones, Smith, Williams, or so on. In Baltimore, I had a lot to learn because the city is a melting pot of ethnicity with many nationalities represented within its population.

Down South, I never truly experienced hunger. I had never seen any of my neighbors or friends go hungry. Yes, we were poor, in terms of not having the finer things in life, but many of us were rich in the spirit of sharing and lifting up one another. As a rookie officer, I worked the beat of East Baltimore around the markets. I would see people go in a dumpster to get food and make a meal out what someone else had thrown away. When I witnessed this in the streets of Baltimore, I was astonished. I knew about poverty, but I had never seen or witnessed folks desperate enough to eat garbage. Every night in the market areas, one would see folks down in the dumpster seeking food that, I would say, was not fit for a dog.

There was really only one assignment that I was given that I found to be very difficult. As a rookie, I was a new face. I was assigned to the vice squad for a while. That type of work is one of the worse parts of law enforcement. It involves such crime control activities as arresting male customers for soliciting male or female prostitutes, arresting prostitutes, arresting pimps, investigating and arresting for narcotics sales and distribution, arresting for adult and child sexual offenses, and policing other unsavory human behavior.

The department had received numerous complaints from residents and businesses in the Mount Vernon area of the city about prostitution and solicitation activity. My vice squad assignment was to serve as a decoy and to stand on various corners in Mount Vernon. When a car would pull up, and a citizen would proceed to solicit any type of sexual participation, I would give a signal and the vice squad officers would rush in and arrest the perpetrator, the "John." I was a church member, and I became very worried that one of my church members would see me standing around and frequenting the Mount Vernon area. I begged to be taken off that assignment, and I was happy when finally I was.

My approach to law enforcement and my philosophical standards have been cited by a variety of news articles. Those articles effectively express my philosophy. For example, in 1975 in a Baltimore *Afro-American* article entitled, "You Got to Like People," reporter Pam Widgeon included my quote, "You have got to like people in order to work in law enforcement. You will never be rich from this job, but you will receive an internal feeling that you are accomplishing something not only for yourself, but the community."

That article told how I joined the police department in 1964, started out as a foot patrolman in East Baltimore, and, in 1966, was asked to join the Recruitment Unit. Ms. Widgeon specified how I was often seen driving around the city in my blue and white police van trying to recruit citizens to join the force and how often I went to schools and gave the Civil Service Examination to students who were interested in joining the force. She quoted me as saying, "Benefits and working conditions were poor in 1966. When Commissioner Pomerleau came, I saw positions opening up for blacks."

I was honored for my service on the police force, by the city, the state, local public schools systems, colleges both in and out of Maryland, civic groups, churches, and local businesses. One recognition award that I am very proud of receiving was when I was named *The Evening Sun's* 1979 Policeman of the Year for my work in the community. Wiley Hall, *Evening Sun* reporter, wrote the article in which he stated, "Agent Fullwood, 39, has worked as a recruiter through two of the police department's biggest manpower crisis: the late 60s, when the force was almost 400 men below strength, and during the last two years, when experienced officers have been resigning faster than the department can find men to replace them. Yet his superior, Major Donald Woods, director of personnel, says, "He was nominated for the newspaper's award as much for his community involvement as for his recruiting efforts." Mr. Hall quoted me as saying, "I have always felt that in order to be effective as a recruiter, I have to be involved in the community. It is a question of credibility. I have gotten tremendous help from local churches, because of my credibility with them." In that article, Major Woods said, "Last year, 21 inner-city high school graduates won scholarships and financial aid assistance through Fullwood's help. During the summer, he helped 25 teenagers find summer jobs. For the past two years, he has coordinated the 'People to People' program which provides 10 inner-city youths with an all-expense paid trip to Ocean City." One of my philosophical standards was included in that article, as I was quoted as saying, "I believe that if a person is in college or working in a job, he or she is not going to be out on the streets committing crimes."

In 1974, the Baltimore *Afro-American* Newspaper named me to its 35th Annual Honor Roll and stated, "If deeds be the measure of the man: Police Officer Harlow Fullwood, then, is a man who should know fulfillment, but doesn't. Officer Fullwood doesn't believe in complacency. There is yet much left undone. His supporters describe him as a model of excellence in the home, church, and in the community. He is a massive stone in the foundation of a great city and a great nation. His recruitment for the Baltimore Police Department has helped immeasurably to improve law enforcement in the city."

Police recruitment was very demanding but rewarding. Currently, the minimum educational level to join the department is twelfth grade. It was eighth grade when I joined in 1964. Nevertheless, I feel that my recruits were some of the finest persons that I have ever met. They exercised diligence, were effective, and served with honor.

The 1960's and 1970's were turbulent times in America, and many communities did not hold police officers in a positive image. One of the most contemptuous words used in referring to police by various political and radical groups during that time was "pig." Quite often, we on the force would hear people yell at us on sight "Kill the pigs!"

We just learned to cope with it. At least, most of us did. Law enforcement is not easy work. Unfortunately, many officers could not cope with the pressure, so they quit the force. Police officers are not perfect. They cry, they bleed, they anguish over conditions in society and in their own families. In the department, there were divorces, nervous breakdowns, and other problems. We just tried to encourage each other to hang in there. Sadly, there were even some suicides. The so-called "men in blue" sometimes function under severe pressure. They often have to suppress their emotions, postpone their stability, and get out there to protect society. Many need counseling and chaplain services. This part of the police work experience is rarely talked about. In the real world, we should praise our law enforcement officers. Their work and sacrifices create a better quality of life for us and our children.

In the 1960's and 1970's, there were numerous socio-political movements in both urban and suburban communities and cultures. There was a widespread antipolice attitude. I believe this syndrome evolved because various anti-establishment factions associated "police" with being part of the so-called "system." This anti-police protest movement was not only experienced by Baltimore officers but also by other uniformed law enforcement officers across the United States. Those times were difficult.

I remember after the assassination of President John F. Kennedy in November 1963, all kinds of cross-generation protests and social consciousness movements began. From anti-Vietnam-War demonstrations...to Civil Rights marches...to college campus building-take-overs — new protest movements were occurring every day. Policing became very, very complex. Police officers were treated with extreme disdain.

During the 1960's and 1970's, some major events changed the mood of America, and most of them had an impact on the way police officers were perceived. Some of these events included the six-day riots in the Los Angeles Watts district in 1965, the Chicago Riot in the summer of 1966, the Harlem, New York, riot, the assassination of Reverend Martin Luther King, Jr. in 1968, the Baltimore riot of 1968, the assassination of Robert F. Kennedy in 1968, and many other drastic incidents and events.

Many groups began to distrust each other. Words like conspiracy, intimidation, police brutality, over-reaction, entrapment, and intolerance were heard every day at work and in the news.

To illustrate how complex our local and national environments were during the 1960's and 1970's, I can recall the variety of "protest buttons" that people wore on their jackets. The mere tone of the messages on those buttons painted a multicolored picture of protests and advocacy. The times were really changing rapidly. It seemed like everyone was polarized, competing, demonstrating, or protesting something. It was wild. Here are some of slogans that I recall seeing on buttons, signs, and posters during those incredible times as I conducted my police work: Student Power; Black Power; Hippie Power; Don't Trust Anyone Over 30; Keep the Faith Baby; Stoned; Turn on - Tune in - Drop out; Flower Power; Black is Beautiful; God is Dead; and Stop the War, to name a few.

During that phase of time, law enforcement officers had to deal with all kinds of incidents that related in some way to the issues and causes that these slogans represented. It became very confusing to some of us in uniform as we had to respond to building-takeovers by students at colleges like Hopkins and Morgan, Black Panther rallies, Hippie peace and love demonstrations, and anti-war protests around Baltimore. Our city was "America in microcosm." The same things were going on in practically every major city in the nation.

I decided to just stay close to the church. I joined Concord

Baptist Church and later became the youngest member of the Board of Trustees. I think my involvement with the church got me through those times. Thank God! Sometimes, like many others officers, I was really nervous as I would put my uniform on in the morning. I did not know what angry group or individuals I might face each day. People were angry, and sometimes they didn't even know why. Those were rough times to be a police officer.

I remember once during the Baltimore Riot in 1968 after Dr. King was killed, I responded to a call by a resident whose car had been stolen. That man was already in an angry frame of mind. When I knocked on the door, the middle-aged white fellow who answered the door and saw me yelled, "Hey, I didn't call for a nigger cop!" I did not feel threatened. At 6 feet 4 inches and 285 pounds, I rarely felt threatened. That man's attitude needed adjustment. I calmly said to him, "Sir, when I took the oath to wear this badge to uphold the mission of the Police Department to protect all neighborhoods of Baltimore and to risk my life in doing so, that oath did not say anything about race. Therefore, you called, and I am here. Now that you've got that off of your chest, how can I help you?" My soft words immediately disarmed that man. It was almost as if I had said, "Drop your weapon." Tears were welling in his eyes, and he apologized to me for his racist outburst. Then we got down to the business of trying to locate his car. Words have power. If they are used in a benevolent way, they can have "healing power."

I had a flip-side, similar experience. One hot, summer afternoon when I was walking my beat in East Baltimore over near Oldtown Mall, a young black teenage boy marched up and stood in front of me, and he was blocking my way. That fellow was dressed in an all-black outfit and had a black beret on, the classic attire of the Black Panthers. The Panthers were extremely anti-police, and they verbally attacked and otherwise targeted white and black police officers. I became very apprehensive. The fellow stood there, put his hands on his hips, and yelled, "You black pig!...What you want?..Black Power!" He was trying to precipitate an incident. In those days, it did not take much to spark a riot. A crowd started forming, and I could already hear some begin to chant "Kill the pig." I was a rookie cop and in real trouble, but I kept my cool.

That fellow then made some kind of karate movements, and he was about to make one of those high karate' leap-kicks. I had seen many Bruce Lee movies, so I knew what to expect, but I did not know karate'. I had just left the Colts, just joined the force, and my body was as hard as steel. Man, I was so physically fit that I could run through a wall and keep running. I had a body-builder's physique. Nevertheless, this was the first time any fool had ever confronted me in such a manner.

That fellow was in his karate' position, and the crowd was waiting for some action. I cautioned him, by saying, "Young man, don't you know that karate' can be considered as a deadly weapon? Therefore, I may be within my rights to use reasonable self-defense." Then, I put my hand on my revolver handle and said, "Karate can't stop a bullet! Man, when you jump in the air, I will empty my gun in your chest before you even hit the the ground!" Of course, I did not really mean that I would use my revolver, but that guy did not know that. When he thought about my warning, he just backed away and broke out running. That crowd laughed, applauded, and yelled, "Don't mess with Officer Fullwood!" I guess that young man was hurting inside and just needed to cry out for help. I never recall ever seeing him again when I walked my beat. As I look back, I wish I had the opportunity to help him reach success in life. I certainly hope that he did.

That incident reminds me of the statement that Dr. Martin Luther King made in 1967 when someone asked him about his views on the issue of the Black Power. He said, "It is necessary to understand that Black Power is a cry of disappointment. The Black Power slogan did not spring full-grown from the head of some philosophical Zeus. It was born from the wounds of despair and disappointment. It is a cry of daily hurt and persistent pain."

I have attempted always to prevent violence. I had an expression that I would tell unruly individuals that I would encounter when I was on my beat and would have to place under arrest. It was, "You have two choices. You can go my way or your way. It will be a lot better for your health, if you go my way!" I have never become accustomed to seeing how vicious humans can treat humans. Unfortunately, police officers have to witness some of the most degrading acts that people commit against each other.

I have presented these two scenarios, the white man's reaction to me and the black radical youth's threat, to illustrate the degree of despair by which we were surrounded in Baltimore during that period of time. That social environment made it even more difficult for me to recruit future police officers. It was a time when police were not held in high esteem in many communities. Unfortunately, there were hundreds of other racial conflict and anti-police incidents that I experienced and could tell about. However, I do not wish to review much negativity about our society. On the contrary, my message is a positive one, intended to lift up our youth and to give them confidence that they can succeed against all of the odds.

I have always been an advocate of non-violence and civil rights. I am proud to note that I was the first-ever police officer in the United States elected to the board of a National Association for the Advancement of Colored People (NAACP) local chapter. It was the Baltimore Chapter, and I received more votes than the legendary Mrs. Enolia McMillan. I served with distinction, but later I decided to resign from my position on the board. I am sure you are asking why? Unfortunately, many NAACP chapter members began to become suspicious of my affiliation with the organization. The fact that a police officer was on the board precipitated rumors that I was a plant, an informer, or a spy for the Baltimore Police Department or perhaps some other agency. This hurt me, but I was able to understand. Unfortunately, during that period in our society, police officers were not universally trusted, to say the least. On a national scale, there were rumors and conspiracy theories about who killed Dr. Martin Luther King, Jr., and many thought that some of Dr. King's own associates were informers for the FBI. Some even thought that the FBI had a role in King's assassination. Again, I say, the 1960's and 1970's were turbulent times. As ironic as it may seem, the NAACP later honored me. In recognition of my service on its board and my dedication, the Baltimore NAACP Chapter established The Harlow Fullwood, Jr. Award, a permanent award in my honor. This award is presented each year to a citizen who has distinguished himself or herself by outstanding civic deeds.

Human kindness should be unconditional. There was one rainy, cold night when we were riding in the patrol car. My partner and I stopped because we noticed a lady lying in the gutter. She was elderly and was very intoxicated. She was also very filthy. The rain and mud was just streaming all over her.

My partner was white. Once he realized what was happening, he quickly went over to the woman, carefully picked her up, and helped her to her feet. Another white officer saw this and immediately yelled, "Hey man! Don't touch that dirty piece of trash! How can you put your hands on that woman? Just let her stay right in the gutter where she belongs!" My partner turned to the other white officer and said, "Listen, this woman could be somebody's mother. If she was my mother, I would hope that some good person would come along and pick up my mother off of the ground." I will never forget that act of compassion. I was very moved by it. The woman was black. True compassion is color-blind.

I was the first African American to be elected to serve on the police department's Personnel Service Board, a unit that met once per month to review and discuss internal grievance matters relating to benefits, work assignments, and other day-to-day issues of concern for the entire 3,000-member police workforce. Policing can be very exhaustive. The daily grind can produce a lot of anxiety and uncertainty for some officers. There were many who had alcoholism problems. The wear and tear of law enforcement can drive some to drink and/or also to experience mild and severe emotional problems. Stress management was a priority issue at the Personnel Service Board meetings.

I never had to use my revolver. I am grateful for that. There tends to be much controversy when a police officer shoots a person. On this issue, I must emphasize that in the academy police officers are trained only to pull their revolvers to protect themselves or innocent citizens. We were trained that when and if we were forced to shoot, it should be to kill on the first shot not to wound or disable. I know that this sounds extreme; however, the rationale is that you may not have a second chance to get off a second shot. It is as simple as that.

Police must often make split-second decisions. In emergencies, an officer will not always have time to consider the long-term United States Supreme Court ramifications of how he or she responds in an instant to rectify a problem and to restore order. An officer must act immediately. Officers cannot pause and conduct syllogisms on the appropriateness of their response. Anyway, who is to say that the issue would go to the Supreme Court and still come back a 5-4 decision in favor of the department?

Some of the saddest moments in my life have been when I attended a funeral service for a fallen officer, an officer who gave his life so that the rest of us could live in peace and harmony. Police are killed in-the-line-of-duty through a variety of tragic circumstances. I can only say one thing. The department really knows how to put an officer away with dignity, with a magnificent ceremony. Of course, this is no consolation for the grieving families of deceased officers. It represents the solemn respect and love that officers have for each other.

One of my role models on the force was Major Lon F. Rowlett, the Director of Personnel. He and I worked together on many recruitment assignments. He was from Texas and had a master's degree. His often-stated credo was, "I think if a young man wants to make a contribution to society today, then there is no greater opportunity afforded than in the law enforcement field." One day, Major Lon F. Rowlett called me to his office, and he said, "Fullwood, you are one of my best recruiters, but I want you to be in a position to be more marketable; therefore, I want you to go back to school and earn your college degree." I was very insulted. When I went home, I told Elnora, "Guess what Major Rowlett told me today. He said..." I could always count on Elnora for the supportive advice I needed. Elnora quickly said, "Major Rowlett was right. You should." Oh well, so much for support. I was stunned by the speed of her response. I meditated. I thought about what Major Rowlett said, and I later began to think of him as a genius. He saw my potential, and he was impressed.

I enrolled at Baltimore City Community College (formerly the Community College of Baltimore) in 1972. The college had some of the best faculty members that I have had. Faculty members were really knowledgeable and dedicated. I graduated in 1974 and earned an associate degree in urban sociology with highest honors. I took twenty courses and earned nineteen "A" grades and one "C." I got that "C" in philosophy. I was very upset. I could have graduated "Number One" at BCCC. I went to the professor to find out, "Why a 'C'?" The professor explained that I had missed many class sessions. I reminded him that, I had been involved in a car accident, and this caused me to miss classes. Nevertheless, I earned A's in all of my other courses. Where I come from, if you earn an "A," you get an "A." He understood and said, "All right, Mr. Fullwood. You tell me what grade to give you, and I will." I thought about that for a moment and I said, "No. Never mind, I will go with the 'C'. If you think that I really deserve a 'C,' then a 'C' it will be. Thanks for allowing me the opportunity to express myself." So there, nineteen "A's" and one "C."

Thanks to the encouragement from Major Rowlett, I earned my Associate of Arts degree from BCCC with highest honors, summa cum laude. Next, I decided that I wanted to earn my bachelor's degree from Virginia Union University. I needed to know exactly how many additional credits I needed to earn to get my degree, but I was working every day in Baltimore. How could I find time to go to Richmond? Major Rowlett again came up with a genius solution. He put me on a three-day assignment to do some police recruiting in Richmond. He asked me, "Who is your boss?" I said, "You." He said, "O.K. then. I will give you a car to use, expenses, and will pay for your hotel stay. Use your time wisely, and go over to VUU and talk to the officials about what you need to do to get your degree." I did that.

I learned that if I could enroll in and complete a sociological research course that was offered by Morgan State, VUU would award me my degree. However, I discovered that the course was only offered in the day. When I went back to Baltimore, I told Major Rowlett this. I said, "Thanks for helping me by sending me to Richmond and all, but Morgan only offers this course during the day, so I will not be able to earn my VUU degree." Major Rowlett asked me, "Who runs this outfit?" I said, "You." He said, "If you only need that one course, and it is offered only in the day, you go to school, and I will cover for you." I was really impressed by his humility. I took the course and earned an "A." I notified Virginia Union.

I went to Richmond to VUU's Commencement to get my degree. When I was walking across campus, I saw the college president, Dr. Allix B. James, at his car. The trunk was open, and he was putting a box in that contained diplomas. I said, "Good afternoon, Dr. James. Can you please give me my diploma now so that I can get back to Baltimore?" He said, "Yes," and he did. I drove back to Baltimore with my Bachelor of Science Degree in Sociology from Virginia Union University.

Shortly after that, I was up for consideration for promotion. I had to go before a four-member Interview Board, and Major Rowlett was on that board. When I went in for my interview, I saluted. Major Rowlett said to the members of the board, "This is one of the best guys I have worked with in my life. You can't ask him any questions." He told me that I was dismissed and that he would see me in the morning. The next morning, I was informed that I had been promoted to Police Agent.

Approximately one year later, Major Rowlett died of leukemia. When I learned that he suffered from that disease, I remembered that definition that we were required to learn in the ninth grade, Leukemia: a malignant disease of the blood-forming tissues characterized by large increases in the numbers of leukocytes (white blood cells) in the circulation. I was deeply sorrowful about his death. Major Rowlett inspired me in many ways. He was a tireless leader, a mentor, a scholar, and a friend. He never looked at the color of a person's skin. He judged everyone by his or her character. He was good to me, and I was good to him. When he had to travel out of town, he took me with him, and we always flew first class. This was unique because I had officer rank. Typically, only the upper-ranked officers were allowed to fly out-of-state, but the major took me everywhere with him. Often, after we would return to Baltimore from a recruitment trip or a convention, the major would say, "Fullwood, take the next two to three days off!"

He was not perfect. He drank alcohol quite a bit, and he smoked big cigars. I guess one reason that he took me with him so often was that he knew that I did not drink. I was his "designated traveler" so to speak. The major also loved to play golf, and we had some great times on the greens. When he died, it felt like I had lost a father. Whenever we went on a recruitment assignment, he would always say, "Fullwood, it is in your hands!" There was a nickname that he gave me, and he only used it in private. Major Rowlett called me his "Ace-Hole." I really miss him. He inspired me to excel.

In March 1975, the Baltimore *Sunday Sun* ran an article entitled, "A Big, Genial Policeman is Dean of Recruiters." That article had a photo of me in uniform, standing in front of my recruitment van. *The Sun* said, "Officer Harlow Fullwood, Jr. likes what he sells, and because of that, he is an excellent salesman." Major Lon L. Rowlett was quoted as saying, "Harlow is very truthful and doesn't oversell. He relates very well to the people to whom he is talking---both black and whites. He's one of the finest recruiters I've ever known." Rowlett was a Marine Corps recruiter before he came to Baltimore, so he knew what effective recruiting was.

That article further stated, "Fullwood is hard to overlook, and when he shakes your hand, you not only feel it, but you wonder how anyone's palm can be that large. But, it is in the area of sincerity that Officer Fullwood is so convincing. When he talks about 'fairness' and 'giving' to the community, it is almost impossible not to believe him. Those two words are his watchwords, and they crop up repeatedly in his conversation, and in his work. Fullwood says, 'When I look for men who can carry the badge, I look for someone who will enforce the law impartially, who will represent fairness, compassion and understanding.' ...As a young black man, Fullwood naturally is concerned about increasing the number of minority policemen, and he has worked to convince other, young blacks that being an officer is not selling out to the white world. He even signed up his brother, Everett, 32, now a six-year veteran. He recalls that when he was a recruit, 'I couldn't even ride in a patrol car. I could name all of the few black officers.' Despite the discrimination that he experienced in the past, Officer Fullwood is convinced that, under Commissioner Donald D. Pomerleau, the department has made great progress in racial matters."

I did not mind traveling far to recruit. An article in a 1975 Richmond *Afro-American* celebrated how I returned to Virginia Union to recruit officers. It described me as a combination of army recruiter and evangelist and how I successfully recruited eleven new members from VUU to join the Baltimore City Police Force.

In January 1992, when Commissioner Pomerleau died at age 76, the Baltimore *Afro-American* published an article that included a 1978 photo of which I am very proud. It pictured me being presented the coveted Jimmy Swartz Medallion for my police work by the Commissioner Pomerleau and J. Millard Tawes, the former Maryland governor. It was Commissioner Pomerleau who recommended me for the Jimmy Swartz Medallion. He advocated cultural sensitivity and required all Baltimore City Police Officers and other department employees to take a course in black history.

That article quoted me as saying, "I remember Commissioner Pomerleau for upgrading the education of employees. He brought the department 'all the modern stuff'; the crime lab was one of the best in the country. Before Pomerleau, blacks were assigned to patrol only certain areas, but under him they were assigned on the basis of need in patrol cars and other areas."

Speaking of traveling far to recruit, I will never forget the time, in 1980, when Major Woods and I drove 600 miles to Anderson, Indiana. Yes, 600 miles! About 5,000 workers had been laid off indefinitely from two General Motors plants pushing Anderson's 22 percent jobless rate to near the top of the national unemployment chart. In Anderson, we spoke to a group of young men and women who applied for some of the 200 patrolmen positions available on Baltimore's force, which was then the nation's sixth largest.

A Marion, Indiana newspaper, The *Chronicle-Tribune*, published a major article about our recruitment trip. It reported that 80 people submitted applications; 15 percent were already working in law enforcement, 95 percent were white, and four applicants were women. Major Woods told the group, "In Baltimore, we deal in community policing. Nobody said that policing is easy. I expect you to be trained and put your biases behind you and work for the community."

I served on the force with distinction, and I received many awards. However, there comes a time in life when one realizes a need to discover a new endeavor. It comes time to create a new career path. On Wednesday, May 14, 1986, at age 45, and after 23 and one-half years on the force, I resigned. Commissioner Bishop Robinson saluted me for becoming the department's top recruiter. I brought 1,600 people onto the force. During my tenure, the number of vacancies shrunk from 500 in 1970 to just two the week before I quit. The number of black officers on the force increased from just two percent to twenty percent of the more than 3,000 officers. Prior to resigning from the Police Department, Elnora and I had started our KFC venture. It became very complex to perform both jobs.

On the day that I retired, Michael Powell of the Baltimore *News American*, in an article entitled, "Top Police Recruiter Moving On," wrote, "After 23 years of police work, Sgt. Harlow Fullwood, Jr. is turning to chicken. Fullwood, well known in the streets of Baltimore among young men and women, is devoting full time to his Kentucky Fried Chicken franchises. Fullwood had been through the tough times of recruiting, including the tumultuous police strike of the 1970's that left the ranks depleted. Its salary scale, lower than those in all nearby counties, made it difficult to attract prime candidates. Fullwood says, 'There were tough times, times when I didn't think anyone wanted to be a police officer. But then, I'd find someone who had the quality.'

A May 15, 1986, Baltimore *Evening Sun* article, by Frank D. Roylance, entitled, "His Job was to Recruit the Best," announced my retirement. It stated, "Fullwood believes he has been able to serve his department, his community and young men and women whom he's helped launch to police careers." That article praised my recruitment accomplishments but also included my perspectives on future recruitment challenges that I predicted the department would face. I was quoted as saying, "Recruiting police has grown more difficult over the years, and not only because other jurisdictions can and do lure good people away from the city with better pay and benefits. The department is fighting a war of image. Many young folks don't want to wear a uniform. They don't want to work in certain areas of the city. They don't want to have to arrest their friends who smoke marijuana. They don't want to change their lifestyle. They don't want to make real commitment. Police officers may be popular on television, but they are not in real life. I blame the times, drugs, and the whole breakdown of society. When the homes fail, and the schools fail, then the police become the bad guys. I never arrested a man with a good job and an education, for a crime of violence."

When I was a recruiter, I enjoyed working with young people and helping them get started. Since I left the department, I am still doing that. As a KFC franchise owner, I work with a younger group, but I strive to do something with them, tell them to stay in school, and I get them started with a job. I guess I will never really be out of police work. Many young people who come to work for me hear more than a few words about getting into police work. I can't help it. As I noted, my son in-law once worked for me at my KFC operation, and now, I am proud to say Robert is a Baltimore City police officer.

Well, as a former police recruiter for the Baltimore Police Department would do, I now present some key information to you:

Today, a new police officer in the Baltimore Police Department can earn an annual salary: $31,000 - $45,800 (within 5 years). Minimum Qualifications: On or before the day of examination, each applicant must be a U.S. citizen; have a high school diploma or a General Education Development (GED) Certificate recognized by the Maryland Police and Correctional Training Commission; have a valid driver's license from any state at the time application is made; be within three months of his/her twenty-first birthday; and not have been convicted of a felony.

A Policeman's Prayer

Lord, I ask for courage;

Courage to face and conquer my own fears...

Courage to take me where others will not go.

I ask for strength;

Strength of body to protect others...

Strength of spirit to lead others.

I ask dedication;

Dedication to my job to do it well...

Dedication to my community to keep it safe.

Give me, Lord, concern;

For all those who trust me...

And compassion for those who need me

And, please, Lord, through it all; be at my side.

Dr. Thomas H. Henderson

6th President
Virginia Union University
1960-1970

Chapter Eight

Deathbed Promise and Commitment of Service to Fellowman

Many individuals have asked me why I am so dedicated to supporting charitable causes. Some have criticized me for giving away too much. My answer is a simple one: "I made a promise." I made a promise to Dr. Thomas Howard Henderson who became the first layman and the third VUU alumnus (Class of 1929) to be Virginia Union University's president. Before I explain about my promise, I will present to you some information about Dr. Henderson and his presidency.

Dr. Henderson was a very effective chief executive. He initiated an extensive building program. During his tenure from 1960 until 1970, the university began construction on four new facilities: Mac Vicar Hall, Storer Hall, Ellison Hall, and the Henderson Center. Under Dr. Henderson's leadership, the size of the faculty doubled, and the student enrollment increased by 28 percent. Some of his numerous innovative accomplishments included a faculty exchange program with Concordia College in Moorehead, Minnesota, and he coordinated the merger of Storer College in West Virginia with Virginia Union.

As I previously stated, the 1960's were turbulent times in our society. Dr. Henderson served during that extraordinary period when student unrest was prevalent on college campuses across the nation. Virginia Union was not spared this phenomenon. In 1968, VUU was disrupted by a student takeover of the administration building. That event resulted in a decline in enrollment and some financial difficulties, but President Henderson was courageous. He refused to allow his institution, his alma mater, to concede to student disorder.

In a document on presidents of Virginia Union University entitled: "A Virginia Union Historical View," the following statement describes Dr. Henderson's undaunted reaction to the student protest environment at VUU during that period. It states, "At one time, he expressed the opinion that militancy, rather than intellectual pursuit, was the prevailing mood on the campus but, characteristically, he tempered his remarks with a basic optimism that it was only a phase in student development in an era when students became more concerned about social problems and conditions. Moreover, that concern, he contended, was good."

Dr. Henderson's term of office came to an untimely end when, at the age of 59, he died on January 17, 1970. When I learned that Dr. Henderson was ill, I went to his home to visit him. He had intestinal cancer. He had been hospitalized, but the doctors had done all that they could do. His condition was terminal; therefore, Dr. Henderson's family had brought him home to die.

When I arrived at his house, his wife answered the door. I asked her whether Dr. Henderson could have any visitors, and she said yes. Because of his medical situation, the smell in his home was almost unbearable. Cancer was destroying his body, and the rectal/bowel-related odor was nearly overwhelming. As I walked up the stairs to see Dr. Henderson, I called out, "Dr. Henderson, I'm coming to see you." He immediately recognized my voice, and I heard him say, very faintly, "Harlow, I am glad that you are here."

When I walked into that room and saw him lying in bed, I was astonished to see how his body had become so frail, but I tried not to let him see my reaction. Dr. Henderson looked up at me and he said, "Harlow, I know that I look terrible, and I know that it smells terrible in here. I am dying. However, I do not have a problem with that. I want to thank you for having the courage and concern to visit me. I realize that I do not have much more time." I said, "Dr. Henderson, I just want to personally thank you for the support and inspiration that you have provided to me."

It was at that moment when Dr. Henderson replied to my statement that my life was changed. He looked up at me and said, "Harlow Fullwood, Jr. if you commit to me today that you will dedicate your life to **lifting up others** as I **lifted you up** and hundreds like you, then my dying will not be in vain." I leaned down and whispered into Dr. Henderson's ear, "Yes I will. I promise you." I tightly gripped his hand, and I then left his home. Dr. Henderson died two days after my visit.

The impact of that incident did not hit me right away. I did not take that promise very seriously until one day when I was home sweeping the floor. I was listening to station: WEBB 1360 AM, a popular black station at that time that played everything, gospel, jazz, rhythm and blues, and talk. At that particular time, a guest was speaking about the Big Brothers/Big Sisters program. The discussion became quite interesting. I put down the broom and listened. I became downhearted as I heard descriptions of how young boys and girls were seeking anyone who cared to help them enjoy basic experiences like going to a museum, the zoo, the movies, a baseball game, or to church. As I continued to listen, I said to myself, "I have got to do something to help these children in need." It was at that exact moment that I realized that I had made a promise.

Before that experience, I was an avid golfer, and I would go straight from the golf course to the card table. Most of my endeavors involved self-gratification. However, after listening to that radio show and reflecting on that solemn promise that I had made to Dr. Henderson, I made a drastic change of priorities. Since that experience in the 1970's, until today, I do not think I have played golf more than three times. I have devoted most of my time to helping others. Love Lifted Me, so, accordingly, I have dedicated my life to Lifting Up Others. That deathbed promise has become my beacon, my inspiration, and my commitment for helping humanity.

PSALM 23

The Lord is my shepherd; I shall not want.

He maketh me to lie down in green pastures: he leadeth
me beside the still waters.

He restoreth my soul: he leadeth me in the paths of
righteousness for his name's sake.

Yea, though I walk through the valley of the shadow of
death, I will fear no evil: for thou art with me; thy rod
and thy staff they comfort me.

Thou prepareth a table before me in the presence of mine
enemies: thou anointest my head with oil; my cup
runneth over.

Surely goodness and mercy shall follow me all the days
of my life: and I will dwell in the house of the Lord for ever.

THE OLD TESTAMENT

Harlow Fullwood, Jr.
President, Fullwood Foods, Inc. (KFC)

Chapter Nine

KFC Years: Becoming An Entrepreneur "From Night Sticks to Drumsticks"

"You make a living by what you get, but you make a life by what you give. Harlow Follwood has been giving to others his entire life, and the story in this book inspires all of us to get serious about service to others."

Steve Provost
Senior Vice President, KFC Corporation

"Harlow, whom I have known for many years, apparently came into this world with a mission and a gift from God."

Osborne Payne
*First African-American McDonald's Franchisee
in Maryland*

When my daughter enrolled at Virginia Union University, I did not have much money. That was the same year I had the opportunity to go into the Kentucky Fried Chicken business. I had worked with dedication and commitment for a Baltimore Police Department that also did much to help me in terms of being exposed to the community and meeting people. I really enjoyed my work. I loved my work.

As a police officer, I was bringing home about $600 every two weeks. I enjoyed my work. When my daughter enrolled in college, and we had very little money, it was then that I was started to face the reality of my situation. Here I had been working for an organization with dedication and commitment for 23 1/2 years, but every morning I woke up broke. I decided that if the right opportunity presented itself, I was going to resign from the police department. It's really something to work a job 23 1/2 years and not be able to provide an adequate education for your children or to be able to afford nice things that you would like your family to have.

There I was. I had two college degrees, and I had recruited more individuals for the Baltimore Police Department than anyone had ever done in its history. I had received the Distinguished Service Award, the highest honor that can be given to anyone not killed in the line of duty. I was recognized as a national expert in police recruiting, and I was the most decorated police officer in terms of community service. I felt really good about that. The day I submitted my resignation, I had one year and a half to wait for full retirement. I had about $30,000 in the pension system. I took it out to help get started in the KFC business. During that time people said, "Man, you're crazy!" Nevertheless, I maintained my faith.

There was a man by the name of George Larkins who was the head of public relations for the Marriott Corporation. He was a neighbor, and I was out tending my lawn. I felt very proud to do yard work because it was my first house. Larkins would drive by and speak. Soon we got to know one another. On one particular afternoon, he told me that Marriott Corporation owned

Kentucky Fried Chicken, and he said that it did not have any KFC stores in the area. The corporation wanted to acquire Gino's, which had been selling KFC chicken and hamburgers, but Marriott did not want to continue to mix the two products. Now defunct, Gino's, Inc., a hamburger restaurant chain, was later acquired by the Marriott Corporation in 1982. Under the territorial agreement, Gino's had operated 69 KFC locations in Baltimore, Washington and Philadelphia. The Louisville, Kentucky-based KFC Corporation wanted more locations within that region; therefore, in 1984, it began a $28.5 million expansion program to add 57 new restaurants and 1,200 employees in Baltimore and up to 35 new stores and 500 employees in suburban Baltimore.

In 1984, KFC had also reached an agreement with the Reverend Jesse Jackson and his Rainbow Coalition organization's People United to Save Humanity (PUSH) to increase minority participation in the KFC chain. At that time, KFC required candidates to pay about $50,000 for store rights and have a net worth of about $400,000. Mr. Larkins said that since KFC was looking for blacks to buy franchises, this was my golden opportunity to make enough money to send my daughter and son to college. Larkins told me that I had the opportunity to become the first African-American KFC franchisee in Baltimore City. I said to Mr. Larkins, "All that's fine, but I don't have much money." He said, "But, you have a prominent community reputation." I always point out to students that there is a vast difference between character and reputation. Reputation is what other people say you are. Character is what you are. I would rather that my character be more notable than my reputation.

Well, at Mr. Larkins's insistence, I called the KFC Headquarters in Louisville to ask for a franchise application. It was sent promptly. I must tell you. I needed five Philadelphia lawyers to fill out that application. It was so complex that I had to use a magnifying glass to read the fine print and a dictionary to comprehend various terms. It was truly an application that lawyers wrote for lawyers.

One day, I was walking down the street, and I saw a friend with whom I worked. I took that application out of my briefcase. I said, "Look, I need some help. I don't have much money." He said, "Fullwood, I will certainly help you, and I won't charge you a dime. I just want to see what is going to happen to a person applying for a KFC franchise who has no money." When he finished analyzing that application, he said, "You go back to your job and pull out of your file of commendations, letters, certificates, newspaper articles, magazine articles. Pull out your letters from the mayor and the governor and all those other important documents." I did as he instructed, but I did not see the relevancy at the time. We completed that application and sent it along with all of that information. It must have been about 12 inches thick. To tell you the truth, I didn't have great expectations of ever hearing from KFC again.

Well, low and behold, about two months later, I received a letter from KFC saying that I was requested to come in for an interview. Somewhat excited, I called the company for details. I was asked to go to company headquarters in Louisville at my own expense. I really wanted to take Elnora because she was part of the decision-making process. When I saw Larkins, I told him that I could not afford to go. He said, "Well, you're going to have to continue doing what you have been doing - make a sacrifice." I called and told KFC that I was coming. I asked for permission to bring Elnora because she was part of the Fullwood family's decision-making process. KFC officials understood. Elnora and I flew to Louisville.

While we were waiting for the interview, a gentleman came out. He was, in my opinion, one of those "down home" hillbilly types that you look at and say, "Oh Lord!" We quickly learned that sometimes we can prejudice a situation, and that our first first impressions do not always have to be right. When we started the interview, his first question was directed to Elnora. "If Kentucky Fried Chicken provides your husband with a franchise, what would your role be?" Elnora, without hesitation, replied with a smile, "The same that it has been for 20 years-- supportive." You know, he never asked her another question during the entire hour and a half that we sat for the interview.

He started to review the 12-inch-thick package. He said, "This is good. This is good." When he got down to the financial statement, he looked and me and said, "You're broke!" I said, "Mister, I could have told you that on the telephone." He went on to say, "Don't be disturbed. We know about your reputation and your exemplary record of caring for your fellow man." As a result of that, we were guaranteed by the Kentucky Fried Chicken for $750,000. Getting a guarantee from KFC meant that if I failed, I could have walked away from the whole thing without being in debt to the company. KFC had enough confidence in me and the business marketing sense to know that I could be an asset to its system. I did not have the capital, but I did have the character and reputation.

I had to go to Louisville for training. I learned quickly that the chicken franchise business is a science. It was something that I endeavored to work at, but I had not realized that there was so much involved. I looked around at what other guys were doing in my particular field. I learned that the best thing that you can have, the essential ingredient for a successful franchise is, ...location, location, location. Then, you can apply management techniques. You cannot survive if you do not have a good location. Eventually, the survivor will need exceptional management skills.

When I went to Louisville, there were about 25 participants in the class. Most of them had tremendous backgrounds in the KFC system. They came from New York and other major cities from around the nation. There were only four blacks in the class, a psychologist, an accountant, an attorney, and I---a police officer. We studied together. When the training ended, I finished second in the class of 25. Yes, second, but that time I did not protest. I rejoiced.

It was the first time outside of the police department that I had ever been in a class with so many white Americans. We would go to class from 8:30-4:30 every day except for Sunday when I would go to church. I recall that when I first went to the training center, man, was it frustrating. I didn't know that there was so much involved in learning all about the product, service, and cleanliness. I finished second place at the KFC National Training Center and earned a 96.3 academic average. Wow! I also received the Director's Award given in recognition of being the one most likely to succeed.

A man named Walter Simon, the highest-ranked black in KFC, assisted me in getting my first franchise. He died several years later after his retirement. Mr. Simon was a very influential guy with KFC and helped the first minority franchisers realize a life-long dream...sharing a piece of the "American Pie"...economic success.

So, I opened up my first store in 1984 on Harford Road. We purchased the property. There was a building already there. We took that building and brought it up to KFC standards. Elnora was still teaching school. I wanted to do something to uplift my mother. She was the first person that I put on the payroll. She had been doing domestic work for two Johns Hopkins Hospital physicians and taking care of their children.

Ka-Ching! Ka-Ching! Ka-Ching! The cash registers rang incessantly. It was opening day for my first KFC franchise. My mother was terrified. I said, "Momma, I'm opening up my doors soon, and I just want you to be with me so that we can experience this special moment together." My mother looked at me and said, "I'm so afraid because you've worked so hard. Do you think that they will buy chicken from a black man?" I remember telling Momma, "I'm not selling Fullwood. I'm selling Kentucky Fried Chicken, a national brand." But, I was scared too.

My Harford Road location was in a community made up of blue-collar workers who were 99 percent white. It was 1984, and I felt like a stranger in a strange, strange land. I really didn't know what to expect. I did not know that I was embarking upon an experience that would transform my life and finances so dramatically. Within three months from our opening day, I had my initial $30,000 investment back in the bank. I was saving $10,000 a month. It had taken me 23 years to save the $30,000 in the pension system while working for the Baltimore Police Department. I thought I was in another world. The company expected the store to generate about $500,000 in first-year sales. However, we generated $850,000.

On that first day when we looked out the window, there was a long line of people waiting for us to open the doors. There were so many people waiting to get their chicken from KFC that the police department had to control traffic. Now, isn't that ironic? I needed police assistance for crowd control. The first two customers to come through the doors were Osborne Payne, Maryland's first African-American McDonald's franchisee, and William Anderson, one of the best volunteers I've ever met.

As I stated, when I started my KFC franchise, I was still a police officer. I would get off from the police department and go to work at the Kentucky Fried Chicken store every single day for one year and a half. When I wanted to expand, I was informed by KFC that I would have to leave my police department job. I had one and one half years left before retirement. That first store operated very well for the first two or three years, and then we saw a decline in sales. It wasn't that we were doing anything wrong. It was that KFC was really, really saturating the market, and I was surrounded by new stores, modern stores. We saw a drastic decline in our sales.

At the same time, it came to my attention that KFC wanted a store in West Baltimore on Franklin Street. The person who owned the property was black. That owner said to KFC, "We will sell the property to you on the condition that you will select a black franchisee. Of course, I was called by KFC. I consented, and we established an $800,000-store on that location which later became a million-dollar store. Our Franklin Street operation later led the state in volume sales for 15 years, and it was second or third in the other years. That was a very successful location. Later, I met with the lady who owned the property. I let her know that I appreciated her courage and steadfastness by insisting that an African American be given the chance to pursue the American dream.

Two Faces You Can Trust In Baltimore.

KFC.

Harlow
Fullwood, Jr.

Presenting a Bucket to Maryland
Governor, Parris N. Glendening

"Top KFC Awards"

Holding Portrait of Walter Simon
KFC Executive

Opening of my
First Franchise

Later, I opened a location at Pennsylvania Avenue and North Avenue, in the Tickner Building, a former funeral home. We gutted the structure and developed a new KFC location. It became one of the top locations not only in the state but also in the country. It became a top money generator.

Then, George Larkins, who planted the seed for me to enter the world of business, passed away. Shortly after opening my first KFC store, he had a heart attack while driving in the Cherry Hill community of Baltimore. His car careened into the river, and he drowned. I never had the opportunity to thank him for his encouragement and confidence.

Since Elnora and I started our business in 1984, our phenomenal achievements have been highly recognized by The Kentucky Fried Chicken Corporation. In our first year of operation, we were awarded the company's prestigious "Five Star Award," which recognizes those franchisees who successfully adopt and use the greatest number of Kentucky Fried Chicken's operation systems and programs. It was the highest award given franchisees at that time. We were the recipients of the "State Sales Award," presented to the franchisee that had the highest dollar volume restaurant in each state. We were the 1987 winners in Maryland, making us the first blacks in the history of Kentucky Fried Chicken Corporation to lead a whole state in gross sales. During 1987 and 1988, we received the "Million Dollar Award." This award was presented to the restaurant with gross sales of over $1 million. Our restaurants have also received the "QSC Excellence Award" and KFC's "Triple Crown Award," in recognition of providing excellence in quality products, fast friendly service, and cleanliness of our restaurants.

Things suddenly changed. Inflation hit. The illegal drug trade became prevalent in neighborhoods where our stores were located. All of a sudden, crime hit to the extent that people were not comfortable. People were afraid to get out of their cars. These environmental conditions affected my business so drastically that I had to close a location in the Walbrook Shopping Center in a section that Baltimoreans refer to as "The Junction." We became business victims of the drug and violence culture that affects our city. People were afraid to come out at night because they were gripped by the meanness of crime. That nearly broke my heart. As a result of the influx of crime and drugs in the communities, we lost $500,000 to $600,000. Unemployment and factory closings were other economic occurrences that had a negative impact on our business.

One of the things that we learned was not to live above our means. I would probably be out of business today if we had not had the long-range vision to see that: Times may be good for now, but when you are operating a business, times change, and things are going to get lean. This is an important maxim that any aspiring businessperson should know and understand.

I was able to put a substantial amount of money back into my business. I've been very fortunate to have angels standing over me. When I was thinking about franchising, I sort of felt I had a good opportunity to get one, but I was scared to death. I didn't know what to do and in what direction to turn. So, I turned to Osborne A. Payne, an African American, who was the first McDonald's franchisee in Baltimore. Then, I turned to William March who was perhaps the most successful funeral home owner and director on the East Coast. Next, I sought advice from Mrs. Dorothy Brunson, an African-American media executive who owned a radio station and who is currently owner of a television station in the Philadelphia area.

These dynamic people were very supportive. I know that I worried them to death, but they gave me good advice and encouragement every step of the way. I will be forever indebted to them for their kind and candid advice. Osborne even went as far as to take me into his office, close the door, and he opened up his personal books. He pointed out certain things that he thought I should know. He placed a lot of emphasis on paying yourself first because he felt everyone else is going to get paid. Pay Yourself First! Additionally, he emphasized: Understand the percentages of your business. If you are in business, and you do not understand and are unable to control what we call the "controllables," such as product costs, gas and electric, and your labor, you are doomed to fail.

God blessed me at a time when I really, really needed help. There was a lady in the police department whose son worked in the Kentucky Fried chicken business. She said, "I think he would like to work with and for you." I called him, and we had lunch together. I was very impressed with him. Later, I selected him to be head of operations. Lord, because of my ill health, I do not know where I would have been without Tony Cameron.

Tony was with my operations for 12 years and was outstanding. As a matter of fact, by knowing the KFC business, he was one of the best people with whom I had contact. With his high school education, he is far, far ahead of many young people who went on to receive their college degrees. Not only is he good at what he does, he is loyal, honest, and he works hard. The truth of the matter is, as I began to suffer health problems, I became unable to do a lot of things that I could normally do. Tony picked up the tasks, and he really kept the business rolling.

I cannot put a price on what Tony Cameron has meant to me because of his commitment, devotion to duty, and his loyalty. He's not just loyal. He is also honest. I know, without any reservations, the business could not have survived without his devotion. For that, I will always be indebted to him. I am hopeful that one day I will be able to repay him for his hard work and sense of great loyalty. He's one of the finest young men that I have ever met, and I love him as I love my brother. Tony has now moved on to launch his own business. He has my blessings.

I have heard that if you have a need for medical advice, never use a doctor who is also a friend. It is often felt that if people are too close to the situation, they are incapable of giving you the professional, impartial advice and answers that you really need and deserve to keep the business viable. I think that rule is a matter of judgment. I have been very fortunate to have other individuals like Tony Cameron to work with me.

For example, there is also a young man named Allen Schiff who started out with me in an accounting firm where he is now one of the partners. Allen is one of the closest friends I have. I am prefacing this by saying that he is Jewish. Friendship, to me, has no color or ethnic background. He is one friend that I can honestly say, I love and respect as a brother.

In starting up a business, the best thing that you can do is to surround yourself with good people because you cannot be in the store 24 hours a day. Training is important. Location is important. You have to have a good attorney who understands the fast-food business, and you must have a very good accounting firm behind you. A franchising business can present excellent opportunities. On many occasions as a KFC franchisee, my greatest competition really did not come from other franchise outlets such as Burger King, McDonald's, etc. My biggest competitor was the KFC Corporation itself.

You could have a real good store doing good volume, and then all of a sudden the KFC Corporation would surround your outlet with other outlets within a mile and one half radius. It is very difficult to compete against the corporation because of the leverage that it has financially. Nevertheless, this is something with which you have to deal. That is one of the reasons why if you are going to be successful, you have just got to have a good location that can fight off those other obstacles.

A worthy principle is to save your money because there will be times when you are going to have difficulties. Normally, those difficulties are built around expansion, renovations, and new equipment, etc. The only way that you can acquire the money is through the banking institutions. I must hasten to say that the banks are very reluctant about lending you money if you are not making money. While you're making money, banking institutions from all over are calling you and wanting you to do this, do that, and making everything available to you. I understand the banking institutions, and that is something else that you have to deal with in business.

KFC has been good to me, but I have been good to it too. I don't think anyone in the entire system on a day-to-day basis, on a month-to-month, or even on a year-to-year basis has marketed the brand any more or any better than I have. I take pride in that fact. The KFC Corporation and I have had a good partnership. I know many other franchise operators cannot say that same thing. However, I'm still in business because I always tried to do it the right way. In business, I can't say I did not make mistakes; nevertheless, trial and error is the worst and the best way to learn. Still, I can honestly say that the mistakes that I made were honest mistakes. Mistakes can cost a lot of money, but at the same time, you should always try to avoid making the same mistake twice. I once heard a person say: "To make one mistake is human, to make the same mistake twice is foolish."

When you make a mistake, you have to use it as a stepping-sstone to continue because every day there's going to be an obstacle. How you reach a solution to obstacles is by staying on top of them every day, constantly trying to eliminate them. It is extremely difficult when you go into business and do not have a business background. Then, trial and error become very expensive. It can cost you. That is why it is so important for you to save your money. Before you pay anyone else, pay yourself first because there will come a time when you have to reach up for it. If it's not there, then you have big, big, big problems.

I can recall when I had a need for operating funds and had to consider consolidating all my loans. I had put hundreds of thousands of dollars back in my business to stabilize it during those bad economic periods. I am always mindful of what the KFC officials told me at the table when they were determining whether they could assist me. They said, "You know, if you had not invested back into your business, if you had not saved your money or lived within your means, then we would not be at the table to assist you. You didn't go out and buy yachts and condominiums, Rolls Royces, etc.; so you put yourself in a position where we can help you." A good track record and a good credit rating mean a lot in business especially when times get lean.

Yes, I was given an opportunity in franchising, but I must add, I was not really, really trained adequately to run a franchise operation. I was just very fortunate to have some good people at the intervals when I needed real help. So, I'm saying to all who aspire to business success, try to surround yourself with good people.

I never had a problem with sitting down, on a monthly basis, and sharing with my key people where we were financially. I let them know how we were doing, how we were not doing, and what we could do to improve. I feel that they cannot buy into the business, if they do not know what you're doing and how you're doing it. Otherwise, all they see is a lot of money coming coming in, but they do not see all the money that is going out.

Quite often in the franchise business, ten or fifteen percent of your receipts leave before you even start dealing with the basic operation items. You must make sure that your staff understands that. How do you go about that? Communication, training, and follow up are the essentials, and you must be prepared and willing to listen to your staff's suggestions. Sometimes employees see many things that you do not. Often, they see situations about which you may not even have thought. Therefore, it pays to have an open ear, and in my opinion, it pays to sit down with your employees and communicate with them as often as you can.

If you see something going wrong, you should not wait two days or three days. You should strive to correct it right then and there. Always remember that loyalty begets loyalty. As your business grows, try to let your key people grow also because they are the heart and the pulse of your business. This might be a surprise to those who read these words. Having been in business for over fifteen years, it was my plan to stay in business only ten years, to bow out, and just place a lot of interest on the development of the Fullwood Foundation.

During one period, I went five or six years without a vacation. There was another time when I went a number of years without days off. Sometimes I have worked without any pay. People see the successes, but they do not see the sacrifices.

The franchising business has been good to me, but I had to take my lumps too. When I look at the overall picture and consider what I've gained and what I've lost, I do not feel that if I could do it over I would ever go in business. Even when I'm away, I feel so uncomfortable. When my illness set in, and I was unable to do things that I normally do, that became very frustrating.

One of the greatest enemies in the world is stress and worry. When you have invested everything to provide for your family, a lot of stress factors are in the picture. Before I went into business, I was able to do many things, things with my family and all that. It just seems like I did not find the time while running a business.

Yes, I had planned to stay in it for ten years, but the "best-set plan" can sometimes go astray. If I had looked down the road to do it again, I do not think I would have taken this route. My wife and I were moving along. I was in law enforcement, and she was teaching. Together, we could have made a good living as we moved along. By the same token, if l had known then what I know now and if I had to do this thing all over again, I don't believe I would want to do it.

My children were interested in this business when I started. My daughter worked with me for ten years after she graduated from college. But, she was born to teach. She is like my Elnora, born to teach. I believe that in the game of life, some people are born to do certain things. After ten years, Paquita decided that she wanted to teach math. I said "Honey, go get it!" She is currently teaching business math and is real content with it.

Later, my son worked with me for several years. At that time, he did not want to go to college. He graduated from the Baltimore School for the Arts, and he became an outstanding artist. Things happened with him that really broke me down. I was striving so hard to try to give my family a quality standard of living. In some ways, my son suffered because people always looked upon him as Mr. Fullwood's son; therefore, the expectations on him were, unfortunately, always very, very high.

We can experience a lot of problems because of how we treat employees. Many of them have the tendency to believe that what you own belongs to them. So, they may start taking two for them and one for you; and, after a while, they wonder how you got there. It's tough enough having customers coming in, using drugs and dropping the syringes down the toilet. Then, you have to call the plumber. Truthfully speaking, over the years, I guess I have called the plumber enough — because of that situation. Drugs are a prevailing problem, but at the same time, it is one that we have learned to deal with. It is not good for a business when you have those kinds of people hanging around.

In 1986, *Black Enterprise* magazine published an article that celebrated my achievements. I wish to share that article with you because it effectively chronicles the advancement of my KFC experience. It stated:

> Harlow Fullwood may be living proof that community service can be as good as money in the bank. In fact, the story of his rise from a job as recruiter for the Baltimore Police Department to ownership of two Kentucky Fried Chicken franchises stems directly from his having given far more to the public than he took for himself.
>
> His is an up-by-the-bootstraps story, one in which life experiences and countless hours as a tireless community volunteer were parlayed into a compelling sales pitch that convinced the Kentucky Fried Chicken Corp. (KFC) to award the inexperienced, under-financed Fullwood with a fast-food restaurant.
>
> "It was a blessing," says Fullwood. "I had no notion of what I was doing, but I had the desire to do it. KFC was willing to take a chance on me, and I wasn't about to let it down." Indeed, KFC officials acknowledge that sponsoring Fullwood's venture was a gamble on their part. He had no business experience whatsoever, and almost no capital. But, on the strength of his personality and an extraordinary show of support from his friends (many of them in high places), the company took the chance, and it worked. For the past two and a half years, Fullwood has built a growing, award-winning business out of an uncertain start, which included having to convert an Arthur Treacher's Fish & Chips restaurant in Parkville, MD, a predominantly white suburb of Baltimore. The Parkville store, which opened in July 1984, generated first-year sales of nearly $1 million. "That's about $400,000 more than KFC expected, he says with button-bursting pride. "KFC considers any franchise that earns $500,000 successful. I guess we were doubly successful in our first year."

This feat earned the brand-new franchise the KFC Five Star Award, the company's highest honor for sales achievement, and the White Glove Award was also given to the store, for cleanliness. When the franchise, which was selected for Fullwood by KFC officials because of its potential for reasonably good sales, turned out to be a continuing huge success, he was able to convince the executives at KFC's headquarters in Louisville, KY, to give him a second location. Last year both stores grossed almost $2 million in sales.

He opened his new restaurant last May. This time, Fullwood launched into his venture with confidence and an ulterior motive: He wanted it located in a black neighborhood, which is located on Franklin Street in West Baltimore. "I wanted a store in the inner city," he explains. "That's where I came from, and the people who live there have been responsible for my success." It is Fullwood's goal to build a business that will become so profitable that it can sustain itself, enabling him to devote more time to a favorite avocation: raising money for predominantly black colleges. In fact, Fullwood credits his current success to his long-time work for black colleges.

During much of the past 22 years, Fullwood presided over the Baltimore Chapter 62 of the Virginia Union University Alumni Association, a group responsible for raising millions of dollars for the traditionally black university in Richmond, Va. Ironically, he made the decision to go into business in 1983 while he was struggling to figure out a way to afford college tuition for his daughter, Paquita, now 22. At the time, he was a highly decorated police agent responsible primarily for recruiting black officers onto the force. He earned about $20,000 a year, and he felt that he was being underpaid, probably because the family was beginning to feel the strain financially as Paquita and her brother, Harlow III, now 10, got older.

During his own college days at Virginia Union, where he was an all-CIAA tackle and met Elnora Bassett, his wife-to-be, Fullwood developed a close attachment to the university. And, like his marriage of 24 years, his love affair with black colleges has endured.

The Fullwood family has been responsible for raffles, fashion shows, concerts, sales of souvenir books, speeches and a myriad of other activities that have helped to promote and raise funds for Virginia Union. The basement walls of their new home, in a quiet community on the outskirts of Baltimore, are decorated with medals of honor, awards, photographs and certificates of appreciation for Fullwood's having raised millions of scholarship dollars for his alma mater. "I've gotten so many awards, I stopped counting them years ago," he says with genuine modesty.

"But it was strange, I thought at the time, that I had helped send hundreds of kids to college, but I didn't have the money to send my own daughter," Fullwood adds. "That kind of depressed me."

A neighbor, however, came to his rescue with the news that Kentucky Fried Chicken was looking for minority members who wanted to own their own restaurants. Fullwood's neighbor persuaded him to apply for a KFC franchise, reminding him that KFC was one of the companies that had signed a deal with Rev. Jesse Jackson and Operation PUSH to boost the number of minority franchisees in its operation. The news coincided with KFC's announcement of a $28.5 million expansion program, which would include the building of about 50 new stores and the hiring of 1,200 additional employees in Baltimore and its suburbs.

But, after he expressed his desire to have a piece of that action, Fullwood quickly learned that it was neither easy nor inexpensive to acquire a KFC franchise. According to Walt Simon, vice president of business development at KFC's headquarters, individual franchise operators own about 4,000 of the company's restaurants, and it operates an additional 1,000 facilities. Before most KFC candidates are offered a franchise, they must meet the company's stringent managerial and financial requirements.

"We usually require franchisers to pay between $30,000 and $50,000 for store rights, and they must have about $125,000 in liquid assets and a net worth between $350,000 and $400,000," says Simon. Fullwood was unable to complete the financial section of the KFC franchise application. "I didn't have that kind of money," he says.

Rather than document his meager financial holdings, Fullwood attempted to impress the KFC executives with the only capital he owned: his community service record. Fullwood's application included a five inch-thick stack of newspaper clippings and letters documenting his volunteer work and the honors he was awarded by the police department. He asked his friends to send Kentucky Fried Chicken letters of recommendation. Simon says that when Fullwood's application first landed on his desk and he glanced at the financial statement section, "I wasn't impressed, since he failed to meet the company's standards for minority franchises." Simon was about to send Fullwood a 'thanks, but no thanks' form letter when "my office was flooded with letters," he says. "I got one from the Governor, the Mayor of Baltimore, the City Council President, City Council Members, the Chief of Police, community groups, college teachers and one from a college president. Then I got a letter from Congressman Parren Mitchell's office. "That's when I said, 'Who is this guy?' I wasn't convinced I would give him a franchise, but I wanted to know who this person was who commanded such respect from so wide a range of people."

He set up a series of interviews between Fullwood and KFC management. Fullwood insisted his wife participate "because we're a team. Whatever I have is hers too." Initially the company expressed reluctance to grant a franchise to someone who lacked the practical experience and the financial resources to run a restaurant.

"They told me during the interviews they were impressed with my community service," says Fullwood. "But they said they had a problem with me - I didn't have enough money. "I said, 'Mister, I told you that before I came here. I know I don't have money. That's why I want the franchise. I'm trying to make some money.' That's when they all smiled and told me that my commitment to the community was worth more than money to them. I got the franchise."

Simon is pleased that KFC took a chance on Fullwood and won. It was an especially big risk, he notes, because the company provided him with almost all of the financing necessary to set up his business. "He's so plainspoken, down-to-earth," says Simon, "He's not a slickster or very polished. That's what persuaded me to say, 'What the heck? Let's give him a chance. Every once in a while you go with a gut reaction.' Fullwood says he contributed about $10,000 of his personal savings and borrowed another $4,000 to go into business. The rest came from bank loans underwritten by KFC.

They guaranteed his loans, he says, because "they had enough faith in me and my record of community involvement. They wanted me to do well, and they put up the money to back me." Fullwood now controls two separate corporations, Fullwood Foods Inc., which is the parent company for the Parkville franchise, and El Pa Ha, Inc., which owns the franchise rights to the Franklin Street location. (The El Pa Ha Foods title comes from combining the first two initials of the names Elnora, Paquita and Harlow.)

The reason for his keeping the operations separate is prudent business management, says Fullwood. "I felt that it was to my my best advantage to form separate companies. My first franchise was successful, but I didn't know if the second would be, too. If something went wrong with one, nobody could take away the other. My long-term plan is eventually to put both companies under the Fullwood Foods company. But I'm not ready to do that yet.

"Although he plunged boldly into the business world, it is Fullwood's general inclination to be cautious. For most of the past two years, despite booming sales at his first Baltimore-area KFC franchise, he was reluctant to give up the security of his job on the police force. Last spring, after he found it impossible to run two franchises, oversee some 55 employees and work full-time as a police officer, he finally summoned the courage to retire from the Baltimore Police Department.

Now Fullwood works 18-hour days, shuttling between the two stores and attending to the numerous details of food management. Says Elnora Fullwood: "He spends more time away from home now than he did when he was on the police force. In a way, I don't mind because he's doing what he enjoys, but in a way I would rather have him home more."

Fullwood admits the fast-food restaurant business is demanding and far more time-consuming than police work. "As a recruiter on the force, I was promoting the police department, and I was promoting myself by making contacts with people I wouldn't have otherwise met," he says.

But, operating a franchised business requires just as much self-promotion, and he has also developed the fiscal and managerial skills necessary to turn a profit. "Man, this restaurant business is harder work than I ever imagined," he says. "You know, I thought all there was to this business was cooking chicken and selling it over the counter. With the way Kentucky Fried Chicken makes us follow rules and require-ments, running this place is not just a business it's a science."

Business does enable Fullwood to bring his family to work, though. Elnora, who is by profession an administrator for the Baltimore school system, is also vice president of both corporations. And, during the summer, when the schools are closed, the entire family often works together at one or the other of the restaurants. Elnora often dons the KFC khaki-and-red uniform to work behind the counter. Paquita, who recently graduated from Virginia Union with a degree in business administration, works the night management shift. She has, with her father's strong support, set her sights on becoming an officer in the two-family owned corporations, and from there she plans to work her way up into senior management at KFC's headquarters. Even young Harlow III has been seen in a company uniform, pushing a broom or mop to earn spending money for tennis shoes or his extensive collection of He-Man and Masters of the Universe toy figurines.

"Can you believe what this old country boy has done?" says Fullwood. "In the two years that I've been in business for myself, I've been able to see the American dream come true."

During my career, or I might say, my various three-career experiences (football player/police officer/KFC franchisee), I have aimed to demonstrate and devote my time to helping people while leading my teammates across the goal line. I have attempted to exhibit strong leadership skills.

I am very proud of the numerous awards that I have received for business achievements. For example, *The Baltimore Sun* honored me for several years as one of the 50 leading black businessmen in Maryland; I was selected by the Maryland Department of Economic and Employment Development as one of five successful Small Minority Businesses in Maryland; and I received the Governor's Recognition Award for Growth and Development. In 1992, the United States Chamber of Commerce and *Nation's Business* magazine designated Fullwood Foods, Inc., as a Blue Chip Enterprise for underscoring that small business is truly the engine that drives the American economy.

However, above all of these accolades, I am happy to be merely known as a minority KFC franchisee committed to the philosophy that an important part of doing business is to give support, either in volunteer services or in cash grants to the community we serve. To that end, Elnora and I established our Annual Fullwood Benefit and Recognition Breakfast in January, 1989. Its purpose is to bring together the recipients of our charitable contributions. Our breakfast is an annual affair to distribute publicly scholarships to promising students and cash grants to local non-profit organizations that are making a difference.

Our philanthropic objective has been to give hundreds of thousands of dollars to organizations where our money can make the greatest impact, whether it is in the area of culture and the arts, religion, education, or human service. With regard to education, we have awarded and helped provide several million dollars in college scholarships to more than 500 students. We hope that our support to organizations and humanitarian concepts will remain viable long after we are gone.

Actually, we cared about others and our community long before we became involved with KFC entrepreneur activity. Elnora and I are overjoyed that our financial success as entrepreneurs has given us this blessed opportunity to share God-given wealth with worthy citizens and causes. In addition, in the area of education, I served five years as President of the Miles W. Connor Chapter of the Virginia Union University Alumni Association, Baltimore, Maryland Chapter. I have personally recruited more students to attend and ultimately graduate from VUU than any other alumnus. During my tenure as alumni chapter president, I helped raise over $300,000 to provide scholarships to enable Baltimore City youths to pursue scholastic excellence at VUU. With me at the helm, the chapter became VUU's most active financially supportive and productive alumni group in the nation.

I am equally proud to note that I received the first Presidential Citation issued by Dr. S. Dallas Simmons, VUU's former president, in recognition of my financial support, strong volunteer recruitment leadership as Chairman of the Board of Trustees' Student Affairs Committee, and my valuable assistance in enhancing alumni relations. For my dedication to black colleges, in 1990, I was inducted into the National Black College Alumni Hall of Fame in Atlanta, Georgia.

I would have not been able accomplish any of my success without some help from others. That fact is the true essence of my entire story. Yes, I have been blessed by being able to distinguish myself in the classroom, on the gridiron, in the police department, the business community and as a father and husband. However, others helped place me on the correct highway.

It is true that I have been the recipient of a lengthy list of awards, certificates and citations for honorable service to Baltimore City, to Maryland, local public school systems, colleges, both in and out of Maryland, civic groups, fraternal organizations, churches and local businesses. However, without the guidance and ethics that my grandmother, parents, teachers, coaches, and many others provided to me, none of these awards would have come forward.

Words like best, highest, first, and outstanding are usually found on these awards to describe me. When I read those words, I think of my own role models and mentors who were my "shining stars."

My personal philosophy is best described in the words of George Washington Carver who said, "How far you go in life depends upon your being tender with the young, compassionate with the aged, sympathetic with the striving, and tolerant of both the weak and the strong because someday in life you will have been one or all of these."

After being put through the application process by KFC, I was told that hundreds of blacks all over the country had been interviewed but few had come close to my stature. "Community involvement is money to us," said Mr. Kolasis, a high-ranking black executive in the Kentucky Fried Chicken operations. "Therefore, we are willing to guarantee your first loan," I was told.

I trained my workers to understand that loyalty begets loyalty, and I required them to make a covenant with me at the beginning of their employment making certain they understood my rules about attitude, lateness, dishonesty, and insubordination. Customers are number one in my stores. I have worked side by side with employees and promoted from within. I believe that once employees recognize that an employer is sincere and observes his or her record of accomplishment -- the employee is more productive. I very rarely have had to fire anyone; the person just realizes that he or she simply does not fit in, and the person just leaves at his or her own accord. I credit all of my successes to "blessings." Throughout my life, I was blessed to meet individuals who helped to form my character and who helped me make progress in my career. It is also a blessing that Kentucky Fried Chicken was willing to take a chance on me. I will be eternally grateful for that.

I can count many blessings including the blessing of the college president who saved me from being sent home from college; my boss on the police force who made me go back, finish college, and earn my two degrees; and the lawyer who helped me without charging me a fee. Most of all, I credit Elnora and my family for being the greatest blessing bestowed on me by God.

In 1990, Baltimore's *Daily Record*, a legal and financial journal, published an article entitled, "Minority Area Loans Found To Be Lacking." That article by Bill McConnell described a reality of small business enterprise having extreme difficulty in getting financing. The article stated,

> *"By the time Fullwood decided to open his third KFC restaurant, at the corner of Pennsylvania and North Avenues, even the success of his first two stores was not enough to convince bankers to give him the $400,000 he needed to build on the site, located in a crime-ridden neighborhood."*
>
> *"They said nobody ever goes to that corner, but I said 'They've got nothing to go to,'" Fullwood said. He said only one bank offered to finance the restaurant, and it would have required him to pay a high interest rate, put up both his stores and his house as collateral and take out a $100,000 life insurance policy. "If I can't get a loan with my track record, who the hell are they giving it to?" he asked. Instead, Fullwood took his business to a bank in New York State, which was recommended by KFC. Now that he has proven his success, local banks may be out of luck.*
>
> *Fullwood said minority areas are misread by banks because they have never been given the chance to show their economic worth. The store at North and Pennsylvania is his best example. Fullwood said, "There are two subway stops there, and the bus stops every fifteen minutes. If you go to the*

suburbs, you see fast foods stores with no one in them on a Saturday night. That store is packed at midnight, and I have to keep it open until four in the morning."

A 1992, *USA Today* published an article entitled, "Securing a Dream Through Persistence." It defined a predicament that I found myself in --- after the KFC loan guarantee. The reporter, Peter Pavillonis, stated,

"Fullwood was lucky. He got his start-up money through a guaranteed loan program developed by KFC to encourage more minority ownership of the company's franchises. The loan program was just one of several initiatives the company undertook after a meeting between KFC corporate officers and Jesse Jackson, who asked the company to open its franchising opportunities to more minorities. While the loan guarantee program provides the crucial start-up capital to budding minority entrepreneurs who pass KFC's rigorous selection process, highly successful franchisees who want to expand their operations must eventually resort to conventional lending institutions. KFC guarantees loans for only two stores, and loans must be refinanced after five years."

Coming out of the security of KFC's loan program into the harsh reality of banks' own lending criteria can be a rude awakening to minority owners. It is a feeling Fullwood knows all to well. After turning his first two KFC franchises into the highest-volume stores in Maryland, Fullwood thought his track record was good enough to approach Baltimore's banks for the money he needed to open a third store. The answer was a resounding 'no.' Fullwood's story is typical among minority entrepreneurs. 'It is difficult for minorities to get financing,' says Fullwood. 'I mean, here I was a five-year operator, one of my stores led the whole state in volume, and I couldn't get anywhere with banks.'"Once again, Fullwood turned for suggestions to KFC, which provided him with a list of out-of-state banks with which the company has good relations. He had his money in no time. Though Fullwood praises the opportunity KFC provided him, he admits the opportunities came with a price. 'If I had the capital, I would have finished paying for the stores in five to seven years --- instead of taking 10 years to pay,' says Fullwood, who figures he probably paid about $200,000 more for each store under the terms of the KFC-sponsored loans. 'If I did not have good volume, no way I could have survived.'"

Enough said. The franchise business is a very challenging endeavor, but **love lifted me**.

Colonel Harland Sanders, born September 9, 1890, actively began franchising his chicken business at the age of 65. Now, the Kentucky Fried Chicken business he started has grown to be one of the largest retail food service systems in the world. Internationally, the KFC Corporation has 2,624 corporate-run facilities, 7,585 franchised facilities, and 290,779 employees. The colonel's cooking is available in more than 82 countries around the world.

√ KFC had 55 percent of all chicken quick-service restaurant sales in the U.S. in 1999 -- nearly seven times more than our nearest national competitor.

√ After just three months of selling sandwiches, KFC owned eight percent of the $5 billion sandwich category.

√ Lined side by side, the nearly 67,400,000 KFC chicken sandwiches sold in the U.S. in 1999 (most in the last three months of the year) would march from Manhattan to Los Angeles and on to Dallas.

√ Laid head-to-claw, KFC chickens consumed worldwide in 1999 would reach 209,000 miles -- encircling the earth at the equator 8.5 times.

√ In the United States, KFC sold just over nine pieces of chicken for every man, woman, and child in the country.

√ The 46,000 miles of fresh-baked biscuits sold in the U.S. in 1999 would stretch in 15 solid lines between Boston and Los Angeles.

FULLWOOD FOUNDATION, INC.

Chapter Ten

Fullwood
Foundation, Inc.

I n 1988, Elnora and I formed The Fullwood Foundation, Inc. We saw the need to highlight the achievements of the unsung people in the Baltimore community who care and share for others every day in hopes of making Maryland a better place to live. We practice the tenets inferred by our logo that shows a big-hearted adult holding one youngster and lifting another. We did not go into the KFC business just to make a profit. We went into the business to give something back. Our foundation and its charity programs and events provide us with a method for putting something back into the lifeline of our community.

The foundation is a non-profit IRS 501(c)(3) tax-exempt corporation and Registered Maryland Charitable Organization. The mission of the foundation is to raise funds to support numerous educational initiatives. These initiatives are designed to provide youth with scholarships for higher education and to empower them to successful careers. The foundation presents awards and special grants to organizations that provide vital and exemplary human services. Additionally, it publicly honors individuals whose humanitarian deeds substantially improve the quality of life of the citizens of Maryland.

Our foundation's charitable support to organizations and institutions is intended to provide: 1) restricted-purpose grants for continuation and enhancement of successful methods; 2) start-up, seed-money for new community improvement initiatives; and 3) one-time grants and recognition awards to individuals or organizations who perform outstanding services that contribute to the betterment of society.

With regard to education, our foundation recognizes the value of scholarships as essential methods for helping students stay on course, discover their full academic potential and talents, develop career objectives, and gain leadership skills. The Fullwood Foundation believes that there is an emerging need in the inner-city for youth to be prepared, aware, and competitive, if they hope to achieve the best quality higher education and career opportunities. Fullwood Foundation scholarships are awarded in accordance with restricted selection criteria. Ideally, it is our wish that Fullwood Scholars will one day continue our tradition of providing some scholarship help to meet the needs of others. Our philosophy is "Caring and Sharing." Fullwood Foundation scholarships are awarded year-round. The foundation has generated and awarded more than $6 million of college scholarships to more than 500 students.

Our foundation's major charity projects include The Annual Fullwood Benefit and Recognition Breakfast, which was started in 1989, and is now held each January. This event raises thousands of dollars to support a variety of community-wide causes and has awarded hundreds of thousands of dollars and scholarships during its fourteen years. Today, our breakfast is held at Martin's West in Woodlawn - Baltimore County, Maryland. With an annual attendance of more than 2,000 persons, our event is acclaimed as the largest and most spectacular fundraising event of its kind in Maryland and the nation. It is particularly noteworthy that our Annual Breakfast occurs close to the birthday of the late Dr. Martin Luther King, Jr., who dedicated his life to caring and sharing. His endowment of service makes us more devoted to reach out and help others achieve a better quality of life.

Our "First-Time Experiences For Children Project" reaches out to at-risk inner-city youth to broaden their knowledge, social, and cultural awareness by taking them on their first bus ride, boat ride, Amtrak train ride, plane ride, first trip to Annapolis, Maryland, and other dynamic cultural enrichment endeavors. When I was a member of the Baltimore Police Department, I was fortunate to be involved with an innovative program that benefited inner-city youth. That program was based upon the same philosophy on which I base my First-Time Experiences for Children Project.

Throughout the last fourteen years, The Fullwood Foundation, Inc. has awarded a total of several hundred thousand dollars to hundreds of non-profit community organizations and educational institutions such as The Children's Cancer Foundation and Big Brothers and Big Sisters of Maryland, just to name a few. Furthermore, it continues to encourage citizen volunteerism and corporate philanthropy for community programs that serve the broad spectrum of the people of Maryland. Most of the foundation's activities are made possible by more than 100 volunteers who provide essential support for numerous activities that relate to a variety of foundation initiatives. They function as chaperones for trips, tutorial mentors, essay contest readers, judges, breakfast host/hostesses, team leaders, choir event coordinators, and in other important roles.

In the 1980s, a group of ten inner-city youngsters from Baltimore was taken to Ocean City, Maryland for a one-week experience. The "People To People" program was jointly created and sponsored by Maryland District Court Judge Dale Cathell, Ocean City Mayor Harry Kelley and me. The participating children were given "red carpet" treatment. Mayor Kelley gave them keys to the city, marlin pins, basketballs, and other souvenirs. During their stay, the youngsters were also treated to many recreational activities in the resort. Others sponsors were District Court Judge Robert Sweeney and Detective Harry McDonald. Detective McDonald accompanied me, and he was a master at gaining cooperation from children.

The youth enjoyed amusements, swam, played miniature golf, and went to the movies. The object was to provide under-privileged children from Baltimore the opportunity to have a vacation away from inner-city life. Detective McDonald and I selected the boys with the help of friends who worked with various youth programs.

The black and white youngsters began their week with worship at St. Paul's Methodist Church in Berlin, Maryland. They stayed in the Boca Grande Condominiums and had dinner at the famed Phillips Crab House, Mario's Pier One, Blue Hawaii, English's Chicken and Steak House, and Gunning's House of Seafood. They were also entertained at an elegant cookout. They enjoyed an educational scenic boat ride on Captain Jack Bunting's "Miss Ocean City" and a "nature walk" at the world-famous Assateaque Park. They also went deep-sea fishing.

The youth all received passes to movies, new tennis shoes, tennis lessons, tennis racquets, skateboard lessons, new skate-boards, kite-flying lessons, kites, wristwatches, T-shirts, went indoor skating, visited Frontier Town, took a twelve-mile canoe trip down the Pocomoke River, and enjoyed an airplane flight. About fifteen resort businesses donated their services to the program. The trip was an incentive for the children to get out of poverty by seeing what was available for them. Expenses and gifts came from the Ocean City Council, McDonald's operator Osborne A. Payne, Concord Baptist Church, Wendy's, Coca Cola, WMAR-TV, Cox Cable, Allegheny Pepsi Cola, the Afro-American Newspapers, and the Miles W. Connor Alumni Association of VUU.

A 1979 Baltimore *Sun* editorial entitled, "Visit Begins Ocean City Program: Resort to Host City Teenagers" stated, *"Ocean City Mayor Harry W. Kelley announced yesterday that 10 Baltimore teenagers who cannot afford to visit this resort will 'live it up' for a week. The young people have been individually selected for what is described as a 'seed program' organized by Mayor Kelley, a committee of the District Court system headed by Chief Judge Robert F. Sweeney, and Agent Harlow Fullwood, Jr. of the Baltimore Police Department.*

About 15 resort businesses have contributed part or all of their services or products, and an exuberant Mayor Kelley, anticipating the arrival of the young people, called the project 'the best thing I've done as a mayor.' Mayor Kelley and Judge Sweeney thought up the 'People to People' program. Agent Fullwood was drawn into it after Judge Sweeney saw his resume and met him a few months ago when he received the Sunpapers 'Policeman of the Year Award.' Agent Fullwood agreed to select the participants, he said, because he has seen 'so many programs abused.' He said that he wanted to select personally teen-agers who would benefit from the experience and whose parents could not afford to give them such an opportunity."

In their own words, some participants in the program stated, in a 1979 letter to Mayor Kelley that was published in the Ocean City Times, "Dear Mayor Kelley: We are very lucky to have been selected for the 1979 People-to-People program. As a result of your interest and concern, we have had the opportunity to experience some of the finer things of life. This trip helped to solve many of our problems. It is our hope that the new experience will help each of us to become a better person in the future. "We would also like to express our thanks to Mr. Dale Cathell who gave his time to us and our counselors, Police Agent Harlow Fullwood, Jr. and Detective Harry McDonald, who handled our problems and gave us confidence in ourselves when we needed it. We also want to salute the local businessmen and all the other wonderful people involved in the program. All of you have helped make the past week in Ocean City one of the greatest weeks of our lives. Mr. Mayor, thank you for caring. Sincerely yours."

The letter was signed by Elgin Porter, Jeffrey Johnson, Kenneth Elder, Darren Hayes, Charles Stanley, Eddie Gilchrest, Thomas Outing, Darrell Williams, Monroe Johnson, and William Easter.

THE FULLWOOD FOUNDATION, INC.   0591

                                    FEB. 3, 19 95

PAY TO THE ORDER OF   UNITED BAPTIST MISSIONARY CONVENTION OF MD. $ 10,000.00

TEN THOUSAND DOLLARS & NO CENTS _____ DOLLARS

Nation

FOR _____

''000591'' ':0520000161: ''002-3309959''

THE FULLWOOD FOUNDATION, INC.   JANUARY 14, 1995   275
"A CELEBRATION OF CARING & SHARING"
13 COUNTRY MILL CT
BALTIMORE, MD. 21228

PAY AMOUNT OF   FIVE THOUSAND DOLLARS   CHECK AMOUNT

DATE
1/14/95   THE BALTIMORE CITY COMMUNITY COLLEGE FOUNDATION INC. $ 5,000

NationsBank

''000 275'' ':055002341: 59 0250 5''

"Giving Until It Helps"

176

A particular focus of our foundation is on the positive development of African-American young men. It is our concern that young black males need extra attention, nurturing, encouragement, and recognition of their need to realize that they do have the potential to achieve and to excel. Efforts are made to include black adult male chaperones, mentors, and role models so that they can lead our black youths by example. We believe it is urgently important for all of our participants to meet African-American professionals such as lawyers, judges, politicians, doctors, and other businesspeople. Our aim is for long-term mentor relationships to evolve for youth from their first time experiences of meeting these respective role models.

Our foundation believes it is not good enough to merely teach children to "Say No to Drugs." We provide learning support and counseling for youth to gain knowledge and acquire ethical decision-making skills necessary for them to take control of their lives. We feel that our young people's ability to say "no" to drugs and other harmful behavior depends on their self-assurance that they are important, valued, and capable. The Fullwood Foundation's educational mission is to recognize the value of each child and to provide comprehensive programs that inspire students to discover their full academic potential, talents, career objectives, leadership ability, initiative, and sensitivity to meeting the needs of others. Seeking charitable support is vital to the Fullwood Foundation's continuous future operation.

Our aim is to foster a philosophy of working together in relationships based on equality and respect. Through an organized and fun process of support systems provided through cultural and recreational "First-Time Experiences" involving discipline and quality assurance methods, our youth can aspire to advance to new levels of appreciation of themselves and of others.

Fullwood Foundation
"Changing the Lives of Youth"

Teaching our youth better problem-solving skills and decision-making skills instills within them vital talent in relationship building. It is becoming increasingly important to develop structured ways to identify and to praise positive youth behavior, correct problems when they occur, and prepare youth and their parents to deal successfully with difficult situations. The result can be significantly fewer incidents of serious behavior problems and significantly better academic achievement.

Today's youths are growing up in a world that seems to hold more dangers and opportunities for disaster than in the past. Today's youths are much more at risk of becoming teen parents, being addicted to drugs and alcohol, dropping out of school, and becoming involved in gangs than their parents were. They face many other dangers that their parents did not. As the variety of negative forces and problems facing today's youth becomes more challenging for them and their parents, there is a growing need for new and alternative attempts to be made to steer youth in positive directions.

Through various Fullwood Foundation initiatives, youth gain skills in leadership and goal setting. Drugs, teen pregnancy, academic failure and a lack of positive role models are just some of the pressures that have left inner-city children in a condition of distress, low self-esteem, and probable failure as they seek to achieve a quality education that can lead to acquiring employable skills. To assist youth in avoiding this negative syndrome, the Fullwood Foundation seeks to combat these problems by using a comprehensive series of activities targeted for elementary, middle, and high school students, to encourage youth to utilize their potential to strive for academic success and a productive life.

Through our unique philanthropic process, The Fullwood Foundation aims 1) to motivate individuals to excel in education that will serve as a gateway to their success, 2) to strengthen the effectiveness of community programs that work, and 3) to create new "first-time" educational enrichment, recreational, and personal development activities for our youth, thus providing them with social growth, confidence, cultural diversity awareness, spiritual focus, and hope.

The Fullwood Foundation strives to make one-on-one investments in the future intellectual and social growth of each child by offering educational and cultural enrichment experiences that cultivate and maximize success. Our objective is to maintain a student-centered learning environment that allows discovery of both talents as well as areas in need of reinforcement in each student. We strive to empower students to manage their own learning process, by working closely with a variety of selected schools.

A fundamental strategy within the Fullwood Foundation's comprehensive fund-raising process is to seek and secure charitable partnerships and sponsorships with corporations, charitable foundations, colleges and universities, individual philanthropists, banks, and private sector businesses that have common goals and compatibility with our foundation's beliefs. Our foundation's corporate sponsorship solicitations invite joint support for educational and community-wide initiatives that fulfill the charity objectives, philosophies, and missions of both parties.

Our foundation's ultimate objective is to contribute to the quality of urban life by developing effective learning skills in students and enhancing their ambition to succeed. Providing quality educational and cultural experiences for at-risk children is our primary mission. However, not only do we focus on each child, we also encourage parents to be involved. Our foundation feels that the linkage and partnership between and among the schoolteacher, parents, and our foundation serve as a vital network for fostering the success of each child.

Through the years, our annual breakfast has served as the focal point occasion for Elnora and I to award a considerable amount of scholarships and grants. Our first breakfast was held on Saturday, January 21, 1989. In the ten-page souvenir program for that event, we included a statement in the inside cover that symbolically states the philosophy of all fourteen breakfast events to date. It stated:

****

Fullwood Foods, Inc.
"Sharing With Our Community"
Fullwood Grants of Love, Sharing and Caring

Fullwood Foods is a minority Kentucky Fried Chicken franchise committed to the philosophy that an important part of doing business is to give support, either in volunteer services or in cash grants to the community we serve.

This year is the first of what will be an annual affair to distribute cash grants to local non-profit organizations that will be meaningful to people for generations to come.

The objective is to give to organizations where our dollars can make the greatest impact, whether it is in the area of culture and the arts, religion, education or human service.

Please be remindful that we cared about others and our community long before we entered the KFC entrepreneurship.

We are overjoyed to have this blessed opportunity to share this glorious occasion with so many of our friends and supporters.

Thank you for your prayers and your good wishes. We will continue to go forth as one of the highest-rated Kentucky Fried Chicken operations in the nation.

HARLOW FULLWOOD, JR.

Recipient of the
THE GERI AWARD
The "Nobel Prize" for Extraordinary Humanitarian Community Service

Inducted Into the
Maryland Senior Citizens Hall of Fame
October 25, 2001

The Story of GERI

A group of distinguished citizens of varying ages, including senior activists, gathered on September 18, 1987 to promote the founding of a Hall of Fame dedicated to honoring senior citizens of the State of Maryland who have made exemplary contributions to society. Those selected by a special panel of judges would be inducted into the Senior Citizens Hall of Fame and have their names inscribed in the archives of the Hall of Fame located in the Ethel Percy Andrus Library at the Bayview Medical Center of the Johns Hopkins Medical System.

As the arts and sciences have their Grammy, Emmy, Tony and Oscar so the seniors of Maryland have their GERI – the geriatric "Nobel Prize" for extraordinary humanitarian community service.

The GERI sculpture – a baby's hand in the palm of an adult hand – was specially designed to represent the admired philosophy of our maturing population, namely, to give meaning and worth to the later years. Thus, the hand of the older person holding the hand of the child signifies understanding and love between generations. The GERI symbol depicts the intrinsic value of service to others regardless of race, creed, color, national origin, or handicapping condition.

GERI is a tangible expression of the leaving of a memory, a legacy, indeed a shining symbol of the fundamental value of giving and service. The tenderness of the child is entwined with the strength and wisdom of the older person.

The Maryland Senior Citizens Hall of Fame seeks to immortalize men and women and to record their names in the archives of the Hall of Fame for all time because of their caring and volunteer efforts in improving the lives of others.

"The gift without the giver is bare; who gives himself with his alms feeds thee, — himself, his hungering neighbor, and me."

James Russell Lowell

****

The First Annual Fullwood Benefit and Recognition Breakfast held on Saturday, January 21, 1989, at The Forum, a catering hall in Baltimore, had about 100 attendees, and more than 100 organizations were honored. The Fullwood family members were involved in the program. My daughter Paquita presided; she was a KFC Restaurant Manager at that time at our Harford Road location. My son, Harlow Fullwood, III, provided the welcome; he was at that time President of the Student Council at Johnnycake Middle School. Elnora stated the occasion of the event.

That first breakfast started a tradition that we have continued through the years, recognizing the outstanding deeds of individuals and organizations, and awarding scholarships. Some of the first honorees included Osborne A. Payne, CEO of Broadway-Payne, Inc.; Catherine Pugh, then a writer for the Baltimore *Sun* and now a member of the Baltimore City Council; and Agnes Welch, who was then and is now a member of the Baltimore City Council.

Some of the organizations that were honored at our first breakfast were African-American Heritage Tour of Black Landmarks; African-American Empowerment Project; Arena Players, Inc.; Associated Black Charities; Baltimore Council on Adolescent Pregnancy; Baltimore Symphony Orchestra; Baltimore City Police Youth Clubs; Boy Scouts of America - Baltimore Area Council; Community College of Baltimore (BCCC) Foundation, Inc.; Concord Baptist Church Family Outreach Ministry; Baltimore Alumnae Chapter, Delta Sigma Theta Sorority, Inc. (Delta House); Elite Giants Boys Clubs, Inc.; Fuel Fund of Central Maryland; Girl Scouts of Central Maryland; Great Blacks in Wax Museum, Inc.; Grant-A-Wish

Foundation; Juvenile Diabetes Foundation; Children's Home of Johns Hopkins Hospital; The United Negro College Fund; Harford Park Little League; Life Line Ministries, Inc.; Maryland Special Olympics; Morgan State University - Phi Eta Sigma Honor Society; NAACP; National Aquarium in Baltimore; Patterson Park Emergency Food Center, Inc.; Rotary Foundation of Rotary International; Sojourner-Douglass College; Virginia Union University; Walters Art Gallery Foundation, Inc.; and YMCA - Druid Hill Branch. While the above list is lengthy, it is representative of the hundreds of individuals and organizations that the foundation has honored through the years.

Through the years, our breakfast events have received sponsorships from a significant variety of local, national, and international corporations and businesses. A brief summary, in no ranking order, includes: KFC; WMAR-TV 2; WJZ-TV 13; Pepsi; Bank of America; Gillette; AllFirst; Mano Swartz Furriers; American Airlines; Coors; Nabisco; TWA; AT&T; JC Penney; Burger King; Coca Cola; Verizon; The Larry Beck Company; Grabush, Newman & Company, P.A.; State Farm Insurance; and Pimlico Race Course, to name a few.

Some notable, nationally recognized individuals honored at our breakfast events through the years were the late Coach Earl C. Banks, legendary football coach at Morgan State University; the late James W. Rouse, real estate developer; Cathy Hughes, CEO Radio One, Inc.; Dr. Levi Watkins, cardiologist, Johns Hopkins Hospital; Kweisi Mfume, former U.S. Congressman and current President/CEO of the NAACP; the late Dr. Florence Griffith Joyner, Olympic Gold medalist; Lawrence Douglas Wilder, former governor of Virginia; Robert M. Bell, chief judge, Court of Appeals of Maryland; Dr. Earl S. Richardson, president of Morgan State University; Dr. James D. Tschechtelin, president of Baltimore City Community College; Elijah Cummings, United States Congressman; Kathleen Kennedy Townsend, Maryland Lieutenant Governor; William Donald Schaefer, Comptroller of Maryland, former Governor of Maryland, and former Mayor of Baltimore; Dr. Calvin W. Burnett, president of Coppin State College; Dr. S. Dallas Simmons, retired president of Virginia Union

University; the late Dr. Rebecca E. Carroll, educator; Dr. Benjamin S. Carson, surgeon, Johns Hopkins Hospital; and many others.

I wish to cite one organization in particular of which I am a proud member: Rotary International Club of Woodlawn-Westview. Rotary International is an organization of business and professiobnal leaders united worldwide, who provide humanitarian service, encourage high ethical standards in all vocations, and help build goodwill and peace in the world. There are apprpximately 1.2 million Rotarians, members of more then 29,000 Rotary clubs in 161 countries. Rotary Club of Woodlawn-Westview sponsors a variety of outreach activities that include: Financial support for A Place for Children, which provides homes for children at risk or without homes; contributions to the Little Sisters of the Poor to help provide care for the needy; and financial support to the Community Assistance Network that provides shelter for the homeless.

One important way to show the dynamic impact of our charitable efforts is to share testimonial statements made by some Fullwood Scholars. We have received numerous letters, notes, and faxes of appreciation from students who attend a variety of colleges and universities. Here are a few statements by some Fullwood Scholars and supporters:

That there are angels on earth is a very true statement which I have personally experienced: Mr. Harlow. Because of him, I was given a full scholarship to Virginia Union University. My sister was in college at the time that I was about to enter, so money was real tight in my household. If it had not been for the tremendous blessing that Mr. Fullwood gave me, my parents would have been deeper in debt, and their financial struggle made harder.

I thank God each and every day for sending Mr. Fullwood into my life. He has truly been an angel to me and my family.

Alicia Reid, Future Cardiologist

How I Met Mr. Harlow Fullwood, Jr. *One evening during my senior year in high school while dining at Applebee's Restaurant on* the day nine-week report cards were issued, I met Mr. Harlow Fullwood Jr. While waiting for our dinner, my parents and I were discussing plans for funding college. I told them that although there were a lot of scholarships available, the qualifications were so stringent for some of them, and there was not that much money available for my intended major - economics. I told my parents of my college choices and what school was at the top of the list, and we conceded that it would take a miracle for me to go to that school, seeing as how we had no money for me to attend any college.

Our conversation led away from colleges and universities for a moment, while waiting for our dinner. When we were on a totally different subject, my mother looked up and saw Mr. & Mrs. Fullwood and stated that he just gave away five $10,000 scholarships to high school students to attend college, and that I should ask him if he could help me. I thought that he could help me out in that way since we had just confirmed that I had no money to attend college.

I wrestled within myself to approach Mr. Fullwood and decided to be bold and ask him a question. So, I approached him and asked him if he could help me attend school, citing that he helped others by issuing five $10,000 scholarships. After seeing my grades, he was very pleased and gave me his phone number. I called him, and we talked a long time about my college choices, and he narrowed it down to one school - Virginia Union University. He said he would put me in touch with the admissions director there, and we could see what would happen. The admissions director called me back and said that I qualified for a scholarship that paid for my tuition, room, and board. I accepted that offer and thanked God for leading me to Mr. Harlow Fullwood, Jr. and providing me with a way to attend college.

Jamin Keene, Junior, VUU

I had the privilege of hearing you speak. I was very touched by your support and dedication...to the importance and role of the Historically Black Colleges and Universities (HBCU's). As I was sitting in my seat listening to you, tears came to my eyes. Like yourself, I am a great supporter of African Americans attending HBCU's. It is my belief that these institutions are our roots and foundation of our leaders both past *and present as well as future leaders to come.*

As I left Martin's West and traveled home, I reflected on the positive message you shared with us; however, I still did not realize the extent of your warm heart. Before we departed, you said that you would send me some literature in the mail. What I received cannot be called a souvenir journal but should be titled - "A Testament: Unconditional Commitment to Care and Share with Others." God is truly a strong force in your life.

It is my belief that success is when preparation meets opportunity. The success of our youth lies in our wisdom to support them and be positive role models. The children are our future, and we must teach them well so they can lead the way. Your foundation is giving many students of all creeds, races, and religions the opportunity to succeed.

Marsha Diane Worrell, Executive Committee
Morgan State University, Tri-State Alumni
Association

One Sunday afternoon, at the age of eighteen, I received the phone call that would change my life. The voice on the other end of the telephone was Harlow Fullwood. Mr. Fullwood called me to find out if I would attend his alma mater, Virginia Union University. I was hesitant, and he could tell. He had worked hard to make a way for me to attend VUU on scholarship, and Mr. Fullwood made it happen. I attended Virginia Union, and I like many others past, present, and future became a Fullwood beneficiary.

Based on the Fullwood influence, I finished at the top of my class under his watchful eye. Harlow always left an impression. When I first met Harlow, he was a police officer, but he was not just a police officer. He was the most well-known police officer on the force, working every day on community issues. His character, commitment, and tenacity are unmatched in my experience. The stories which come from the pages of this book are reflective of a special person who has lived a rich life which began long before he accumulated financial wealth as a businessperson. Harlow's life speaks volumes about the ability of one person to change the lives of many."

Scott Phillips, attorney-at-law

On Being Cast in Wax

On Wednesday, April 4, 2001, it was my distinct honor to be recognized in a very spectacular way. The wax figures of three Maryland businessmen were unveiled to be installed at the Great Blacks in Wax Museum, becoming part of its permanent collection. The honorees were Osborne Payne, a Baltimore entrepreneur and my business mentor; Isaac Myers, who was born in 1835 and was founder in 1865 of the Chesapeake Marine Railway and Drydock Company of Baltimore, and one of the nation's first black labor union; and I.

The unveiling was held at the Engineers Club in Mount Vernon Place, and more than 500 persons attended. It was one of the greatest tributes that I have ever witnessed. The event was sponsored by the museum and the Presidents' Roundtable, and it was entitled, "Men in History: Three Baltimore Legends."

In an April 7, 2001, Baltimore *Sun* article by Frederick N. Rasmussen, Osborne Payne was described as, "A well-known champion of charitable causes and a role model for many young people whom he inspired and hired. Payne, who was one of the nation's leading African-American fast-food executives until he left the industry in 1997, had owned and operated several McDonald's franchises in Baltimore." The article further stated, "Isaac Myers was the proprietor of one of the first independent black-owned businesses in Maryland; was inspired to found his own company after a dock strike in 1865 left 1,000 black mechanics and longshoremen unemployed; and employed several hundred men. He died January 27, 1891." The founders of the Great Blacks in Wax Museum, Elmer P. and Joanne Martin, were quoted in that article as saying, "Mr. Fullwood and Mr. Payne are certainly deserving of this honor. They were willing to take risks and get into business. They had guts, spirit, and the foresight to see that one day franchises would open up and create opportunities for other African Americans. They truly represent the entrepreneurial spirit in the highest form."

At the exact moment when my son Harlow III and my brother Everett unveiled my wax figure, I experienced a feeling of extreme gratitude for all of the support and guidance that I have received from so many persons that enabled me to qualify for and gain this supreme honor. When I saw my figure, I could not believe its remarkable resemblance to me. I remain astonished.

I am exceedingly proud and humbled that my wax figure joins those of such famous African Americans as Harriet Tubman, Dr. Martin Luther King, Jr., General Colin Powell, and many others that are on display at the museum. I encourage all to visit the Great Blacks in Wax Museum at 1601-03 E. North Avenue in Baltimore, Maryland. This unique institution is an American treasure. It is the first wax museum of African-American history in the nation, and it serves visitors from throughout the United States, and international visitors have hailed from such countries as Canada, France, Africa, England, Japan, and Israel.

A Baltimore *Times*, April 14, 2001 article by Ursula Battle quoted me as saying, as I admired my wax figure at the unveiling, "Man, I tell you, that looks just like me. I got a smile like I just got finished a piece of KFC." A Baltimore *Afro-American*, April 14, 2001 article also by Ms. Battle quoted Mr. James "Winky" Camphor, Vice President of the Coppin State College Alumni Association, as saying, "Harlow Fullwood lives up to his credo. You make a living by what you get, but you make a life by what you give. Harlow gives a lot. He has made a good life for many a young person." I am very grateful for this complimentary statement and for the generous comments of many others.

When Elnora and I formed the Fullwood Foundation, we established a mission not to merely give money away but to instill in others the desire and commitment to care and share. I hope that my wax figure will be symbolic to remind individuals who visit the Great Blacks in Wax Museum to strive to make this commitment and to help ensure that those in need can attain a better quality of life.

The Fullwood Foundation caring and sharing with our youth.

Harlow Fullwood, Jr.

Chapter Eleven

Fullwood's Philosophy

S o often we fail to share and care for others. Many of us are poor because we do not give more. If you have a financial problem, start giving to others. If you have a psychological problem, start sharing of yourself with others. Jesus once said that whatever mercy you deal out to others, it will be dealt to you in return. You should always strive to give more than you receive. Whether you plant money, love, or hope, the abundant life is only for him who gives abundantly. I feel that there are many forms of wealth that are not monetary-based. The more we give freely, the more abundantly it comes back to us freely. The measure of a life is not its duration but its donation.

I realize that the above statements may be considered to be a collection of over-general corollaries by some; however, my philosophy represents a combination of all of the lessons that I have learned. The word philosophy can be described as a study of truth, a systematic view, a theory, a reasoned doctrine, or a set of logical concepts. These thoughts that I will share represent a collection of all of the above that I describe as Fullwood's Philosophy:

On Education

A good education can, most times, guarantee a lifetime of success. I feel that if a child acquires a good education, that child can realize the value of it. The value can be experienced in many forms. I was a scholarship student. I feel that money spent on education is an investment in our future; that is why I advocate and award college scholarships. I also believe that a good education can prepare students for world-class participation.

In a 1998 speech entitled "The 21st Century Must be the Century of Education," President William Jefferson Clinton said, *"The best way to strengthen democracy worldwide and to meet the challenges of the 21st century is to guarantee universal, excellent education for every child on our planet. A world-class education for all children is essential to combating the fear, the ignorance, the prejudice that undermine freedom all across the globe today in the form of ethnic, religious and racial hatreds. A technological revolution is sweeping across the globe and changing the way we live, work, and relate to each other. It is binding our economies closer together, whether we like it or not. It is making our world smaller. One hundred million people are logging onto the Internet each day, and within three years that number is expected to be about 700 million. With all these changes come new challenges."*

In 1976, an editorial that I wrote was published by *Baltimore's News-American* newspaper in a column called **Voice of the People**. I stated, *"It is my hope that all of the children's educational needs may be lifted up, not only by their own efforts, but by the inspiration and help they receive from those of us who have achieved the highest and are in a position to challenge inequalities.*

In developing new educational ideas and concepts, as in all human experiences, we win and lose; we try and fail and try again; and we get knocked down, get up, and learn. However, I hope we never give up on looking for a workable answer to the educational needs for our children.

Problems are not roadblocks; they are challenges. Sincere black and white citizens have responded to challenges, and we will do it again. The strength of our community is never tested under the easiest conditions. It is always tested under adversity.

The community leader or elected official who aggressively and uncompromisingly proclaims changes in the racial makeup of schools is bound to make waves. He threatens established powers and values.

Preparing for change in the educational system calls for teamwork and dedication to the educational needs of all children, with all sharing according to our talents and resources. To be able to work for equal education, all of us must examine our lives for grudges and unfair attitudes.

In the words of John Ruskin: *"when love and skill work together, expect a masterpiece."*

* * * * * *

As President Theodore Roosevelt once said, *'The credit in life goes not to the critic who stands on the sideline and points out where the strong stumble, but rather the real credit in life goes to the man who is actually in the arena, whose face may get marred by sweat and dust, who knows great enthusiasm and great devotion and learns to spend himself in a worthy cause, who at best if he wins knows the thrill of high achievement and if he fails, at least fails while daring greatly, so that in his life his place will never be with those very cold and timid souls who know neither victory nor defeat."*

On Charitable Giving

If a person has never been taught to give and share early, unless he has some traumatic experience in his life, he will never willingly and cheerfully give. I belong to a church that places a lot of emphasis on tithing and personal giving. I am one who believes that there is nothing in God's word that says support the church with bake sales, car washes, raffles, chicken dinners, or fish dinners. Someone once said that there are three types of givers: the flint, the sponge, and the honeycomb. To get anything out of a flint, you must hammer it; but, for the most part, you only get chips and sparks. To get water out of a sponge, you must squeeze it; the harder you squeeze, the more you get. But the honeycomb is full and overflowing with sweetness. I trust that everyone will become a honeycomb if we pass the word along to the flint and the sponge.

Much of my philosophy is derived from the words of George Washington Carver. "How far you go in life depends on your being tender with the young, compassionate with the aged, sympathetic with the striving and tolerant of both the weak and the strong, because someday in life, you will have been one or all of these." The hardest job that I have ever had is the constant challenge of being a good father, good husband, and a good provider.

On the Church

I have often questioned the practice of shouting and running around the church hollering the Lord's name. I spoke to a theologian who was highly respected in his profession. I expressed to him my concern that I was very religious but had never gotten to the point where I wanted to run around the church and holler out very loudly. My grandmother taught me that religion is something personal and special. This theologian said, "Fullwood, tithing is one, if not the most important aspect of service. As long as I have been in the church, I have never seen anyone shout at the offering plate." We must look at ourselves and determine what kind of giver we are. These are the words of the Lord Jesus, "It is more blessed to give than to receive."

With regard to the black church, I must admit, it is one of the most prejudiced institutions, especially in terms of folks seeking to sit in special places. Many members like to be able to say something such as, "I've been a member here for 40 years, or 50 years," or they like to say that "This is the way we've been doing it all along." I often have to remind them that the word of our Lord and Savior Jesus Christ will always remain the same.

In the church, I also find that we have members who like to

play down the pastor in meetings, etc. I am not implying that the pastor is perfect, but I am saying he is our leader, and I respect that. I have never questioned a man's calling, but I do stand in a position to correct him once he has been called. If I have anything helpful, detrimental, or otherwise to offer, I will not stand on the floor at a meeting and say, "Brother pastor you're not doing this, you're not doing that...." If there is a difference in opinion or strategies, I prefer to sit down with him and explain my points. I recognize that God didn't give the pastors all the brains. We place pastors in positions to lead, and it is up to us to follow. Wherever we can make the path a lot clearer, we should join hands and work together in harmony.

I think that there is a tremendous strength in the black church, and it is a guardian of our heritage; however, I feel that we are not taking advantage of the opportunity. So often, I see churches being built with no classrooms. I have a concern about that. Often, I see churches so big, with so many memberships, that it seems to me that it takes the personalization away from it. But again, that is one's choice. I think the bottom line is when you find a person who is willing to accept the Lord Savior Jesus Christ as his guardian. It would then help to open up and focus on what the church really is. As far as I am concerned, it is about sharing and caring and lifting one another up. If we are unable to do this, I think we are missing the true meaning of religion.

Often the black church could do more than any other institution that I can think of in terms of providing spiritual and economic guidance. When I say economic guidance, I am saying that it sure could make a difference if all the churches would pool their resources for economic development. We could hire more folks and do things that are more positive for our community. However, I find that there is a jealousy even within the black church community: "I have this many members, I bring in this many members, we deposit this much money in the bank, etc."

I truly and honestly feel that if a church is really doing something, it should always be in debt. I think it is a crime for churches to stockpile monies when there are so many ills and evils going on in our community. Yes, I say the church I attend cannot save Baltimore, but I honestly and truly believe that the church can make an impact in the community where it is. If you have a church in an area where there are drug transactions on the corner, homeless persons, etc., then the church in that particular area **can and must** make a difference.

When you look at all the churches in Baltimore and realize that there seems to be a church on one corner and a liquor store on the other - the evil against the good – often it looks like the evil is winning. However, if the good people who are **quiet** in church would **stand up** and **speak out**, there would be many dynamic changes. Can you see the impact of a coalition of a community of churches coming together to pool their resources to provide jobs and businesses and otherwise? When you strengthen the person, you strengthen the community. Isn't that what religion should be about? We should be able to look at the least of us and *lift them up*. As my grandfather said, "When we *lift up others*, the rest of us will be all right."

I always had problems with a church where you have trained ministers who build churches without classrooms and where memberships are satisfied with taking over an old church that someone else didn't want. Many churches are very satisfied with hand-me-downs. However, the Jesus I serve is an organized Jesus. He did everything in order, and I feel the church should represent the body of Christ which is the church. We should be able to recognize the fact that we are all in the army of the Lord, and we should make it work.

It seems with any major projects upon which Afro Americans embark, we look to see who the leadership is. There is always the question, who is going to be in charge? Who is the leader? We must be mindful of the fact that we should put in place the best available person who understands what is going on, and let that person take the lead as we follow. You will find out that the venture would be a lot more successful when we all are working on one accord. There is nothing, in my opinion that black churches cannot accomplish collectively. Individually, we'll be hitting and missing forever and never making a real impact that we could make for our people throughout the city, the state, and this nation.

On Helping Our Youth

A young fellow once told me something after I gave him and a group of other inner-city youths an experience he had never had before - a vacation for a week with everything included. They lived for a week like millionaires lived. I recall the symbolic comment he made when I brought him home; he lived in the worse conditions that you would ever want to see a child live. I brought him home in my station wagon; he was the last one that I took home. When I looked over at him, he was crying. When I looked around at where he lived I said, "Lord, this is a tough situation." I said, "You gave me a fit for a whole week in Ocean City, MD. You were very disrespectful and a real troublemaker. You're crying on me now?" This is what he said, and I will remember it for as long as I live: "Mr. Fullwood, I want you to know I had a good time. I also want you to know I want to be somebody, but I need some help."

Hearing that, you should see what he is now, a nice family guy with a good job. He recognized from that experience that he wanted to be somebody. In addition, that is the cry of many our young people throughout the City of Baltimore, throughout the State of Maryland, and this country. Many young men and women are saying, "I want to be somebody, but I need some help." I hope all of us are willing to accept the challenge enough to care and to share and give the least of us an opportunity to reap the fruit of this outstanding society of ours. As an African American, I know that all is not well in America, but we can help our youth toward a brighter future for them and us. Let's all do that.

On Humanitarianism

I understand about slavery, about bigotry, about prejudice, and discrimination. I understand all of those things, but I'm here to say that I am not a traveling person. I have not been to any of the Third World countries, but I have read of the suffering that is going on throughout the world. Understanding all the problems that we have in America, I still consider myself one of the luckiest persons in the world to be able to stand up proudly and say that this is the greatest country in the world. I am happy to have the opportunity and the blessing to be part of it. Of course, it could be better, but nothing gets better sitting on the sideline and wishing it to happen. In order for it to happen, we have to join hands in love, devotion, and harmony for one another. I often say, "Everything I do, I try to do it for the children." You never hear me say I am doing it for white children or black children. I love to think that I am doing it for all of our children. It just happens to be that in many instances our black children need it the most.

Thomas Edison and Abraham Lincoln

Thomas Edison was a successful man of his time. Part of his philosophy really impressed me. He said, "Show me a completely satisfied man, and I will show you a complete failure." In essence, what he is saying is that none of us should be completely satisfied with where we are in life. We can always be better. I recall a story of a lady who was illiterate. Her grandson was in college; she had someone write him to see how he was doing and to ask him to write back. He wrote back and said he had made all B's. His grandmother responded, "Well, he can do better." Two or three years went by and in his senior year, he had all A's. His grandmother wrote back "Well, you can do better." I recall that my grandfather said when I graduated from college with a B.A. degree: "Son, sit down and let me teach you the rest of the alphabet."

Giving up is the easiest thing to do. I think that is what impressed me about Abraham Lincoln. He pursued different offices in politics, and he never won an election until he was elected president of the United States. After every loss, he would say to himself, "I will continue to study and prepare myself, and one day, my chance will come." What I learned from this is that giving up is the easiest thing to do. Sometimes giving up can be our worst enemy. In life, there are times when you are going to fail. You have to look at it pragmatically. If you are flat on your back, you can always be reminded of the fact that if you can look up, then you can get up. The biggest tragedy is to give up.

Meetings, Meetings, Meetings

I go to many affairs, dinners, and breakfast events which normally benefit the organization sponsoring the same. So often, at those types of affairs and at the church, they become long and uninteresting with boring speeches and prayers. Let's look at prayers first. The officers of the church where I attend, when called to pray, go on and on and on. They are trying to out-pray the master of prayer, Our Lord Savior, Jesus Christ. He gave us the Lord's Prayer. The Ten Commandments have 297 words. The Gettysberg Address has 267 words. Moreover, the Lord's Prayer has less than 100 words. Pretty good and impressive words! I once read a report on the pricing of cabbage which contained 26,900 words. Speaker that I am, I prefer to confine my remarks to somewhere between the Lord's Prayer and the cabbage pricing report.

Often in many organizations to which I have belonged, everyone strives for recognition, and some, for false recognition. We often recognize folks who are not deserving. It cheapens the people who have worked hard to be recognized.

At our annual Benefit and Recognition Breakfast, one of the greatest feelings in the world is to see other people feel good about their accomplishments. We honor them for the contributions that they have made to help make a positive difference in the lives of those in need. **People who are self-confident do not fight for recognition**. They will gladly give unto others. This is one reason why they are self-confident people. Do not wait until a person is dead before you recognize him for his accomplishments to his fellowman. If we are going to give recognition, let us give our flowers while the person can smell them.

I would say the most powerful motivation force in the world is personal praise. This is not the same thing as cheap flattery. I used to hear folks in my hometown say that flattery is made up of "ten percent soap and ninety percent lye." For a person who works faithfully for his family and organization, yet never receives personal recognition, a lack of productivity will mark his life. I feel very secure when I am leading anything simply because I learned a long time ago to understand that if I am in charge I am the motivator. Those individuals who work with me or under me accept their charge with the greatest of enthusiasm; they are doing what it takes to make me look good. As a result, if they are making me look good, then I pass all accolades down. Why? I feel secure because I am in charge. When Fullwood is in charge, it means that I am going to get most of the credit. However, it is up to me to see that the other workers can feel some appreciation and, at the same time, feel that they made a contribution to whatever we might be doing.

Encouragement is the most effective performance enhancer. Not very many of us do a better job merely because we are expected to do so or are even paid to do so. I know that money is not the best motivator, at least, for long. I once sponsored an event that included 12,000 people at the Baltimore Arena. It was a wonderful occasion. Young people who had never missed a day of school were accompanied by their parents. At one stage during the program, I asked them to turn the house lights on. I asked every male who had brought a child to please stand. I would say that it was something for the eyes to see because I had never seen that many African-American men in one place with a child.

On Worrying

One of my pet peeves is that people worry too much. I see it in a lot of young people, old people, and sometimes in myself. I am often worried about many things over which I have no control. If we have no control, then we have to look to faith for an answer and a solution to whatever we are worried about. Worry saps our energy. Worrying is self poisoning. Worry takes the place of prayer, planning, and practical pleasure of living. Someone said jokingly, "Why pray, when we can worry." We must learn to cut off the worrying habit.

Worrying is the number one enemy of mankind. Worrying is

like a rocking chair; it will give you something to do, but it will not get you anywhere. Worry, worry, worry, worry, and worry. We should not spend one second worrying about anything that we do not control. Instead, we must concentrate on those things in our lives that we control and invest our time striving and working to strengthen those areas. Young people worry about their grades. They worry about keeping up with the Joneses. They worry about becoming successful. I think the only thing that can knock out worry is working it to death.

We must always be reminded that God gave man two things that made him different from other species. He gave us something on which to sit and something with which to think. We have the ability to determine which one we are going to do. Are we going to sit on it, or are we going to think on it? God gave man a mind, brains to distinguish himself from the creatures around him. Again, the question is, "What are we going to do, sit on it or think on it?" If we think on it, we can do a lot to enhance our fellow man.

Greek-letter Organizations

There are quite a few Greek-letter organizations in Baltimore, and of course, nationwide. I had the privilege to join Delta Lambda Chapter, Alpha Phi Alpha Fraternity, Inc. Since its founding in 1906, Alpha Phi Alpha Fraternity, Inc. has supplied voice and vision to the struggle of African Americans and people of color around the world. It was the first intercollegiate Greek-letter fraternity established for African Americans and was founded at Cornell University in Ithaca, New York by seven college men who recognized the need for a strong bond of brotherhood among African descendants in this country. The fraternity initially served as a study and support group for minority students who faced racial prejudice, both educationally and socially, at Cornell.

Alpha Phi Alpha's principles include scholarship, fellowship, good character, and the uplifting of humanity. Alpha Phi Alpha has long stood at the forefront of the African-American community's fight for civil rights through leaders such as W.E.B.

203

DuBois, Adam Clayton Powell, Jr., Edward Brooke, Martin Luther King, Jr., Thurgood Marshall, Andrew Young, William Gray, Paul Robeson, and many others.

It seems very difficult to get all of the fraternities and sororities to come together under one umbrella - once every four years, once every three years, or once whenever so that we could do things together to make an impact on the community. I personally do not believe in Alpha House, Delta Center, or whatever. I believe that together we could come together and develop a Greek Center to house educational facilities where we could work with the children on computers, after school, or a designated time. We could even have our own barbershop, beauty parlor, and provide other services. Many of us have our Alpha House, AKA Center, and Delta Center and all that, but when we really look at the total picture, we are really, really not doing anything to benefit the community.

The name of the game is economics, and how do you develop that? Pool your resources and make it happen. When you employ people, we change their lives. I notice that our KFC employees include many young folks making minimum wage, but at the same, I see a big difference in the expression on their faces when they get their paycheck. We should be about developing young people spiritually, socially, and economically. We have the power. God gave all of us two things, one thing on which to sit and one thing with which to think. He also gave us a choice. The question is, "What are we going to continue to do think on it or sit on it?" The need is truly great. Working together and pooling our resources, I would almost guarantee, can make a difference.

Can you imagine how beautiful, how wonderful it could be if the black church and the fraternal organizations would come together and say, "This is the plan for the future, and this is how each one of our organizations can contribute to that plan." Oh, I'm telling you, it could and would be awesome to have something of which we all could be proud if we all could work together to achieve. It sounds wonderful, but the plan does not mean anything, unless folk buy into it.

We are divided. As long as we are divided, we will be easy to conquer. I think Thomas Edison said it, and I mentioned it before, "Show me a thoroughly satisfied anything, and I'll show you a complete failure." We can never, as a people, be satisfied about where we are. We must learn to do things **on our own** and not be dependent upon anyone else to do what we should be doing.

As a result of integration, few of us have climbed the ladder. On the other hand, many of us have climbed the ladder of progress and forgot to look back and reach down. As long as one of us is suffering, all of us should bear the cross. The need is so great. I think somewhere, someone said that there is a lot of work to be done, but there are few workers committed to doing it. With commitment and faith, one can build anything.

Once I heard a story about the pig that had gotten together with the chicken and with the cow. They all wanted to contribute to breakfast. The cow said, "I'll give the milk," and the chicken said, "I'll provide the eggs." Both of them said, "Now Mr. Pig, you can provide the ham." The pig looked at them and said, "What you want me to do is make the supreme sacrifice." That's the way it is with many of our organizations; we want a few people to make the sacrifice, and we all live off of their efforts. It can't work that way. It has to be a team effort. One of the things I liked about sports was that it taught you how to follow. I guarantee you, when you find yourself a good follower, you're going eventually to have yourself a good and effective leader because they go hand in hand. One cannot exist without the other.

Sometimes words of encouragement can fan the spark of a genius into the flame of achievement. I once heard a story that Lincoln's dying mother called her small son to her bedside and whispered, "Be somebody Abe." Well, folks all across my life have whispered to me on so many different occasions, "You are going to be somebody." Thank God, I am somebody.

I am most encouraged by the words of Secretary of State Colin Powell when he said, "There are no secrets to success. Don't waste time looking for them. Success is the result of perfection, hard work, learning from failure, loyalty to those for whom you work, and persistence." We all can learn from these words. Yes, in my life, I have done all of these. Even with that, there are no guarantees. Success is based upon hard work and loyalty and the fact that I have never forgotten from where I came. I worked hard to acknowledge those folks who helped me along the way.

On Achievement

I once had the privilege to speak to a group of honor graduates at Morgan State University. I was so impressed. They had so many students from across the country that had excelled academically. Oh, what a wonderful occasions it was. I told the young people, "You are smarter than I ever hoped to be. You have everything going for you academically. I was not perhaps as good academically at this stage of my life, but I was persistent. I worked hard and I was persistent."

There are so many unsuccessful men with talent. However, there are so many educated folk who are derelicts. I have always been full of persistence and determination. I had the will to press on, press on to help solve many problems. As I said to the young people at Morgan, "You are smart, and you know it; I have to work at it all the time. I even have to work at it while you're sleeping. The big difference is that you know you are smart. However, if you and I were competing against each other for jobs with all your smartness, I'm here to tell you my commitment and desire for hard work would be as competitive as your book sense. If we were competing for a job, you would wake up one morning, and I'd have it, and you'd never know the real reason why. Persistence, hard work, integrity, and loyalty to those who have been supportive of you will always surface to the top."

Booker T. Washington, one of this country's greatest educators, stated that success is to be measured not so much by the position that one has reached in life as by the obstacles that one has overcome while trying to succeed. There are so many obstacles, and often when we are faced with obstacles, we have a tendency to give up. As mentioned previously, the easiest thing in the world to do is to quit. Anyone can do that.

Relevant to marriage, I was always impressed by something that I heard years ago and it is that: The most important thing a father can do for his children is to love their mother. That is one of the greatest examples that one can give.

On Finding Your Way

Dr. Billy Graham tells of a time early in his career when he arrived in a small town to preach a sermon. Wanting to mail a letter, he asked a young boy where was the post office. When the boy told him, Dr Graham thanked him and said, "If you'll come to the Baptist Church this evening, you can hear me telling everyone how to get to Heaven." The boy looked at him befuddled and said, "I don't think I'll be there. You don't even know your way to the post office." In finding your way in the game of life you have to prepare to meet its challenges. And you do that with training, love, and a spiritual, forgiving heart.

The road is clear. There is an upper road and a lower road, and you have a choice. What will it be, the upper road to success or the lower road to destruction? Be mindful that no man is an island; no man goes his or her way alone. All that one sends into the lives of others shall come back into one's very own. Praise God. Be mindful that there are splinters on the ladder of success, but you will never notice it unless you're sliding down.

To make one mistake is human; to make the same mistake twice is to be a fool. I often say to young folk that you can't do it for momma, for daddy, for brother or sister, uncle or aunt until you first do it for yourself. Once you do it for yourself, you can pass the torch on in caring and sharing and uplifting one another. Remember, you've got to do it for yourself before you can pass it on. The greatest feeling in the world is when you can look in the mirror and say without a reservation of a doubt, "I have done the best I can do, and the best I can do is all that can be expected." Then too, I have heard older people say sometimes the best you do is not good enough.

That is why those words of Thomas Edison are so meaningful. I would like to look at myself as a diamond in the rough that was polished by a number of different people from all walks of life. Those who used the polish didn't have any regard for color or creed, but they had a lot of hope that the diamond would shine upon all of us. A diamond in the rough!

On Forgiveness

I know whatever transgressions I have caused, I can always sit back and think of the three men on the cross. There was one who said, "Lord, you are not worthy of what is happening to you. Me, I am a sinner and I know I'm worthy of what is happening to me. Please remember me in Paradise." On the cross, the man asked for forgiveness, and he was forgiven. To me, that is the greatest passage in the Bible, when the Lord said, "Ask and yea shall receive." This poor man on the cross asked to see Jesus and to be admitted into His Kingdom. By merely asking, it was granted. The good news for all of us who have sinned and have fallen short is to know that we can ask our Lord and Savior to forgive us at any point in our lives. Forgiveness. Forgiveness. When one says to a person, "I'm sorry, please forgive me," you can judge that person's sincerity by what he does after he has said I am sorry, please forgive me. Sometimes in life, it is not the mistake that wipes us out; it is what we do after we realize we have made a mistake.

On Sharing

Even in business when you give and share, there is a blessing in store for you. Sometimes you are not able to always see it, but it comes back in proportion. This reminds me of a story of a lady who visited one of my KFC stores. She had four or five children with her that she was babysitting for their working mothers. She brought them in the store, and she ordered some food. The cashier said that the amount was about $20 or $25, and the lady said, "I don't have any money, but you all have to feed these kids." The cashier came to me and explained that there was a woman who had these children who were hungry, but she did not have any money. I told him to go ahead and feed them.

The manager at the time told me that I would have a hard time making it in business because I am always giving, giving, and giving; a business cannot exist that way. I told him that there was a blessing in store. Well, about two hours later, a fellow came in that represented a big organization that was working with children. He ordered 500 box lunches. He asked me not to discount them because the organization could afford to pay. We gave away that day $25 worth of chicken and in turn received over $2,500 in sales. Therefore, that led me to believe that it is good business to **share and care**. For a number of years, when our business was thriving, I got employees to volunteer their time on Thanksgiving and Christmas. My family and I worked and fed free meals to folk during the holidays, and that made all of us feel really, really good.

Pay the Debt

The policy in my store was if a person walked in and said, "Mr. Fullwood, I don't have any money and I'm hungry. Will you please give me something to eat,?" I would not run that person out of the store. In the business, we waste a lot of chicken, and I would always find a way to feed a person at no cost who honestly says he's hungry. Sometimes they are **just** getting over, but I know there is a blessing down the road because I try to do what's right for a person. Often people take goodness for weakness. But I can assure you that I have to be tough. I can be tough. I am tough.

There have been occasions when folk called me late hours of the morning to say, "Mr. Fullwood I need money for my rent; they're going to put me out." I know you've got to be way behind before you get put out. They come and we work out an agreement. I do not believe in signing forms or anything like that because a person is no better than his word.

On one occasion, a fellow borrowed money, and I told him he did not have to pay it back until he got his tax return. He did not even have to pay interest on the money. I asked him to have it in at a certain time, and I gave him ample time. Well, when the time came for him to pay, he was ducking me. He was a member of my church, so one morning I came to church a little late, and the ushers directed me to a seat right beside him. He didn't know what to say. He was hemming, hawing, and going on; I told him I did not want to deal with him then. Well, to make a long story short, he ducked me and ducked me. I just wanted to show him that his word was not any good, and I was not going to let him get away with it. After I took him to court, he had to pay all the attorney fees; he had to pay me and my attorneys. It really did not make sense. Out of my good heart, I loaned him the money with no interest, and he could pay me back when he said he could pay me back. When he gave me the date, and we agreed on it, I held him to it.

On Saying Thanks

There have been many, many occasions when folk in need made approaches. I was able to accommodate some of them. I recognized that you just could not stay in business without an open and compassionate heart. I always said there is a business side and a conscience side; sometimes they have to go together in order to have equity.

A lady called me stressed out, needing $1,000 to keep her son in school. She vowed that she would repay me. I sent the money to the young fellow. I never heard anymore from her nor did I get a thank you letter from him, not that I'm looking for it. I guess ninety percent of young people go through life taking, holding their hand out, never, never even thinking about saying, "Thank you, I appreciate it." What they have to realize is you never know when you have to go back to the well.

On Seeking Something for Nothing

In business, you always have to be aware that there are a number of people out there who are always trying to get something for nothing. They say they ate a bad piece of chicken. They would call in and say they did not like the chicken, and we would ask them to bring it back. When they brought it back, there was nothing but bones. It is amazing what folk will do to try to get something for nothing. Many will sell their own souls to get a piece of chicken. However, it is understandable because if they have never been taught the difference between right and wrong, then those kinds of things are expected. Many folk say they fell in front of the store; what they are really trying to do is **get something for nothing.**

There are many rewards for being in business, but there are many heartaches too. I have learned that there are a lot of good people, but there are many folk who by their own nature make every effort to try to get something for nothing. They have never been taught anything about integrity or hard work, those things that get us to the top. Whenever you are in business, and you are hanging around the top, it took a lot of effort to get there. I am here to tell you that you have to work twice as hard to try to stay there. You can take years to build a business, and then you can destroy it overnight.

I have worked very hard to try to keep my outlets looking as good or better as those located in the suburban areas, but it is so difficult. I remember on one occasion I put $10,000 worth of landscaping in my business, and within 60 days, it did not look as if I had put anything in it. Inside the building, people would steal toilet paper, and the hanging plants; anything that they could take, they would take it. Many of the folks in the neighborhood would come in and steal sugar out of the bins. It made it so difficult to try to maintain your business and make a profit and watch much of it go out the door simply because folks do not have any respect.

I had a store in the county, and this was the difference. I had some young ladies working for the first time. It was their first job, and they were a little slow. The folks would say to them, "Take your time because we know you're learning." They would be just as patient as they could be. In the store that I had in the inner city, customers would walk in where the same young girls were working hard, trying to learn, being a little slow in the learning process; impatient customers would call them every-thing but a child of God. The children would come to me crying, saying, "Mr. Fullwood, I just can't take this." They would leave.

However, when I would be in the presence of the young people and a customer would curse them, I would intervene because I am not going to let any customer do that. I will be the first to tell you that the customer is *Not* always right. When they come in being abusive to my employees and my management team, I will not condone it. I am in business to make money, but not at all costs, and that is one of the costs that I am not willing to patronize.

I have to stand by my young people because I want them to see that making money is important, but being courteous and being respectful are just as important. I cannot stand idly by and watch a customer abuse an employee, nor can I stand by and watch an employee abuse a customer. However, for the most part, it is a learning experience for all involved.

Edwin & Eldonia Bassett

Happy 62nd Anniversary!

1939-2002

The Greatest Gift: Love
"And now abideth Faith, hope, charity,
these three; but the greatest of these is charity."
—1 Corinthians 13:13

My Mother in-law and Father in-law.

Dr. Bernard W. Franklin   Dr. Matthew L. Jones

Frantz C. Wilson   Everett C. Fullwood

Chapter Twelve

Impact "What They Say About Harlow Fullwood, Jr."

Steve Provost, *Senior Vice President, KFC Corporation*
You make a living by what you get, but you make a life by what you give. Harlow Fullwood has been giving to others his entire life, and the story in this book inspires all of us to get serious about service to others.

Anthony "Tony" Cameron, *Former KFC Manager for Fullwood Foods, Inc.*

My relationship with Harlow Fullwood began in the summer of 1988. I ran the KFC on Frederick Avenue, and Harlow came in to borrow soda cups because his KFC on Franklin Street ran out. I heard rumors that a retired police officer owned a KFC in the neighborhood, but I never had the opportunity to meet him. I will never forget when he walked in the door. His presence filled the room. When he introduced himself, I immediately felt a sense of compassion. That was the closest I have ever come to being in awe of someone.

Over the next few months, we struck a friendship. I would call him to ask his opinion on certain matters, and he did the same. During this time, Harlow was in the process of opening a KFC on Pennsylvania and North Avenues. Our conversations over this time began to focus on me running this new store. So, on

October 16, 1988, I walked away from ten years of service, stock options, four weeks' vacation, and a great health plan to help Harlow build a company.

Since I worked for a company for ten years, it took some time for me to adjust to working for an individual. I would soon learn making money was not Harlow's first priority. In fact, during those first weeks, I was introduced to Harlow's philosophy: "We want to make money. That's why we're in business, but I will not make money at all costs." He taught me that integrity and fair play were the most important things. If you treat people fairly (your staff and customers), the loyalty will come and also the money. Over the next ten years, I began to look to Harlow as my mentor.

During this time, I was going through a divorce and custody battle over my six--year-old daughter. I was going to give up on custody until I talked to Harlow. I still remember the words he said to me. He told me the hardest job he ever had wasn't playing football, recruiting police officers, or even starting his own business. He said, "Cameron, the hardest job I ever had was rearing Paquita and little Harlow." Those words continue to stay with me. Ariel, my daughter, graduated with honors from high school and currently attends Xavier University in Ohio.

The lasting legacy that Harlow passed on to me is not business skills-related, but rather it is the mission of making the rearing of your children your most important job and instilling in them values and morals that you want their children and community to have. Harlow exemplifies the African proverb: "*It takes a village to raise a child.*"

William Donald Schaefer, *Comptroller of Maryland, former Maryland Governor, former Mayor of Baltimore*

The Fullwood name is synonymous with community service. Time and time again, you inspire your peers and our public at-large to follow your lead. Maryland truly appreciates what you do for people.

Senator Paul Sarbanes, *United States Senator, Democrat, MD*

I believe the service you have contributed to Baltimore has been responsible, in large measure, for the physical and spiritual renaissance which has earned our city national and international recognition. As your United States Senator, and as a fellow Baltimorean, I want to express my own deep appreciation for your efforts and interest in our city. Your concern and activism inspire us all to reaffirm our commitment to a Baltimore that is best because it reflects the finest in its people.

Dr. Matthew L. Jones, *Pastor, Concord Baptist Church*

I speak of a man who is a loyal friend, who has high moral character, a good steward, and a committed ambassador for Christ, and a man who has committed his life to helping others and, in doing so, making the world his friend.

Someone has stated, "A life lived with friends is a life well-lived." I speak of a man whose humble beginnings did not afford him much, yet out of the depths of his heart he has given so much to so many. I salute my friend and parishioner -- Harlow Fullwood, Jr.

Rev. Dr. William C. Calhoun, Sr., *Pastor, Trinity Baptist Church, Baltimore, Producer/Host "Lift Every Voice," WMAR TV2*

Harlow Fullwood continues to tenaciously value humankind at every level of society. His Christian faith and character allow him never to forget from whence he comes and the bridges that have brought him and his over. Fullwood's commitment to make an opportunity for others is based on the many who helped him along the way. Along with others, I have witnessed undergirding of students, persons who often are overlooked and undervalued, and people who just need another chance to overcome life's vicissitudes. As the Lord lifted him, he lifts others. He is a dear Christian comrade, fraternity brother, and alumni brother who deserves your undivided attention to his autobiography *Love Lifted Me.*

Osborne A. Payne

Dr. Calvin W. Burnett

William Donald Schaeffer, Esquire

Dr. James D. Tschechtelin

Miss Lucy Mae Harrison (94 years old), *Harlow Fullwood's Homeroom Teacher at Stephens-Lee High School, Asheville, North Carolina*

Harlow always wanted to do what was right. He was elected Mayor of the Student Council. He had unusual integrity at an early age. His charitable giving is wonderful and significant. I think he has done a tremendous amount of good. As a teacher, I grade Harlow an "A" for how he has lived his life. In one word, I describe Harlow Fullwood, Jr. as "compassionate."

Rev. Matthew R. Silver, *Pastor, Piney Wood Chapel Baptist Church, Ahoskie, North Carolina (Reverend Silver was previously Pastor of Concord Baptist Church, my first church in Baltimore.)*

Harlow Fullwood has a love for humanity. He is a man with restlessness for causes in his heart. He has found, in the course of living, that he could uplift humanity by helping others develop their spirituality and education. He is methodical, and he has vigorously pursued endeavors that would benefit humanity as well as himself. He is a dedicated family man. He was a devoted Public Relations Man for the Baltimore Police Department, and he carried out his duties while counseling others to succeed. He is a lover of humanity. His transition to becoming a KFC franchisee involved him being selected from a host of applicants. Harlow is a "People Man." I feel that his mission is, from a theological standpoint, to be a servant of God for the purpose of uplifting humanity, and he lives his life in a humble way to accomplish that mission.

Dr. S. Dallas Simmons, *former President, Virginia Union University*

First of all, it is difficult to describe Harlow in a few words, but I will try. Harlow has a certain insight and legendary charisma that motivates young people to follow his lead. He is a person who does not, in any capacity, think of self first. He thinks of others before he thinks of himself.

I remember the first day that I met him, when I began my posi-

Samuel T. Daniels   Dr. S. Dallas Simmons

Alicia Reid   N. Scott Phillips, Esquire

tion as President of Virginia Union, on the day that the board named me president. Prior to then, I had never heard of or seen Harlow Fullwood. After the board meeting, he came over to me and said, "Mr. President, this is my school. I'm going to be watching you. But, at the same time, I will help you, with whatever you try to do...,but I will be watching you." He expressed his love for Virginia Union. Every year, he brought many, many high school students to the university to see his alma mater. He would express how much it meant to him and to his life. He would give them a tour of the campus and help instill in their minds that VUU was where they wanted to go to college.

I have said to others that Harlow Fullwood recruited more students for Virginia Union University than any other alumnus that we have. I reminded the board that anytime you have an individual recruiting students for the university...it means money. The reality is that colleges are enrollment-driven. As a result of the generous, personal philanthropy of Harlow and Elnora Fullwood, as well as Harlow's customized student recruitment techniques, Virginia Union has significantly benefited.

Drew Berry, *Vice President / General Manager, WMAR TV2 / ABC*
Harlow Fullwood is an amazing man with an incredible story. His drive, dedication, and determination to help others help themselves are sincere and consistent. Harlow knows the power of asking and the rewards of giving. I have seen the fruits of his labor warm the coldest of hearts. Once you see his work and the positive impact it has on thousands of children, you will be hooked on Harlow. He is a man of his word, a man with a vision, and a man of great deeds. Harlow and his silent but powerful partner, Elnora, his wife, are extraordinary people whose extraordinary works are legendary in Baltimore.

Joan Marshall, *Executive Director, Maryland Prepaid College Trust*

Harlow Fullwood Jr. cares deeply about helping all children to get their best possible start in life. He not only helps hundreds of young people to get a good education, but he serves as a living example of how faith, trust, commitment, respect and pride matter in living one's life and in giving back to the community.

J. Millard Tawes, *former Governor of Maryland (deceased)*

"Harlow Fullwood, Jr. is a natural-born achiever, organizer, a leader, giving every waking hour of his private life, without remuneration or acclaim, to some 30 community projects and services." Stated by Governor Tawes, upon presentation of the first prestigious Jimmy Swartz Medallion Award to Harlow Fullwood, Jr.

Stanley I. Morstein, *Esquire*

The first time I met Harlow, I said, "This guy is bigger than life. He is warm, hospitable, and bright." It was a privilege for me to assist Harlow in developing his relationship with KFC. He has been an inspiration to me. When I met Harlow and Elnora, he was on the police force. Harlow learned that Operation Push was seeking minority franchise applicants to KFC. He endeavored to submit a franchise application, and he sought help from me and my then law partner Theodore Losin. We were delighted to help Harlow. He was honest and ambitious, and his community service accomplishments were exemplary. I am proud that Harlow gained his franchise. I am privileged to know such a fine gentleman, successful businessman, humanitarian, and philanthropist.

Samuel T. Daniels, *Grand Master Emeritus, Most Worshipful Prince Hall Masons Grand Lodge, F & A.M. of MD*

In more than 55 years of community and military involvement, I have encountered only a very few persons who have demonstrated the level of commitment and competent organizational skills as I know Dr. Harlow Fullwood possesses and constantly implements. His development of his program to provide support annually to dozens of young students is unmatched by any program of which I have knowledge. His financial undergirding of community service organizations has been extremely broad, and for the most part, without the public's knowledge. Dr. Fullwood is very special, and his commitment has served to fill a tremendous void across this state.

Dr. Ruth N. Swann, *Professor, Norfolk State University*

One has only to look at the incredible legacy of Harlow Fullwood Jr. to realize the magical and profound impact his work has had on others. He is a striking force in a monumental initiative to expand opportunities for youth to obtain a college education. An ongoing proliferation of youngsters are the beneficiaries of his visions, talents and generosity. Our country has been greatly served by his leadership and philanthropic contributions to educational, health and human service organizations.

His achievements are more remarkable because he does not operate from a corporate base or with great fortune. He has done what he has done in the spirit of caring and sharing, while earning his living as an employee, employer, and entrepreneur and through the creation---by choice---of the Fullwood Foundation. This ordinary, gracious man is unique among humankind. His story is phenomenal.

Bernard W. Franklin, Ph.D., *President, Virginia Union University*

Mr. Harlow Fullwood's life story is an inspiring odyssey of a man who has become a bright star in the constellation of humanity. His is the story of a man who has excelled at every endeavor he has tackled. He has been an All-American athlete, a highly decorated law enforcement officer, a successful entrepreneur and a generous, caring philanthropist.

Mr. Fullwood is a man who believes that young people represent the future of our country and world. Through his foundation, he has awarded more than $6 million in college scholarships. His investment in young people reflects his deep commitment to providing educational opportunities for deserving students. His efforts have made a reality of the dreams of attending college for over 500 Baltimore-area students.

There is much that we can learn from Mr. Fullwood. He offers forthright wisdom that challenges us to become better human beings. He is a living sermon on caring, and he reminds us that it is quite true that one person can make a difference.

Virginia Union University is proud to claim Mr. Fullwood as a heralded alumnus. He is one of our most active recruiters. When he tells the story of how Virginia Union University shaped his life, prospective students are attracted to the unique academic culture that produced graduates like him.

Mr. Fullwood's story is a legacy of greatness. Through his words, he is now passing this legacy on to future generations that will undoubtedly be blessed and inspired.

Stephen Green, *Playwright, Composer, Virginia Union University Alumnus*

It has been my extreme pleasure to know Mr. Harlow Full-wood. I am a 1976 graduate of Virginia Union University and an active member in its alumni association. It was his caring for the survival of the university that has inspired many other students to become successful graduates of the school. If Harlow were an ambassador to the United Nations, like he is for Virginia Union, we would have world peace and the end of world poverty. It was hearing one of his speeches at my church that inspired me to write one of my favorite songs which went on to become the last song of my first play. I now have 54 copyrights and counting because of the inspiration of Harlow Fullwood, Jr. The last chorus of my song "True Measure of a Man" describes my feelings about Harlow. "What's the characteristic that sets us all apart — what's in your checkbook, but what is in your heart? It's only when you follow in the master's plan, that is where you find the true measure of a man."

James D. Tschechtelin, *President, Baltimore City Community College*

I have learned so much from Harlow Fullwood, Jr. Maybe that says it all. He is a teacher. He may not be in the classroom, but he educates. He inspires. He is a wonderful storyteller, and he teaches his lessons about life in the stories that he tells. When he spoke at our commencement, he taught about punctuality by telling a story about a young man who was late for an appointment with him for a job interview.

He teaches about the work ethic when he tells students, "Honest work has dignity." He teaches about reaching out to help others when he says, "I can honestly say that I have never met a successful person who can say that he or she did it on his or her own." He teaches about high standards when he says, "I believe in second chances, but I don't pay for them. I pay for success. You get D's; you get a job."

I have known Harlow Fullwood for ten years since becoming president of Baltimore City Community College. He has been a loyal and generous friend at every turn. Harlow is the type of person who, when he calls, cannot be turned down. His caring is contagious, and he is one of the most generous people that I have ever met.

Harlow Fullwood has touched the lives of thousands of people over the years. Many of those people he has touched directly and personally received an award, a trophy, a college visit, or a scholarship. More difficult to estimate, however, is the number of men and women who have quietly watched Harlow Fullwood, applauded at his annual Caring and Sharing Breakfasts, marveled at his loving generosity, and drove home vowing to change their lives for the better because of his powerful example.

Calvin W. Burnett, *President, Coppin State College*

There are many, many things that one learns while traveling the paths of life. As I have walked many pathways in my 30 years as president of Coppin State, I have learned that there are few, in this world, of the character and humbleness of Harlow

Fullwood, Jr.

The "joy of giving" is a noteworthy and familiar quote that has become this man's motto, for it seems that he derives such enormous pleasure from giving to others. Giving has become his life's work — to do for others what was not done for him.

For one who received so very little financial help while struggling through college to earn his degree, Harlow Fullwood, Jr. works hard to help alleviate the prospect of that same kind of struggle from the lives of many college-bound students.

Harlow Fullwood, Jr. has done so much for so many for so long that the number of students who have attended Coppin (as well as many other colleges) because of his commitment and generosity, is staggering.

I am proud to call him a friend. And, I will be forever grateful for the support that he has and continues to provide to students who need help to attend college.

We are all much better off because Harlow Fullwood, Jr. passed this way. In short, Harlow Fullwood, Jr. is an outstanding individual of character and a great American.

Earl S. Richardson, *President, Morgan State University*

William Osler wrote, "We are here to add what we can to life, not to get what we can from it." Truer words have not been written. This statement categorically applys to the life you have lived and the work you have done as an advocate for the poor and disadvantaged and a philanthropist, among other things. In addition, your commitment to family is obvious and noble.

The ongoing charitable support of Morgan State University and other such entities by your foundation is extensive and admirable. Supporting higher education and Historically Black Colleges and Universities, obiviously, has its short-term rewards, particularly for the immediate beneficiaries, but the far-reaching effect of such philanthrophy is immeasureable and untold.

Your children and the children you have nurtured by your charitable deeds are indeed blessed to have a role model such as you. As a role model, you are unparalleled. The contributions you have made to our society are a testimony illustrated in the words of an old spiritual, "Let the work I have done speak for me."

Mr. Fullwood, your work speaks volumes. The spirit of living embodied in your stated philosophy of caring and sharing and in your work and deeds will reverberate throughout this millennium. You have truly added to the lives of many, and I salute you.

Clyde Rucker, *Vice President, Central Region, Burger King Corporation*

I met Harlow Fullwood during the winter of 1994. He has been a well-known and well-respected person, not only in the KFC system as a franchisee but also within the communities in which he serves. Once we officially met, for the first time, it seemed as though we had known one another for years. I credit this to Harlow's personable approach and enthusiasm toward people.

Harlow sets the pace for all retail organizations when it comes to accentuating a brand's identification within local communities. His pride of ownership is well beyond reproach. Simply said, Harlow made my job easier as his franchise operations manager, when it came to his representation and positive recognition of the KFC brand. Today, I continue to use Harlow as a model for excellence and achievement for entrepreneurship.

Of course, there are always challenges that any independent businessman encounters, but the quality that always prevails is a good attitude, perseverance, and flexibility. This has enabled Harlow to penetrate through any and all obstacles. After all, these are the daily tools in his tool belt of success.

Dr. Edna May Merson, *Retired Principal, Baltimore County Public Schools*

Harlow Fullwood Jr. possesses a genuine feeling for others without thought of race, religion, or ethnic origin. During the 1970's, his leadership in helping to stabilize a community, which was changing rapidly both economically and socially, was of tremendous assistance. Working in the PTA and visiting homes in the evening, he helped unify the many organizations and interest groups together with the parents and citizens always with the common purpose of promoting an excellent educational program for the boys and girls.

Throughout his life, he has served others as demonstrated in his work with the Baltimore Police Department, scouting, Boys' Clubs, church, and the educational community. No task was too large or too small to be undertaken and carried through to a successful conclusion.

After his retirement from the police department, his efforts extended to establishing a foundation, which again exemplified the same values and ideals of caring for others while promoting educational excellence.

My Friendship with Harlow Fullwood by Napoleon Barbosa

I have been a friend of Harlow's since I arrived at Virginia Union University (VUU) as a freshman football player in August, 1959. I met Harlow for the first time at football practice. Prior to the academic year, all of the football players roomed in the basement of Kinsley Hall, which was nicknamed "The Hole." We were assigned as roommates at the beginning of the academic year to a dorm room on the third floor of Kinsley Hall. Both of us hit it off very well because we had a couple of things in common: we were both freshman players anxious to make a contribution to the VUU Panthers football team, and we were "country boys." Harlow was from Asheville, NC, and I was from North Canton, Ohio. Harlow was also very serious about academics, and I also detected that he was destined to help others.

As freshmen football players, I was the quarterback, and Harlow played both defensive tackle and offensive tackle. Harlow was a big man, very quick and fast on the football field. He was also what one of our coaches described as "mo-bile, ag-ile, and hos-tile." As freshman players, we had to be strong to stand up to the antics of our upperclassmen teammates. Many of them served in the military prior to enrolling in VUU, and they would always intimidate the freshmen. Harlow and I wouldn't let that happen because we stood up to them to show that we would not be intimidated. After that, the entire team pulled together to play, and we won nine consecutive games for an undefeated season.

Harlow also contributed to a significant part of my life, not just as a teammate but also as a friend, which I will never forget. One day, Harlow came to our dorm room to wake me up and inform me that he wanted to introduce me to the young lady who later became my wife. Her name was Dorothy Butler, a senior business major at VUU. I later learned that Dorothy found out that I was Harlow's roommate and wanted to be introduced to me. Dorothy and I married in February, 1963, and we have been together ever since. While Harlow was playing matchmaker, he met Elnora, a fellow student, who became his future wife.

I will always be forever grateful to Harlow as a friend. Over the years, I have kept in touch with him, and ours is a friendship that I will always cherish.

Dr. E. Lee Lassiter, *Associate Professor of Journalism (Ret.), Coppin State College; Former Editorial Writer, Columnist, The Baltimore News-American*

Things are indeed different. But where it counts, nothing has changed. And that too is phenomenal. Fullwood's focus is still what it has always been - the promising young and the "extraordinary" ordinary little people. He is still playing Robin Hood to hundreds while masquerading as just a "po' ole country boy."

Hattie N. Washington, *Ed.D., Vice President, Division of Institutional Advancement, Coppin State College, Executive Director, The Coppin State College Development Foundation*

As I journey through the recesses of my mind to pull forth any recollection of persons who have garnered my admiration and respect in my life encounters, based solely upon how they lived lives, one of the names that emerges is that of Harlow Fullwood, Jr.

Harlow Fullwood Jr., who came from a family of meager

means, has touched the lives of thousands of young people in a way that will benefit the whole of society. He is one who understands, as I do, that we must invest in and provide opportunities for our young people. Harlow Fullwood Jr., through his stellar entrepreneurial endeavors, has done just that. He has created a not-for-profit foundation, the Fullwood Foundation, which has only one mandate - to raise money to support the education of our young people. Harlow Fullwood, Jr. is a person who does not just "talk the talk," but he definitely "walks the walk." Undoubtedly, he is a role model for others to emulate.

Evelyn J. Chatmon, *Retired Educator*

Harlow Fullwood's story is the quintessential saga of a man, who from meager beginnings, developed into one of the great philanthropists of our time. His message of "caring and sharing" is a living message as he publicly recognizes outstanding role models of all ages and in all fields of endeavor. A major focal point for Harlow and his wife Elnora are the young people who demonstrate academic excellence in school and personal excellence in their daily lives. Because of their initiatives, hundreds of students have had their college education supported or paid for in full. The Fullwoods are living examples of how to live unselfish yet rewarding lives. What a wonderful world this would be if we all could replicate just a portion of the good for which the Fullwoods are responsible.

Stanley W. Tucker, *C.E.O., Meridian Management Group, Inc.*

Over the past fifteen years, I have seen Harlow Fullwood function successfully in several areas. I have seen him function as a mentor and recruiter of students for his beloved alma mater, Virginia Union University. He has set the standard for caring and sharing in our community through his tireless fundraising efforts that help disadvantaged youths obtain a college education.

Notwithstanding Harlow's success as a drum major for caring and sharing, I am more impressed with his success as a business owner. His business approach is unique in America because he makes money and makes a difference in people's lives at the same time. He has not only built a successful business, but he has also developed a cause that puts the lives of people before profit. Our world would be a much better place if we had more business owners like Harlow Fullwood, Jr.

Dee Evelyn Matthews, *Immediate Past President National, Continental Societies, Inc., Officer of Administration, Columbia University*

The author of this book is a compassionate, compelling figure, an individual who has shown that the courage to love does not have to be modified. Always focused, always steadfast, he displays a deep compassion and understanding that the reader can grasp as a blueprint for integrity and honesty. Thankfully, the parameters of his gifts are not reserved for a few but are generously, graciously and unselfishly offered to many. His "take the high road" attitude and excellent concept for applying these modalities to community social principles are recorded in this publication. He has done more in practice, applying these than most—for he truly does "walk the walk."

Fullwood's approach to the perception of life has been that of service to humankind, advocating change through his well-defined role of leadership, his continued strength, God-sustained faith, and solid understanding of responsibility. You will find these and other qualities of talent interwoven in the fabric of his life's work and in his biography. The book is stimulating, thought-provoking, and argues well the platform for the courage to live and the benefits derived from the fulfillment of that legacy.

The quality of this man is real indeed. This book and his life will have a significant impact on the reader.

Wanda Q. Draper, *Executive in Charge of Production, WBAL-TV11, Baltimore, Maryland*

There are some people that you know. There are some people that you respect. There are some people you appreciate, and there are some people you love. Harlow Fullwood is all of the

Evelyn J. Chatmon

Brock Abernathy

Minnie I. Carter

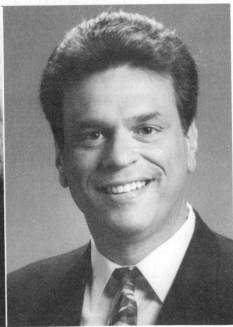

Tony Pagnotti

232

above. You know him because of the wonderful work he does. You respect him because he takes humanity to a whole new level. You appreciate him because the world is certainly a better place because he walked among us. Consequently, you just have to love him.

Tony Pagnotti, *TV Personality WMAR-TV2, Baltimore*

Some folks may observe that the life of Harlow Fullwood is a typical rags to riches story. After all, he came from a small-town family of modest means and went on to become one of the country's most successful African-American entrepreneurs. Although there are similar stories of achievement and inspiration, few can match his high-spirited and unselfish mission. What sets this extraordinary man apart from the rest is that he has chosen to go well beyond turning riches into gold. Fullwood, with loving support from wife Elnora, converts his riches into golden opportunities for others. He lives by his own philosophy from the early years: "I never wanted a handout from others...just a hand." Every day, Harlow reaches out and touches the lives of those in need of a friend they can turn to for guidance and inspiration.

During the fifteen years I've had the pleasure of being his friend, it's been wonderful to witness first hand the joy he's brought to so many young people, who, without a helping hand from Harlow, might have fallen by the wayside. Despite his ongoing battle with diabetes, his commitment to caring and sharing is as strong as ever. In closing, let met leave you with the words I use when introducing him at his many charitable events... "Ladies and gentle please welcome the KFC king who does chicken right. But who does people even better. Mr. Harlow Fullwood."

Dr. Edmonia T. Yates, *Retired Educator*

Having conquered the handicaps of poverty, Mr. Harlow Fullwood devotes his efforts to helping the poor and underprivileged, and at the same time, he motivates and recognizes other people for their humanitarian efforts. This twofold effort has a major impact on the community.

It is said that, "If you have a dark cloud that looms about you, find Mr. Fullwood and he will bring sunshine." He is a role model, an entrepreneur, a risk-taker, a tireless advocate of education, and he represents a rare combination of good judgement, great administrative ability, and social imagination. He serves the community with energy, enthusiasm, resourcefulness, and skill. It appears that his passionate interest in life is to make a positive difference in the lives of those who are willing to take advantage of his visions and generosity.

Herbert C. Sledge, Jr., J.D., *Writer, Marketing Development Specialist*

I have had the pleasure of knowing Harlow Fullwood, Jr. since 1987. He has been my friend and mentor. His advice is direct, his words are often poetic, and his expectations are always high. I have enjoyed observing him conduct his customized and continuous process of charitable giving and recognizing the accomplishments of others.

How do you describe a person who is a humanitarian and a philanthropist, someone who spends considerable time motivating others to be great, and then exerts much time and effort to promote and celebrate their success once it is achieved? You use such terms as compassionate and altruistic. Harlow Fullwood, Jr. lives up to the full definitions of these words.

Osborne A. Payne, *former McDonald's Owner-Operator*

Harlow, whom I have known for many years, apparently came into this world with a mission and a gift from God. Recognizing the many lives he has touched illustrates he does not plan to let God down.

Allen Schiff, CPA, *Partner, Grabush, Newman & Co., PA*

Since 1984, Harlow and I have been through so many ups and downs. From opening four KFC franchises to celebrating birthdays and weddings to unfortunate circumstances such as Harlow's grandmom's death to my mother's passing to closing two KFC locations.

Our happy times during this period are so many between Harlow and me. We could probably fill this book with all of them. However, there is one time that truly stands out from the rest. It was July, 1984. Fullwood Foods, Inc, was born. This was Harlow's first KFC. It was located in Baltimore County, Maryland. I can remember visiting the location and seeing Harlow greet everyone at the door as each customer entered. I think the customers were as surprised as I was that the owner of a quick serve-restaurant would take the time just to say "Hello!" to every customer.

During our business relationship, I have always worked extremely hard for Harlow and at times "even pushing the envelope." Harlow always reminds me to be truthful and honest, and he always wants to be regarded with high credibility and integrity. For that, I respect this man more than anything.

I hope and pray that God gives Harlow the strength to live another 100 years, so those that are less fortunate will have the opportunity that we have had to be touched by such a great human being.

David S. Jones, *President, The Miles W. Connor Chapter of the Virginia Union University Alumni Association*

Congratulations to you on your autobiography. Your life has demonstrated many pages of concern for the youth of today in preparing them for the leadership roles for tomorrow. You will always be remembered for your role of leadership in our chapter and your love for your alma mater through your work. You must be commended for the lives of many young people you have touched along the roads you have traveled.

Love Lifted Me

Veronica Simmons, *Junior, Morgan State University, Fullwood Foundation Scholar*

We'll remember
How you uplifted us
Saw the gift in us
Gave what was essential
Pushed a little potential
To heights we never dreamed of
We'll remember
Because God sends only a few
To do what you do
To be who you are
That bright shining star
To guide us
We'll remember
All the mountains you climbed
All the doors you broke down
And when you were done
How you turned back around
And reached back
For us
Now that's trust
In a man who surpassed expectation
Build a solid foundation
Made dedication
Look like recreation
Made success look like a craft
With your other half
Right in sync beside you
If we couldn't find you
she always could-
Your legacy will live on
Way after you're gone
Motivation kept

Deep inside your footsteps
Trying to keep still in them
We will try to fulfill them
You're loved by many, so
We won't ever let go
Rich in devotion
Wealthy in means
You prosper in elevation
An inspiration you bring
And/or that
We'll Always Remember.

Brock Abernathy, *WBFF-TV45, Baltimore*

When you meet Harlow Fullwood, Jr., you feel as if you have known him all your life. He is instantly a friend, confidante, mentor, and always, larger than life.

You are always happy to see him because he is always happy to see you. Saying "no" to Harlow is never an option. Your only real option is "yes" and to find out how much more you can do for him. Why? Maybe it is the hundreds of young people he has helped through his foundation and his overwhelming charitable nature, or, the thousands of lives he has touched, positively, over the years, or, maybe it is really one's faith in humankind and hope for the future... a future that Harlow sees so much better than most.

My association with Harlow Fullwood, Jr. began ten years ago because we are part of the same Rotary Club. It continues because he epitomizes everything good, positive, and hopeful for the future. And our relationship continues because, happily, I cannot say "no."

Helen L. Dale, *Maryland Department of Transportation*

Harlow's fierce, infectious passion for scholarship and citizenship is eclipsed only by his gentle compassion for those to whom the doors of opportunity have been closed. His dogged persistence, charming persuasion and dedicated vision for "a better world" makes him absolutely irresistible. He reaches out

to local businessmen, national corporations, fledgling entrepreneurs, professionals, and ordinary working people to infuse
and inspire others to open their doors, checkbooks, and hearts to
invest in young people on their way to becoming tomorrow's
leaders.

Harlow and Elnora are the kind of people who never give up.
They challenge us to do more with our lives, give more to noble
causes, and to be better people. Gently, by humble and consistent personal example, they set high standards, giving new
meaning to unselfish love in action, personal discipline, and
exemplary achievement. His legacy is one that will endure and
expand as generations he has touched, inspired, and
empowered grow up and indeed "make a better a world."

Who is Harlow Fullwood? by Wilhemina Nutter

*Who is the man who helps to make the impossible dreams of
young people possible?*
The man who is a true friend and mentor.
The man who is a natural "Big Brother" and a great coach.
The man who is a motivator and an initiator.
The man who is a determined, seemingly tireless worker.
*The man who is always helping and uplifting others while
taking little time for himself.*
*The man who has a heart of gold and the ability to touch
the hearts of many.*
The man who has blazed a trail where few have trod.
*The man who coupled with his wife Elnora built an
organization that shares because they really care.*
*The man who said to himself, "I think I can, I think I can, I
think I can. I thought I could. I thought could.*
I thought I could."
And he did.
He made it (KFC) finger licking-good.

Minnie I. Carter, *Vocalist, Poet and Journalist*

Harlow Fullwood is a sensitive and compassionate man who exemplifies what one's life should be about - "caring and sharing." Although he came from humble beginnings, he did not complain or make excuses, and the word "can't" has never been a part of his vocabulary. In my opinion, he is a survivor, a high achiever, a role model, a philanthropist, a devoted family man and friend, for whom I have the utmost respect. I am thrilled that he has decided to share his story.

SALUTE TO THE FULLWOOD FOUNDATION
By Minnie L. Carter

The State of Maryland has been richly blessed
By the presence of two remarkable individuals
Who stand shoulders above the rest.

"Caring & Sharing" is their motto
Harlow & Elnora Fullwood, a Dynamic Duo!

He is a shining example of the Baltimore City Police Department
from which he retired
The epitome of success, a man inspired.

She is a soft-spoken former teacher with a heart of pure gold
Distinguished and eloquent, a very spiritual soul.

They have such compassion for living
And life has been good to them; now they're committed to giving

Outstanding role models for Paquita and Harlow III
And their little grandsons, Robert and Harlow IV
By the way, have you heard?

Locally and nationally, Harlow is known
He's the "Chicken King," for his KFC franchises have really grown.

With the family's help in 1991,
The Fullwood Foundation was begun.

Annually, its Benefit and Recognition Breakfast seems to attract
Record-breaking crowds, and that's a fact.

This event has been sponsored by KFC,
First National Bank of Maryland, AT&T,
Pepsi-Cola, J.C. Penney, WBAL-TV, Gillette, Comcast and V-103.

Thousands of dollars have been donated to churches and
Non-profit organizations,
The United Negro College Fund, United Way and
Numerous other associations.

The Fullwoods also use this opportunity to present
Awards to public servants and civic leaders
For volunteer time well-spent.

Harlow is the quintessential entrepreneur
With a heart as big as the sun.
With his wife by his side, their work has only just begun.

"Caring and Sharing" is their motto.
God Bless Harlow and Elnora Fullwood, a Dynamic Duo!
©1996

A TRIBUTE TO HARLOW FULLWOOD, JR.
Dr. Jeannette W. Shamwell (Deceased)

It was the year of '41,
In a Carolina town,
That marked the birth of a baby boy
Destined for renown.

The residents of Asheville (And there's no town that's finer)
Lay deep in sleep,
Nor hailed the birth
Of a football-great first liner.

His parents in that Christian home
Taught him to love his neighbor,
Especially each needy one,
And what they did not savor.

Was loafing, loafing on the job
Or shrinking any task;
"Do your best, your very best,"
They said, "is all we ask."

So he applied himself in school.
(Was in the upper tenth)
Each problem was a learning tool.
Ambition urged him higher.
The zeal to climb on up and up
Burned in him like a fire.

And then one day from Union came
A football guy a-scouting,
So Harlow landed on the James.
(You hear the Panthers shouting?)

Their captain great for two fine years,
An answer to their dreams.
(Miss Bassett now has come around:
Oh, Matrimonial Schemes!)

241

But, oh, suppose some other school
Had caught him in its netting?
For Baltimore and Union too,
'Twould been life-long regretting!

To Mr. Harlow Fullwood, Fifth Grade Class 1998
William Pinderhughes Elementary #28
Teachers: Mrs. M. Winston and Mrs. V. Olds Brown

Honesty is the best policy. That's what he believes.
Attain your goals, and you'll be sure to achieve.
Ready to lend a helping hand, loving and kind, a friend to man.
Outgoing and courageous, generous too,
Willing to sacrifice for me and for you.

Full of compassion - free from strife.
Undaunted by all of the obstacles he has met in his life,
Leading the children to a better way.
Light-hearted philanthropist, happy and gay.
What would we do without such a man?
Only trying to help us to be all we can.
Oh, Mr. Fullwood, we thank you so much.
Don't ever forsake us, and do keep in touch.

BALTIMORE MAGAZINE ARTICLE: "HARLOW FULL-WOOD, 'BALTIMOREAN OF THE YEAR': THIS FAST-FOOD MAGNATE USES HIS FUNDS AND CHARM TO HELP LOCAL STUDENTS."

"The difference between me and the man in the penitentiary is that I had a lot of help," says Catonsville resident Harlow Fullwood, one of the nation's highest-earning KFC franchise holders. "I have never met a successful anything who can honestly say they made it on their own."

Those might seem strange words from one of the region's favorite up-by-his bootstraps entrepreneurs, who grew up poor in Asheville, North Carolina. After attending Virginia Union University on an athletic scholarship, Fullwood served on the Baltimore City police force for more than 20 years before starting from scratch in the fast-food business in 1984.

Yet Fullwood is anything but smug about his prosperity. The same year he bought his first KFC franchise, Fullwood and his wife, Elnora, created a foundation to give others a helping hand.

Since then, the Fullwood Foundation has garnered support from 28 national companies--including NationsBank and Nabisco--along with thousands of local supporters. This year's annual fundraising breakfast, to be held January 16 at Martin's West for 2,000 ticket holders, was sold out three months in advance.

Fullwood says he is motivated by a promise he made to the former president of his alma mater, who asked him to seek out youngsters and help them find their way. "I made that commitment to him on his deathbed 35 years ago, and I don't take a backseat to anyone," says Fullwood. "When I do things for kids, I do it with them. We go to field trips with them, because I want them to see there's someone out there who cares." The foundation has disbursed several hundred thousand dollars, supporting a long list of cultural, educational, and social organizations - everything from Artscape to Union Memorial Hospital. It also awards college scholarships and runs field trips and other educational programs for students in some 40 Baltimore City and Baltimore County public schools. No wonder the local chapter the National Society of Fund Executives named Fullwood the Outstanding Volunteer Fundraiser of 1998.

Julius Whitfield Bassett

Mr. Harlow Fullwood, my brother in-law, is a man of major generosity. He possesses an expertise in how to deal with people and the ability to understand the worthiness of individuals and their need to be successful. Harlow is one of the greatest men that I have ever seen and have had the privilege to know. It is my pleasure to congratulate him on his endeavors. I wish him continued success in doing all of the things he does to help other people. He has encouraged many, including me, to be the best that they can be and to encourage others to do the same. Thank you Harlow, for all of the wonderful things that you have done to motivate me in my life. It is a blessing for me to know you, and I wish that people could be like you – always.

Everett Fullwood

As the oldest child in our family, and my big brother, Harlow has been an inspiration to me. Throughout my life, I have followed in his footsteps, in education, college and professional football, law enforcement, family life, and in the spirit of caring and sharing. I love my brother, and I am thankful for the positive footpaths that he created for me to follow.

Elnora Bassett Fullwood

My 37 years of marriage with Harlow have been rewarding. I have seen him develop from a very young man to a mature, inspiring man. When he makes his mind up to tackle a task, he sticks with it until it is done – with perfection. God has given him insurmountable strength and guidance. He is a warrior.

Paquita Fullwood-Stokes

Dad, you are my mentor. I remember, as I was growing up, you would always say, "Do your best, no matter what you choose to do in life. Always try first. Just don't quit!" Thanks Dad, for your support. The following poem effectively expresses my tribute to you.

With Love,
Your Daughter, Paquita

DON'T QUIT

When things go wrong, as they sometimes will,
When the road you're trudging seems all up hill,
When the funds are low, and the debts are high,
And you want to smile, but you have to sigh,
When care is pressing you down a bit,
Rest, if you must--but don't you quit.

Life is queer with its twists and turns,

As each of us sometimes learns,
And many a failure turns about
When he might have won had he stuck it out;
Don't give up, though the pace seems slow—
You may succeed with another blow.

Often the goal is nearer than
It seems to a faint and faltering man.
Often the struggler has given up
When he might have captured the victor's cup.
And he learned too late, when the night slipped down,
How close he was to the golden crown.

Success is a failure turned inside out—
The silver tint of the clouds in doubt.
And you can never tell how close you are;
It may be near when it seems afar;
So stick to the fight when you're hardest hit—
It's when things seem worst that you mustn't quit.
                    Author unknown

Harlow Fullwood, III

Hey Dad! Congratulations, on your book. There are a few things that I want to say. You are the most magnificent, energized man that I think I have ever known in my lifetime. You energize with love. You energize with care. You are a true human being. You are not fake. You are my role-model, for sure; and, no one can take your place. Nobody knows you better than I. This is not like watching someone on TV that you want to be your role-model because they can act or play ball real good. No! I live with you 24/7. I have known you for 25 years. I grew up with you, in my heart. How you care about your family and how you care about others is remarkable.

What truly amazes me is that you have not even reached the zenith of your career yet. You are not at the peak. You are still going, and going, and going. You are like a snowball rolling down a mountain, just getting bigger, and bigger, and bigger.

I admire you for the guidance you gave me, and for the things you have gone through — with me. You taught me to be caring. You taught me how to be a wonderful father, and I thank God for that. Again, congratulations.

There are three words that I always tell you Dad, and they should always stick with you. And, you know that this is coming from my heart. I Love You! Three strong words, for a strong man...a powerful man. Love is Powerful. That is what you give others: Love. That's it! Gotta Go!

I am deeply gratified by what others have said about me. Their sincerity, respect, and love mean everything to me. Their kind expressions will further motivate me to **lift others up, with love**.

If this book helps even one person to live his or her life with more love and concern for others, then telling my story has not been in vain.

Love to All,
Harlow Fullwood, Jr.

Appendix

Baltimore Afro-American, Life Style, February 13-19, 1999, "The Fullwoods Make a Difference in the Community," Page B-8.

Baltimore Afro-American, Lifestyle, May 29 -June 4, 1999, "The Fullwood Foundation Pays Tribute to Retiring President Dr. Simmons," Page B-3.

The Masonic Family, December, 1999, "The Fullwood Foundation," Page 1.

Baltimore Afro-American, Lifestyle, December 25 1999-January 7, 2000, "Caring And Sharing Begin With Me," Page B-3.

1998
Baltimore Afro-American, January 24, 1998, Lifestyle, "Continentals Do it With a Flair," Page B-2 (photo).

Baltimore Afro-American, January 31, 1998, "Elnora and Harlow Fullwood, Jr., Entrepreneurs and Philanthropists," Bettye Moss, Page B4.

The Baltimore Times, May 1-7, 1998, "Harlow Fullwood Receives Fundraising Award."

The Masonic Family, May-July, 1998, "Fullwood and the Fullwood Foundation: Brother Fullwood Continues to Amaze Us All," Page 11.

Woodlawn Villager, October 1998, "Fullwood Foundation Honors Students," Page 9.

1997
Baltimore Sun, January 12, 1997, "10 Students Receive College Scholarships Worth $50,000," Page B1.

The Baltimore Times, January 17-23, 1997, Ginger Williams, "Fullwood Foundation Presents Awards"

Baltimore Afro-American, January 18, 1997, "The Fullwoods Shine Again at their Caring, Sharing Breakfast," Page B-9.

Rhema, January 26, 1997. "Fullwood Foundation Cares & Shares at Benefit Breakfast," Page 17.

Woodlawn Villager, February 1997. "Woodlawn High Senior Receives Award," (Photo), Page 13.

Baltimore Business Journal, March 14-20, 1997, "Starting With Nothing, Fullwood Builds a Dream," Page 13.

Baltimore Sun, April 17, 1997, "J.C. Penney Gives 21 Awards of $1,000 to People, Charities," Page 4B.

The Catonsville Times, May 14, 1997, "Fullwood Mission Gives Others a Chance for Success," Page 6.

1996
Baltimore Afro-American, March 23, 1996, "The Fullwoods Combine Leadership in Business and Charitable Giving," Page A-12.

The Baltimore Times, April 15-21, 1996, "People Who Make Things Happen," Page 9.

The Baltimore Afro-American, June 28, 1996, "Virginia Union Fetes Fullwood With Honorary Doctorate Degree."

1995
Baltimore Sun, January 29, 1995, "Foundation Funds Nonprofits."

Baltimore Afro-American, January 21, 1995, "Fullwood Foundation Gives $5,000 to Baltimore City Community College," Page B-8.

1994
Baltimore Afro-American, Metro Profile, January 22, 1994, "Sixth Annual Fullwood Foundation Breakfast: A Celebration of Sharing and Caring," Page B-1.

CLOSE, (College, Leaders, Organizations, and Students Evolving), September, 1994, "Harlow Fullwood: Community Service Award."

Upscale Magazine, "Business Partners for Life," page 45, October 1994.

1993
The Catonsville Times, January 13, 1993, "Couple Honors Leaders: Fullwoods Host Annual Banquet," Page 9.

Baltimore Afro-American, "If You Ask Me," January 1 and 23, 1993, "Fullwood Benefit and Recognition Breakfast," Page B-3.

1992
Baltimore Afro-American, January 25, 1992, "A Celebration of Sharing and Caring," Page B-2.

The Sun, January 26, 1992, "Fullwood Foundation Holds Breakfast."

The Baltimore Times, January 27, 1992, "Annual Charity Breakfast a Rousing Success."

USA Today, May 11, 1992, "Securing a Dream Through Persistence."

Baltimore Business Record, August 7, 1992, "Substituting Character for Capital Pays Off for City KFC King."

1990
Baltimore Afro-American, February 24, 1990, "Fullwood Benefit Breakfast," Page A-1.

The Daily Record, April 26, 1990, *"Minority Area Loans Found To Be Lacking."*

The Baltimore Guide, August, 1989, "Harlow Fullwood Makes His Business Chicken."

1989
The Sunday Sun, Baltimore, January 22, 1989, "For Restaurant Owner, Generosity is a Way of Life."

The Baltimore Times, January 30, 1989, "Fullwood Donates $50,000 to Community."

The Baltimore Times, June 5-11, 1989, "Adult Learners Expand College Market: Harlow Fullwood is One Who Finished College as an Adult."

1988
Baltimore Sun, April 12, 1988, "From Nightsticks to Drumsticks: Ex-Policeman Does Well in Fast Food," Page D6.

The Baltimore Afro-American, May 31, 1988, "Fullwoods' Fashion Franchise Success."

1987
The Baltimore Times, September, 1987, "Ex-Cop Doing Chicken Right."

1986

The Baltimore Sun, September 8, 1986, "Ex-Policeman in Business Still Tries to help People."

Baltimore Evening Sun, by Frank D. Roylance, entitled, "His Job Was to Recruit the Best."

Black Enterprise Magazine, November, 1986, "Doing Chicken Right," Page 60.

1985

The Evening Sun, November 20, 1985, "Franchising Happy Alternative For the Ownership."

1983

Baltimore Afro-American, April 16,1983, VUU Weekend event attracts 3,000; 14 Honorees Feted at Reception: Choir Concert Fills Meyerhoff, Page 10.

1980

The Crusader, The Weekly Newspaper for Human Dignity in the Washington-Baltimore-Megalopolis, February 9, 1980, "Fullwood: Leader By Example"

The Evening Sun's 1980 Policeman of the Year, for Work in the Community, by Wiley Hall, *Evening Sun* Reporter.

Christian World, May 25, 1980, "Policemen Cited: Harlow Fullwood, Jr., Outstanding Police Work and Service to Community."

1979

Randallstown Community Times, October 11, 1979, "Hall of Famer Helps Students."

1978

Randallstown Community Times, May 17, 1978, "Fullwood Elected Veep of VUU Alumni Group."

Baltimore Afro-American, June 24, 1978, "Fullwood Elected Chapter President."

Baltimore Sun Editorial, *"Visit Begins Ocean City Program: Resort to Host City Teen-agers."*

1976

The Suburban Times, Baltimore County, March 1976, "Fullwood Recalls Long Ride to School."

1975

Richmond Afro-American, February 8, 1975, "Former Union Football Star Returns as Police Recruiter."

Baltimore Afro-American, "You Got to Like People," Reporter Pam Widgeon.

Baltimore Sunday Sun, "A Big, Genial Policeman is Dean of Recruiters."

Baltimore News-American by Michael Powell, "Top Police Recruiter Moving On."

Baltimore News-American June 7, 1975, "Children's Day at Mt. Lebanon."

1974

Baltimore Afro-American June 15, 1974, "Officer Fullwood Gets Top PTA Membership Award."

Baltimore Afro-American April 20, 1974, "Afro Honor Roll Announced: Harlow Fullwood, Jr., Civic-Minded Citizen."

1968
Camp Lejeune Globe, September 27, 1968, "Future Policemen: Baltimore Police Officer Harlow Fullwood, Jr., Recruits."

1963
Baltimore Sun : "Fullwood---4th Round Pick!"

1958
Asheville Citizens Times December 18, 1958, "Four Players Win Shrine Bowl Bids; Moore is Coach."

1957
Asheville Citizen Times, Bob Terrell, a sportswriter, "Crossing The Alps."

APPENDIX B: Major Salutes to Harlow Fullwood, Jr.

16th Annual Dr. Martin Luther King, Jr. Scholarship Breakfast, January 6, 2001, The Howard L. Cornish Drum Major Award.

Coppin State College
Conferring of Honorary Degree, Doctor of Humane Letters, Baltimore Arena, May 16, 1999.

J.C. Penney
The Fullwood Foundation received a 1997 $1,000 Golden Rule Award.

Virginia Union University
Conferring of Honorary Degree, Doctor of Humane Letters, Virginia University, May 11, 1996.

100 Black Men of Maryland, Inc.
Fifth Anniversary Gala, Friday, April 19, 1996 Martin's West.

Baltimore Marketing Association Presents The 25th Annual Business Awards Dinner, Honoring Harlow Fullwood, Jr., December 2, 1993.

Volunteers of America, Inc.
VOA Anniversary Dinner, Tremont Plaza, Baltimore, MD, 1990 Community Service Award, September 1990.

National Black College Alumni Hall of Fame 5th Anniversary, Dinner, Induction Ceremony, Hyatt Regency, Hotel, Atlanta, Georgia, September 15, 1990.

Druid Hill YMCA The William "Box" Harris Memorial Youth in Government Program, 4th Annual Roast, honoring Harlow Fullwood, Jr., June 14, 1990, Martin's West, To Benefit the Druid Hill YMCA.

Institute for American Business First Annual Community Service Awards Luncheon for Exemplary Blacks in Business, Hyatt Washington on Capitol Hill, Washington, DC 1989.

An Evening With Don and Harlow, honorees: The Honorable William Donald Schaefer (former Governor of Maryland and Mayor of Baltimore City) and **Harlow Fullwood, Jr.,** May 7, 1986.

Miles W. Connor Chapter, Virginia Union Alumni Association, Baltimore, Maryland, 1984, Salutes Harlow W. Fullwood, Jr., President, Most Outstanding Alumnus 1979-1983.

APPENDIX C:
Summary of More Than 500 Awards Received by Harlow Fullwood, Jr.

• Second-Place Essay Winner, "Citizenship is a Process of Gradual Achievement," 1957, awarded by The Civitan Club, Asheville, NC.

- Football All-American, Virginia Union University.

- Drafted by the Baltimore Colts and the Buffalo Bills football teams in the same year.

- Second-Place Ranking at the Baltimore Police Academy.

- Received the Baltimore Police Department's "Distinguished Service Award," the highest-level honor that can be awarded to a living police officer.

- The "Most Decorated Law Enforcement Officer in Maryland in terms of Community Service" by Baltimore Police Department.

- Past President of the Miles W. Connor Chapter of the Virginia Union University Alumni Association, Baltimore, Maryland Chapter.

- Honored by the Baltimore *Sun* as "1979 Policeman of the Year" and upon leaving the department.

- Finished second at the ~~KFC~~ National Training Center at Louisville, Kentucky.

- Mt. Vernon International Optimist Club's Policeman of the Year, 1980.

- Alumnus of the Year, 1980, Miles W. Connor Chapter, Virginia Union University Alumni Association.

- Baltimore City Public Schools (Resolution), 1980.

- Baltimore City Council (Resolution), 1980.

- Maryland Law Enforcement Officers, Inc., Appreciation Award, 1980.

- Coppin State College Century Club Award, 1980.

- Congressional Citation, 1982.

- Virginia Union University First Distinguished Alumni Leader Award, 1982, Plaque.

- United Way of Central Maryland Community Service Award, 1982.

- The Varsity "M" Club, Inc., Morgan State University, Distinguished Community Service Award, 1982.

- Milford Mill High School Appreciation Award, 1982.

- Jefferson Award for Distinguished Public Service, 1983, WBAL-TV, Solid Bronze Medallion.

- "Man of the Year," The National Association of Negro Business and Professional Women's Club, Inc., 1983, Plaque.

- Maryland Educational Opportunity Center, 1983, Certificate of Appreciation.

- Meritorious Service Award, The United Negro College Fund, 1983.

- Baltimore Alumnae Chapter, Delta Sigma Theta Sorority, Inc., Community Service Award, 1983, Plaque.

- Became a Kentucky Fried Chicken franchise owner in 1984.

- In 1988, Harlow Fullwood received the KFC State Sales Award, thereby becoming the first African-American franchise holder to lead Maryland in gross sales and one of the first in the nation.

- The KFC *Five Star Award:* the first black franchisee in the history of Kentucky Fried Chicken Corporation to lead a whole state in gross sales.

- During 1987 and 1988, Harlow Fullwood received the KFC *Million-Dollar Award* presented to the restaurant with gross sales of over $1 million.

- Fullwood's restaurants received the *QSC Excellence Award* and *KFC's Triple Crown* Award in recognition of providing excellence in quality products, fast, friendly service, and cleanliness of the restaurants.

- National Blue Chip Enterprise Award from *Nation's Business* magazine.

- Maryland's 1995 Entrepreneur of the Year.

- Alpha Phi Omega Fraternity Leadership Award.

- Henry G. Parks Business Award.

- Presented the Jimmy Swartz Medallion Award by J. Millard Tawes, former governor of Maryland

- Inducted into the Baltimore City Community College Alumni Hall of Recognition.

- The Governor's Recognition Award to Fullwood Foods, Inc. by the Maryland Department of Economic Development as one of five leading Small Minority Businesses in Maryland.

- Big Brothers/Big Sisters of Central Maryland Distinguished Service Award.

- Inducted by the Howard University School of Business to its Wall of Fame.

- The Alpha Phi Omega Fraternity Leadership Award.

- Phi Delta Kappa Excellence in Education Award.

- Anheuser-Busch Companies Outstanding Achievement Award.

- Institute for American Business Community Service Award.

- Charter member of the Baltimore Chapter of the National Coalition of 100 Black Men.

- Life member of Alpha Phi Alpha Fraternity, Inc.

- Member of the National Association for the Advancement of Colored People (NAACP); he was elected to the Board of the NAACP Baltimore Chapter when he was a Baltimore Police Officer.

- Prince Hall Mason.

- Named to the distinguished Alexis de Tocqueville Society of Maryland.

- The Baltimore *Sun* has honored Fullwood Foods, Inc. for several years as one of the 50 leading black businesses in Maryland.

- Inducted in 1990 into the Central Intercollegiate Athletic Association (CIAA) Hall of Fame.

- Received the first Presidential Citation issued by VUU's President, Dr. S. Dallas Simmons, in recognition of financial support, strong volunteer recruitment leadership as Chairman of the Board of Trustees' Student Affairs Committee and assistance in enhancing alumni relations.

- General Chairman of the AFRAM EXPO for 1992 and 1993, one of the largest ethnic festivals on the East Coast of the United States, he led innovative fundraising campaigns and initiatives that have yet to be matched.

- Listed in the 1992 "Who's Who Among Black Americans."

- The 1992 Austin, Texas Metropolitan Business Resource Center National Minority Franchisee of the Year Award (AMBRC).

- Named 1992 Delta Lambda Chapter, Alpha Phi Alpha Fraternity - Brother of the Year.

- Baltimore City Community College 1998 Lifetime Business Achievement Award.

- 1998 Outstanding Volunteer Fund-Raiser Award by the Baltimore Chapter of the National Society of Fundraising Executives.

- 1999 Baltimorean of the Year by *Baltimore Magazine*.

- 1999 *Baltimore Business Journal's* Most Influential Baltimorean List.

- 1999 Rotary International-Woodlawn/Westview Chapter's Community Service Award.

- Charter Member of the Woodlawn-Westview Rotary International and named a Paul Harris Fellow by the Rotary International Foundation "in appreciation of tangible and significant assistance given for the furtherance of better understanding and friendly relations between people of the world."

- Virginia Union University National Alumni Association Alumnus of the Year.

- October 25, 2001. Inducted into the 15th Annual Maryland Senior Citizens Hall of Fame (MSCHF) for the year 2001, and presented with MSCHF Geri Award, the geriatric "Nobel Prize" for extraordinary humanitarian community service.

- October 18, 2001. Received the Excellence for Minority Achievement "Vanguard" Award, by the Maryland State Department of Education, for having demonstrated extraordinary vision and leadership to advance the success of minority students throughout the State of Maryland.

- September 28, 2001. Received the 2001 CITE Odyssey – Scholarship Honoree Award, by the Consortium of Information & Telecommunications Executives, Inc. (CITE) at its 18th Annual Conference, for having contributed and generated more than $6 million in college scholarships to more than 500 students.

The William "Box" Harris Memorial Youth in Government
ROAST OF HARLOW FULLWOOD, JR.
To Benefit The Druid Hill YMCA

June 14, 1990
Martin's West
(6817 Dogwood Road – Woodlawn)

Hor's d'oeuvres
and
Cash Bar
6:00pm

Program
and
Dinner
7:00pm

Patron Tickets $45 ; Table $450 / Sponsor Tickets $100 ; Tables $1000
To Order Tickets Call Kacy Conley 728–1600

Great Blacks in Wax Museum

Harlow Fullwood, Jr. requires a dusting every day

Congratulations
Harlow and Elnora Fullwood

SERMONS WE SEE

"I'd rather see a sermon than hear one, any day.
I'd rather one should walk with me,
than merely show the way.
For the eye's a better teacher, more willing than the ear.
Fine counsel is confusing, but example's always clear.
I can soon learn how to do it, if you'll let me see it done.
I can watch your hands in action, but your tongue too fast may run.
And the best of all the preachers are the ones who live their creed,
For to see the good in action is what everybody needs.
And the lectures you deliver may be very wise and true,
But I'd rather get my lessons by observing what you do.
For I may misunderstand you, and the high advice you give,
But there's no misunderstanding how you act,
and how you live."

— Edgar A. Guest

Your lives are inspiring sermons we can all see. We respect and admire your consistent record of concern for and service to your fellow man. We are proud of you. Keep up the good work!

Grady and Helen Dale